Mormon Settlement in Arizona

"EL VADO," THE CROSSING OF THE FATHERS

Gateway of the Pioneers Into Arizona

MORMON
SETTLEMENT
in Arizona

James H. McClintock

Foreword by Charles S. Peterson

The University of Arizona Press

TUCSON

About the Author

JAMES H. MCCLINTOCK (1864–1933), a California native, came to Arizona Territory in 1879 as a cub reporter, working for newspapers in Prescott, Globe, Tempe, and Phoenix, as well as serving as the Arizona correspondent for the *Los Angeles Times*. After military service with Theodore Roosevelt's Rough Riders, during which McClintock was wounded at the Battle of San Juan Hill, he returned to Arizona and devoted himself to public service. McClintock was named State Historian in 1919, partly in recognition of the research that led to his *Arizona: The Youngest State* (1916), and he continued in that office until 1928, when he became the Phoenix postmaster.

THE UNIVERSITY OF ARIZONA PRESS

Copyright © 1985
The Arizona Board of Regents
All Rights Reserved

Manufactured in the U.S.A.

Library of Congress Cataloging in Publication Data

McClintock, James H., 1864–1934.
Mormon settlement in Arizona.

Bibliography: p.
Includes index.
1. Mormons—Arizona—History.
2. Arizona—History—To 1950.
I. Title
F820.M8M35   1985   979.1'0088283   85-8458

ISBN 0-8165-0953-0 (pbk.)

SUMMARY OF SUBJECTS

v

Chapter Six

Chapter Seven

Chapter Eight

Chapter Nine

Chapter Ten

Chapter Eleven

viii

Chapter Twenty-three

CIVIC AND CHURCH FEATURES—Troublesome River Conditions, 257; Basic Law in a Mormon Community, 258; Layton, Soldier and Pioneer, 260; A New Leader on the Gila, 262; Church Academies of Learning, 263.

Chapter Twenty-four

MOVEMENT INTO MEXICO—Looking Over the Land, 265; Colonization in Chihuahua, 266; Prosperity in an Alien Land, 268; Abandonment of the Mountain Colonies, 269; Sad Days for the Sonora Colonists, 271; Congressional Inquiry, 273; Repopulation of the Mexican Colonies, 274.

Chapter Twenty-five

MODERN DEVELOPMENT—Oases Have Grown in the Desert, 275; Prosperity Has Succeeded Privation, 276.

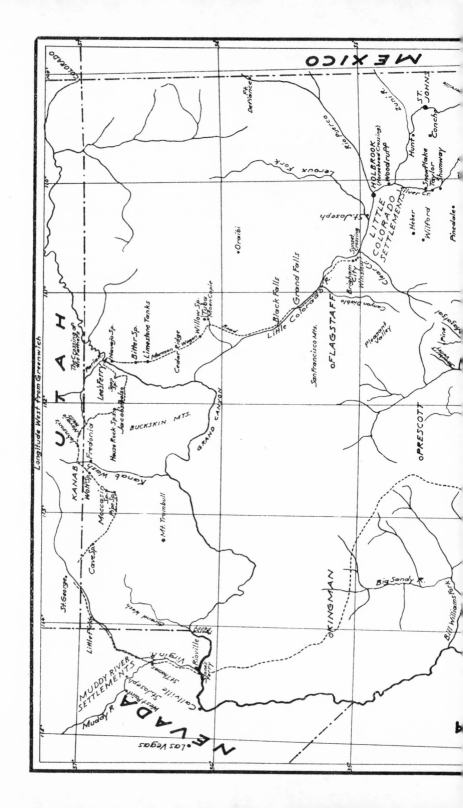

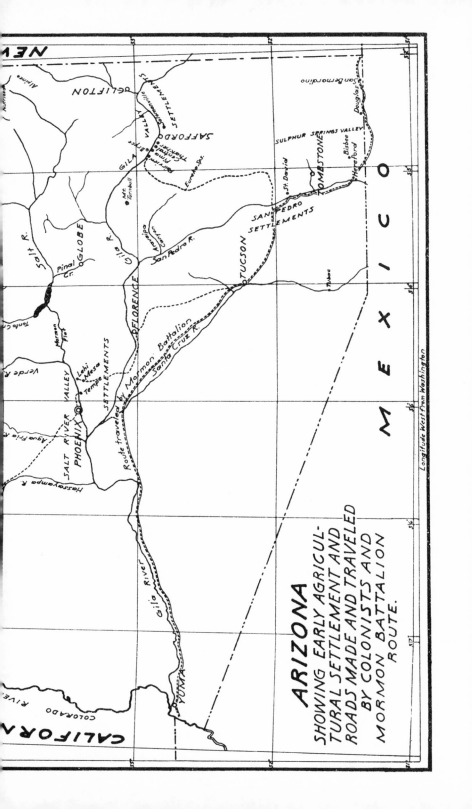

ARIZONA
SHOWING EARLY AGRICUL-
TURAL SETTLEMENT AND
ROADS MADE AND TRAVELED
BY COLONISTS AND
MORMON BATTALION
ROUTE.

FOREWORD

On Sunday, February 6, 1921, Mormons of the Phoenix
area held a meeting that turned out to be a commemoration
of their role in "breaking the wilderness." For the thousand
or so people assembled, it was a day for history. The honored guest was James H. McClintock. The presiding officer
was Mormon Apostle Orson F. Whitney. Both were historians.

Although bristle-bearded and rustic in appearance,
Apostle Whitney was an eloquent speaker and a felicitous
writer who, in a lifetime of church and community service,
had found time to write a stoutly pro-Mormon *History of
Utah* in four volumes and a more popular single-volume
state history. Portly and with a game leg from Spanish-
American War wounds, McClintock was a prominent
member of what may be called the Arizona establishment.
Occupying the State Historian's office since 1919, he had,
among other works, written a well-received, three volume
work entitled *Arizona: The Youngest State* (1916). Together
they were now launching McClintock's newest work, *Mormon Settlement in Arizona: A Record of Peaceful Conquest of the
Desert* (1921). It was a work for which James H. McClintock
would be remembered.

Given that books are generally published amidst all the
fanfare their publishers can generate, the Mormon conference at Phoenix was a pretty good sendoff for *Mormon
Settlement*. Fittingly, Apostle Whitney proceeded first.
Speaking at great length in the morning session, he took as
his text, "Pilgrims of the Desert." McClintock followed in
the afternoon, holding even the sleepiest of the Saints
spellbound as he extolled the valor of their forefathers.
McClintock adapted the name of his speech, "Wilderness

Breakers," from the title of a book by his noted contemporary Frederick S. Dellenbaugh, *Breaking the Wilderness: The Story of the Conquest of the Far West* (1905).

It is the set of mind behind McClintock's "wilderness breakers" idea that interests us here. Then conjuring up few negative images, the term rang truer to the ear of his listeners than it does to our own. But a decade and a half before, when Dellenbaugh coined it, the term caught the precise spirit of the times. Dellenbaugh applied it specifically to Manuel Lisa, a St. Louis trader who was forced by the city's dominant merchants to open new trade frontiers along the wilderness course of the upper Missouri River in the years after 1800. "Wilderness breaker" was descriptive, if poetically romantic, when applied to Manuel Lisa, but the romance of Dellenbaugh's writing reached a high pitch in a subsequent chapter entitled "A Brood of Wilderness Breakers." Here he eulogized "Kit Carson the Dauntless," B. L. E. Bonneville "Captain Courteous," and Nathaniel Wyeth "Leader Hopeful," among others. While Dellenbaugh was less lyrical in his reference to the Mormons, he did set them squarely in what might be called the West's hall of fame — heroic figures among heroic figures, playing an honored role in a grand romantic tradition.

It had not always been so. During most of the nineteenth century, Mormons had billed themselves as God's earthly agents; anti-Mormons had presented them as devilish, conspiratorial, and degenerate; and serious historians had left them largely to themselves. Dellenbaugh reflected a growing tendency to incorporate Mormons into the romantic regionalism that was becoming a stock in trade with Western writers and historians as the new century dawned. If not actually initiated by San Francisco businessman/historian Hubert Howe Bancroft, the tendency to make Mormons an integral part of the larger romantic mosaic was surely given a great boost by his *History of Utah* (1888), a respected volume in the forty-five–volume Bancroft series, which covered the history of the West. Supported by oral statements, diaries, and other primary sources collected by assistants as well as by information supplied by the Mormon Church, Bancroft's *History of Utah* was published at the high tide of the national campaign to reconstruct the Mormons. It foreshadowed a shift in opinion and an awakening sense that the Mormon past could play a useful role in the larger context of Western history.

Bancroft and Dellenbaugh were part of what may be termed the romantic regionalist movement in which Western writers—journalists and novelists as well as historians—memorialized and promoted the West, in effect, creating a place for it in the national tradition and doing what they could to define its role politically, economically, culturally and aesthetically as well. Important throughout the West, the romantic promoters were particularly prominent in the Southwest and in California, where geographic setting and human experience sometimes combined to tempt writers into an effusiveness that has been difficult for critics from other regions to countenance and that has fallen into increasing disuse in recent decades.

Included among those most given to enthusiasm for the Southwest as a region during the decades after 1900 were Charles F. Lummis, Mary Austin, Mary and Dane Coolidge, D. H. Lawrence, Harvey Fergusson, Earle R. Forrest, Harrison Gray Otis (publisher of the *Los Angeles Times*), and (with deference to his influence on James McClintock) Frederick S. Dellenbaugh. The romantic regionalists were a diverse lot, active in a wide variety of things, but sharing an interest in publication and promotion of their region.

Cut from this same general mold, McClintock proved to be a gifted historian. Like most Western writers of the era he was a transplant, having come to Arizona in 1879 from Sacramento at the age of fifteen. He quickly became a promoter of his new home, working with his brother, who was also a journalist, and with newspapers in Prescott,

Globe, Tempe, and Phoenix. In addition, he was for decades the Arizona correspondent for the *Los Angeles Times*. He became a close friend of Harrison Gray Otis and in outlook was his protégé, seeing opportunity and growth for Arizona in water projects, real estate, agricultural development, and in mining and commerce. Along with the flamboyant Buckey O'Neill, McClintock was a prime mover in the organization of the Arizona contingent of the Rough Riders during the Spanish-American War. He was wounded and decorated and returned from the war a bona-fide hero, overshadowed only by O'Neill, whose famous recruiting slogan, "Who would not die to make another star in the flag?" became a guiding light to an entire generation of Arizonans. Like O'Neill, McClintock had something of Teddy Roosevelt's flair for action. He also shared Roosevelt's interest in history and his tendency to make it both the chronicle and the vehicle of progress.

McClintock continued his military interest in the postwar era, serving as president and historian of the national Rough Riders Association and becoming a colonel in the Arizona National Guard. Connections made during the war also served him well when Roosevelt appointed him postmaster at Phoenix in 1902, a position he occupied until Woodrow Wilson became president in 1914. He was again appointed postmaster in 1928, retaining the position until 1933, shortly before his death. He was active politically, serving for years on the state central committee of the Republican Party and running unsuccessfully for the Senate in 1922. He was also an ardent supporter of public education, teaching at the public school level in his early years and later serving as a board member of the Tempe Normal School, now Arizona State University. In short, McClintock was one of Arizona's finest.

More important in the long run than even these contributions was his role in the process by which Arizona strove to create an image for itself. This is a task that Arizona has obviously accomplished successfully, but in territorial days the odds against which image makers contended were impressive indeed. Nature was adverse. The country was rugged, hot and dry. Geographically it was remote. Resistance by Native Americans had been protracted and fierce. It was the "baby state," the runt of the litter, so to speak. This was aggravated by the fact that Arizona had for many years been part of New Mexico, and that, once separated, it had been less successful than the older territory in turning the colorful themes of the Southwest into favorable attention. For Arizona image makers the challenge was simultaneously to put distance between Arizona and New Mexico and to use many of the same themes to Arizona's advantage; to weld the good and the bad into a destiny both fitting and useful for Arizona. To a significant degree the Mormons of Arizona proved useful in this process, if nothing else, in adding a dimension to the Arizona tradition that was not prominent in New Mexico.

By frontier standards, the Arizona image makers with whom McClintock associated were an impressive lot. A few of them merit a quick glance here.

Among the first to begin systematic work toward defining Arizona's place in the West was Mormon Joseph Fish. A pioneer of repeated frontiers himself, Fish worked under unbelievably adverse circumstances to produce by 1900 a seven-volume manuscript on Rocky Mountain settlement, a 700-page manuscript history of territorial Arizona, and numerous Mormon manuscript histories. Although most of Fish's Rocky Mountain and territorial Arizona manuscripts were never published, they became foundation material for every Arizona territorial history written since, including McClintock's *Mormon Settlement* and my own *Take Up Your Mission* (1973).

More important to the official history of Arizona was Sharlot M. Hall. Coming to Arizona from Kansas as a child in 1882, she was educated at the University of Arizona and wrote for various newspapers and periodicals including *Out West*, *The Land of Sunshine*, and an excellent forerunner of *Arizona Highways* named *Arizona: The New State Magazine*, which was published for several years after 1910. In 1909 Hall became territorial historian, a position she occupied until 1913. As state historian she took an active interest in Arizona's Mormons, traveling widely in their communities and devoting special attention to the history of the Arizona Strip, which, lying north of the Grand Canyon, articulates geographically to southern Utah.

Building upon the work of both Fish and Hall but rising above them in accomplishment was historian Thomas E. Farish. Farish had served as private secretary to Governor Conrad Zulick in the late 1880s, making significant contributions toward the settlement of the Mormon conflict in Arizona. Thereafter he continued to play an important role in the development of the territory and the new state. He was state historian from 1913 until the time of his death in 1919. The publication of his eight-volume *History of Arizona* in 1915 distinguished his tenure as state historian.

Other image makers who may more properly be termed newspaper people than historians included writers whose offerings appeared regularly in the pages of *Arizona: The New State Magazine*. Published by John Arden Reaves, *Arizona* was unabashedly devoted to the promotion of the new state. Its pages extolled the Salt River Valley especially and became a major factor in advancing the Salt River Reclamation Project. Its articles had a definite Chamber of Commerce quality, yet they often rose above promotion to help define what Arizona was becoming. Numerous writers contributed, including Sharlot Hall and Thomas Farish. Others less important here but whose writings made lasting contributions included Ernest Douglas, who, like McClintock, was an untiring promoter of irrigation; G. S. Scott, a farm reporter; M. Alice Berry, who, like Hall, took a special interest in northern Arizona; and Bert Haskett, whose articles on livestock interests are of lasting value.

Few if any of these pioneer image makers left more indelible marks on the Arizona image than did James McClintock. Although heavily committed in the years after 1900, he found time to produce a flow of articles and promotional tracts. Typical was an article reporting a trip into the wild country of the Tonto Basin written for *Arizona: The New State Magazine*. Presented with an eye to the development of water resources, it portrayed Maricopa County as one of the great "Empire" counties of the West and did much to attract attention to dam sites along the Salt River and its affluents. After losing the Phoenix postmaster position in the Democratic victory of 1914, McClintock turned his attention squarely to the history of Arizona. By 1916 his largest work, the three-volume *Arizona: The Youngest State*, was ready for publication. It is not clear why this work appeared just at that time, coming as it did on the heels of Farish's official state history. The two works are similar in mood and emphasis, both featuring the military, Indian wars, outlawry, mining, and livestock. McClintock's research must have proceeded concurrently with Farish's, and it seems certain that McClintock must have had Farish's blessing, if indeed his work was not in some degree an official effort of the State Historian's office. It is true that there is a more popular quality to McClintock's writing, and his work is more lavish in format than Farish's. True also is the fact that the third volume of McClintock's *Arizona* is devoted to the biographical sketches of pioneer greats that were so dear to that era. Significantly, McClintock makes Arizonans of the Mormons in this work, claiming them proudly and giving them ample and fair treatment.

Research on something more in the way of Mormon history appears to have been already under way when McClintock took over as state historian in 1919. Farish had taken considerable political risk in supporting the Mormon cause in the 1880s. Thereafter he maintained his interest in them. Not only was he influenced by the pioneering historical work of Joseph Fish but he kept in close touch with friends in Salt Lake City. During his period as state historian he corresponded frequently with the Historian's Office of the Mormon Church and on occasion did research in Salt Lake City. McClintock, whose own interest in Mormon history we have already seen, continued the work. Like Farish he established close contacts in the Church Historian's Office and worked in its records himself. Ably assisted by LeRoi C. Snow, a Mormon appointed especially to the position of assistant state historian, he had readied his book for publication by the winter of 1921.

The Mormons who heard McClintock speak that Sunday in the February of 1921 were ready to hear their tradition recognized as a significant element in the grand effort by which the wilderness had been broken. They were not disappointed when the book appeared later that year. Not only did McClintock claim the Mormons as heroic figures in the emerging Arizona image, but he also pioneered in presenting Mormon history in a secular context, a method that with variation has been employed in most of the successful Mormon histories since. His book is indeed a chronicle of "peaceful conquest"—a celebration in the romantic mold of exploration, migration, town building, conflict, and resolution. Without special pleading, other than his unquestioned enthusiasm for things Arizonan and pioneer, McClintock portrays Arizona's early Mormons as agricultural builders—stable, thrifty, hard-working, and good—worthy figures in the best tradition of romantic regionalism. Sore spots in the Mormon past receive little attention. Polygamy is passed over quickly, almost silently. The Mountain Meadows Massacre is touched only in passing, and then, in keeping with Mormon policy, John D. Lee and the Indians are allowed to carry the onus. There are a few mistakes of fact that may be recognized from the vantage point of today's scholarship. But in the main, *Mormon Settlement* continues to stand the test of time. Readers today will be impressed, as readers were sixty years ago, by the wealth of information James H. McClintock brings together in this book, by the readable, constructive flow of the story he tells, and by his admiration for the indomitable Mormon pioneers.

CHARLES S. PETERSON

Mormon Settlement in Arizona

Chapter One

𝔚𝔦𝔩𝔡𝔢𝔯𝔫𝔢𝔰𝔰 𝔅𝔯𝔢𝔞𝔨𝔢𝔯𝔰

Mormon Colonization in the West

The Author would ask earliest appreciation by the reader that this work on "Mormon Settlement in Arizona" has been written by one entirely outside that faith and that, in no way, has it to do with the doctrines of a sect set aside as distinct and peculiar to itself, though it claims fellowship with any denomination that follows the teachings of the Nazarene. The very word "Mormon" in publications of that denomination usually is put within quotation marks, accepted only as a nickname for the preferred and lengthier title of "Church of Jesus Christ of Latter-day Saints." Outside the Church, the word, at least till within a decade or so, has been one that has formed the foundation for much of denunciation. There was somewhat of pathos in the remark to the Author by a high Mormon official, "There never has been middle ground in literature that affected the Mormons—it either has been written against us or for us." From a religious standpoint, this work is on neutral ground. But, from the standpoint of western colonization and consequent benefit to the Nation, the Author trusts the reader will join with him in appreciation of the wonderful work that has been done by these people. It is this field especially that has been covered in this book.

Occasionally it will be found that the colonizers have been referred to as "Saints." It is a shortening of the preferred title, showing a lofty moral aspiration, at least. It would be hard to imagine wickedness proceeding from such a designation, though the Church itself assuredly

1

would be the first to disclaim assumption of full saintliness within its great membership. Still, there might be testimony from the writer that he has lived near the Mormons of Arizona for more than forty years and in that time has found them law-abiding and industrious, generally of sturdy English, Scotch, Scandinavian or Yankee stock wherein such qualities naturally run with the blood. If there be with such people the further influence of a religion that binds in a union of faith and in works of the most practical sort, surely there must be accomplishment of material and important things.

Pioneers in Agriculture

In general, the Mormon (and the word will be used without quotation marks) always has been agricultural. The Church itself appears to have a foundation idea that its membership shall live by, upon and through the products of the soil. It will be found in this work that Church influence served to turn men from even the gold fields of California to the privations of pioneer Utah. It also will be found that the Church, looking for extension and yet careful of the interests of its membership, directed the expeditions that penetrated every part of the Southwest.

There was a pioneer Mormon period in Arizona, that might as well be called the missionary period. Then came the prairie schooners that bore, from Utah, men and women to people and redeem the arid southland valleys. Most of this colonization was in Arizona, where the field was comparatively open. In California there had been religious persecution and in New Mexico the valleys very generally had been occupied for centuries by agricultural Indians and by native peoples speaking an alien tongue. There was extension over into northern Mexico, with consequent travail when impotent governments crumbled. But in Arizona, in the valleys of the Little Colorado, the Salt, the Gila and the San Pedro and of their tributaries and at points where the white man theretofore had failed, if he had reached them at all, the Mormons set their stakes and, with united effort, soon cleared the land, dug ditches and placed dams in unruly streams, all to the end that farms should smile where the desert had reigned. It all needed imagination and vision, something that, very properly, may be called faith. Sometimes there was failure. Occasionally the brethren failed to live in unity. They were human. But, at all times, back of them were the serenity and judgment and resources of the Church and with them went the engendered confidence that all would be well, whatever befell of finite sort. It has been said that faith removes mountains. The faith that came with these pioneers was well backed and carried with it brawn and industry.

"Mormon Settlement in Arizona" should not carry the idea that Arizona was settled wholly by Mormons. Before them came the Spaniards, who went north of the Gila only as explorers and missionaries and whose agriculture south of that stream assuredly was not of enduring value. There were trappers, prospectors, miners, cattlemen and farmers long before the wagons from Utah first rolled southward, but the fact that Arizona's agricultural development owes enormously to Mormon effort can be appreciated in considering the establishment and development of the fertile areas of Mesa, Lehi, the Safford-Thatcher-Franklin district, St. David on the San Pedro, and the many settlements of northeastern Arizona, with St. Johns and Snowflake as their headquarters.

It is a remarkable fact that Mormon immigrants made even a greater number of agricultural settlements in Arizona than did the numerically preponderating other peoples. However, the explanation is a simple one: The average immigrant, coming without organization, for himself alone, naturally gravitated to the mines—indeed, was brought to the Southwest by the mines. There was little to attract him in the desert plains through which ran intermittent stream flows, and he lacked the vision that showed the

3

desert developed into the oasis. The Mormon, however, came usually from an agricultural environment. Rarely was he a miner.

Of later years there has been much community commingling of the Mormon and the non-Mormon. There even has been a second immigration from Utah, usually of people of means. The day has passed for the ox-bowed wagon and for settlements out in the wilderness. There has been left no wilderness in which to work magic through labor. But the Mormon influence still is strong in agricultural Arizona and the high degree of development of many of her localities is based upon the pioneer settlement and work that are dealt with in the succeeding pages.

First Farmers in Many States

It is a fact little appreciated that the Mormons have been first in agricultural colonization of nearly all the intermountain States of today. This may have been providential, though the western movement of the Church happened in a time of the greatest shifting of population ever known on the continent. It preceded by about a year the discovery of gold in California, and gold, of course, was the lodestone that drew the greatest of west-bound migrations. The Mormons, however, were first. Not drawn by visions of wealth, unless they looked forward to celestial mansions, they sought, particularly, valleys wherein peace and plenty could be secured by labor. Nearly all were farmers and it was from the earth they designed drawing their subsistence and enough wherewith to establish homes.

Of course, the greatest of foundations was that at Salt Lake, July 24, 1847, when Brigham Young led his Pioneers down from the canyons and declared the land good. But there were earlier settlements.

First of the faith on the western slopes of the continent was the settlement at San Francisco by Mormons from the ship Brooklyn. They landed July 31, 1846, to found the

4

first English speaking community of the Golden State, theretofore Mexican. These Mormons established the farming community of New Helvetia, in the San Joaquin Valley, the same fall, while men from the Mormon Battalion, January 24, 1848, participated in the discovery of gold at Sutter's Fort. Mormons also were pioneers in Southern California, where, in 1851, several hundred families of the faith settled at San Bernardino.

The first Anglo-Saxon settlement within the boundaries of the present State of Colorado was at Pueblo, November 15, 1846, by Capt. James Brown and about 150 Mormon men and women who had been sent back from New Mexico, into which they had gone, a part of the Mormon Battalion that marched on to the Pacific Coast.

The first American settlement in Nevada was one of Mormons in the Carson Valley, at Genoa, in 1851.

In Wyoming, as early as 1854, was a Mormon settlement at Green River, near Fort Bridger, known as Fort Supply.

In Idaho, too, preeminence is claimed by virtue of a Mormon settlement at Fort Lemhi, on the Salmon River, in 1855, and at Franklin, in Cache Valley, in 1860.

The earliest Spanish settlement of Arizona, within its present political boundaries, was in the Santa Cruz Valley not far from the southern border. There was a large ranch at Calabasas at a very early date, and at that point Custodian Frank Pinkley of the Tumacacori mission ruins lately discovered the remains of a sizable church. A priest had station at San Xavier in 1701. Tubac as a presidio dates from 1752, Tumacacori from 1754 and Tucson from 1776. These, however, were Spanish settlements, missions or presidios. In the north, Prescott was founded in May, 1864, and the Verde Valley was peopled in February, 1865. Earlier still were Fort Mohave, reestablished by soldiers of the California Column in 1863, and Fort Defiance, on the eastern border line, established in 1849. A temporary

Mormon settlement at Tubac in 1851, is elsewhere described. But in honorable place in point of seniority are to be noted the Mormon settlements on the Muddy and the Virgin, particularly, in the very northwestern corner of the present Arizona and farther westward in the southernmost point of Nevada, once a part of Arizona. In this northwestern Arizona undoubtedly was the first permanent Anglo-Saxon agricultural settlement in Arizona, that at Beaver Dams, now known as Littlefield, on the Virgin, founded at least as early as the fall of 1864.

The Wilderness Has Been Kept Broken

Of the permanence and quality of the Mormon pioneering, strong testimony is offered by F. S. Dellenbaugh in his "Breaking the Wilderness:"

It must be acknowledged that the Mormons were wilderness breakers of high quality. They not only broke it, but they kept it broken; and instead of the gin mill and the gambling hell, as cornerstones of their progress and as examples to the natives of the white men's superiority, they planted orchards, gardens, farms, schoolhouses and peaceful homes. There is today no part of the United States where human life is safer than in the land of the Mormons; no place where there is less lawlessness. A people who have accomplished so much that is good, who have endured danger, privation and suffering, who have withstood the obloquy of more powerful sects, have in them much that is commendable; they deserve more than abuse, they deserve admiration.

6

Chapter Two

𝕿𝖍𝖊 𝕸𝖔𝖗𝖒𝖔𝖓 𝕭𝖆𝖙𝖙𝖆𝖑𝖎𝖔𝖓

Soldiers Who Sought No Strife

The march of the Mormon Battalion to the Pacific sea in 1846-7 created one of the most picturesque features of American history and one without parallel in American military annals. There was incidental creation, through Arizona, of the first southwestern wagon road. Fully as remarkable as its travel was the constitution of the Battalion itself. It was assembled hastily for an emergency that had to do with the seizure of California from Mexico. Save for a few officers detailed from the regular army, not a man had been a soldier, unless in the rude train-bands that held annual muster in that stage of the Nation's progress, however skilled certain members might have been in the handling of hunting arms.

Organization was a matter of only a few days before the column had been put into motion toward the west. There was no drill worthy of the name. There was establishment of companies simply as administrative units. Discipline seems to have been very lax indeed, even if there were periods in which severity of undue sort appears to have been made manifest by the superior officers.

Still more remarkable, the rank and file glorified in being men of peace, to whom strife was abhorrent. They were recruited from a people who had been driven from a home of prosperity and who at the time were encamped in most temporary fashion, awaiting the word of their leaders to pass on to the promised western Land of Canaan. For a part of the way there went with the Battalion parts of families, surely a very unmilitary proceeding, but most of

7

the soldiers for the time severed all connection with their people, whom they were to join later on the shore of the Great Salt Lake of which they knew so little. They were illy clad and shod, were armed mainly with muskets of type even then obsolete, were given wagon transportation from the odds and ends of a military post equipment and thus were set forth upon their great adventure.

Formation of the Mormon Battalion came logically as a part of the determination of the Mormon people to seek a new home in the West, for in 1846 there had come conclusion that no permanent peace could be known in Illinois or in any of the nearby States, owing to religious prejudice. The High Council had made announcement of the intention of the people to move to some good valleys of the Rocky Mountains. President Jesse C. Little of the newly created Eastern States Mission of the Church, was instructed to visit Washington and to secure, if possible, governmental assistance in the western migration. One suggestion was that the Mormons be sent to construct a number of stockade posts along the overland route. But, finally, after President Little had had several conferences with President Polk, there came decision to accept enlistment of a Mormon military command, for dispatch to the Pacific Coast. The final orders cut down the enlistment from a proffered 2000 to 500 individuals.

California Was the Goal

There should be understanding at the outset that the Mormon Battalion was a part of the volunteer soldiery of the Mexican War. At the time there was a regular army of very small proportions, and that was being held for the descent upon the City of Mexico, via Vera Cruz, under General Scott. General Taylor had volunteers for the greater part of his northern army in Mexico. Doniphan in his expedition into Chihuahua mainly had Missouri volunteers.

In California was looming a very serious situation.

8

Only sailors were available to help American settlers in seizing and holding the coast against a very active and exceptionally well-provided and intelligent Mexican, or Spanish-speaking, opposition. Fremont and his "surveying party" hardly had improved the situation in bringing dissension into the American armed forces. General Kearny had been dispatched with all speed from Fort Leavenworth westward, with a small force of dragoons, later narrowly escaping disaster as he approached San Diego. There was necessity for a supporting party for Kearny and for provision of troops to enforce an American peace in California. To fill this breach, resort was had to the harassed and homeless Saints.

The route was taken along the Santa Fe trail, which then, in 1846, was in use mainly by buffalo hunters and western trading and trapping parties. It was long before the western migration of farm seekers, and the lure of gold yet was distant. There were unsatisfactory conditions of administration and travel, as narrated by historians of the command, mainly enlisted men, naturally with the viewpoint of the private soldier. But it happens that the details agree, in general, and indicate that the trip throughout was one of hardship and of denial. There came the loss of a respected commander and the temporary accession of an impolitic leader. Especially there was complaint over the mistaken zeal of an army surgeon, who insisted upon the administration of calomel and who denied the men resort to their own simple remedies, reinforced by expression of what must have been a very sustaining sort of faith.

A more popular, though strict, commander was found in Santa Fe, whence the Battalion was pushed forward again within five days, following Kearny to the Coast. The Rockies were passed through a trackless wilderness, yet on better lines than had been found by Kearny's horsemen. Arizona, as now known, was entered not far from the present city of Douglas. There were fights with wild bulls in the San Pedro valley, there was a bloodless victory in the taking of the ancient pueblo of Tucson, there was travail in the passage of the desert to the Gila and a brief respite in the plenty of the Pima villages before the weary way was taken down the Gila to the Colorado and thence across the sands of the Colorado desert, in California, to the shores of the western ocean.

All this was done on foot. The start from Leavenworth was in the heat of summer, August 12, 1846. Two months later Santa Fe was entered, Tucson was passed in December and on January 27, 1847, "was caught the first and a magnificent view of the great ocean; and by rare chance it was so calm that it shone like a great mirror."

In detail, the following description of the march, as far as Los Angeles, mainly is from the McClintock History of Arizona:

Organization of the Battalion

Col. Stephen W. Kearny, commanding the First Dragoon regiment, then stationed at Fort Leavenworth, selected Capt. James Allen of the same regiment to be commander of the new organization, with volunteer rank as lieutenant-colonel. The orders read: "You will have the Mormons distinctly understand that I wish to have them as volunteers for twelve months; that they will be marched to California, receive pay and allowances during the above time, and at its expiration they will be discharged, and allowed to retain as their private property the guns and accouterments furnished them at this post."

Captain Allen proceeded at once to Mount Pisgah, a Mormon camp 130 miles east of Council Bluffs, where, on June 26, 1846, he issued a recruiting circular in which was stated: "This gives an opportunity of sending a portion of your young and intelligent men to the ultimate destination of your whole people at the expense of the United States, and this advance party can thus pave the way and look out the land for their brethren to come after them."

10

July 16, 1846, five companies were mustered into the service of the United States at Council Bluffs, Iowa Territory. The company officers had been elected by the recruits, including Captains Jefferson Hunt, Jesse B. Hunter, James Brown and Nelson Higgins. George P. Dykes was appointed adjutant and William McIntyre assistant surgeon.

The march westward was started July 20, the route through St. Joseph and Leavenworth, where were found a number of companies of Missouri volunteers. Colonel Allen, who had secured the confidence and affection of his soldiers, had to be left, sick, at Leavenworth, where he died August 23.

At Leavenworth full equipment was secured, including flintlock muskets, with a few caplock guns for sharpshooting and hunting. Pay also was drawn, the paymaster expressing surprise over the fact that every man could write his own name, "something that only one in three of the Missouri volunteers could accomplish." August 12 and 14 two divisions of the Battalion left Leavenworth.

Cooke Succeeds to the Command

The place of Colonel Allen was taken, provisionally, by First Lieut. A. J. Smith of the First Dragoons, who proved unpopular, animus probably starting through his military severity and the desire of the Battalion that Captain Hunt should succeed to the command. The first division arrived at Santa Fe October 9, and was received by Colonel Doniphan, commander of the post, with a salute of 100 guns. Colonel Doniphan was an old friend. He had been a lawyer and militia commander in Clay County, Missouri, when Joseph Smith was tried by court martial at Far West in 1838 and had succeeded in changing a judgment of death passed by the mob. On the contrary, Col. Sterling Price, the brigade commander, was considered an active enemy of the Mormons.

At Santa Fe, Capt. P. St. George Cooke, an officer of dragoons, succeeded to the command, as lieutenant-colonel,

11

under appointment of General Kearny, who already had started westward. Capt. James Brown was ordered to take command of a party of about eighty men, together with about two-score women and children, and with them winter at Pueblo, on the headwaters of the Arkansas River. Fifty-five more men were sent to Pueblo from the Rio Grande when found unable to travel.

Colonel Cooke made a rather discouraging report on the character of the command. He said:

> It was enlisted too much by families; some were too old, some feeble, and some too young; it was embarrassed by too many women; it was undisciplined; it was much worn by travel on foot and marching from Nauvoo, Illinois; clothing was very scant; there was no money to pay them or clothing to issue; their mules were utterly broken down; the quartermaster department was without funds and its credit bad; animals scarce and inferior and deteriorating every hour for lack of forage. So every preparation must be pushed—hurried.

The March Through the Southwest

After the men had sent their pay checks back to their families, the expedition started from Santa Fe, 448 strong. It had rations for only sixty days. The commander wrote on November 19 that he was determined to take along his wagons, though the mules were nearly broken down at the outset, and added a delicate criticism of Fremont's self-centered character, "The only good mules were taken for the express for Fremont's mail, the General's order requiring the 21 best in Santa Fe."

Colonel Cooke soon proved an officer who would enforce discipline. He had secured an able quartermaster in Lieut. George Stoneman, First Dragoons. Lieutenant Smith took office as acting commissary. Three mounted dragoons were taken along, one a trumpeter. An additional mounted company of New Mexican volunteers, planned at Santa Fe, could not be raised.

Before the command got out of the Rio Grande Valley, the condition of the commissary best is to be illustrated by the following extract from verses written by Levi Hancock:

12

We sometimes now lack for bread,
Are less than quarter rations fed,
And soon expect, for all of meat,
Nought less than broke-down mules to eat.

The trip over the Continental Divide was one of hardship, at places tracks for the wagons being made by marching files of men ahead, to tramp down ruts wherein the wheels might run. The command for 48 hours at one time was without water. From the top of the Divide the wagons had to be taken down by hand, with men behind with ropes, the horses driven below.

Finally a more level country was reached, December 2, at the old, ruined ranch of San Bernardino, near the southeastern corner of the present Arizona. The principal interest of the trip, till the Mexican forces at Tucson were encountered, then lay in an attack upon the marching column by a number of wild bulls in the San Pedro Valley. It had been assumed that Cooke would follow down the San Pedro to the Gila, but, on learning that the better and shorter route was by way of Tucson, he determined upon a more southerly course.

Capture of the Pueblo of Tucson

Tucson was garrisoned by about 200 Mexican soldiers, with two small brass fieldpieces, a concentration of the garrisons of Tubac, Santa Cruz and Fronteras. After some brief parley, the Mexican commander, Captain Comaduron, refusing to surrender, left the village, compelling most of its inhabitants to accompany him. No resistance whatever was made. When the Battalion marched in, the Colonel took pains to assure the populace that all would be treated with kindness. He sent the Mexican commander a courteous letter for the Governor of Sonora, Don Manuel Gandara, who was reported "disgusted and disaffected to the imbecile central government." Little food was found for the men, but several thousand bushels of grain had been left and were drawn upon. On December 17, the day

13

after the arrival of the command, the Colonel and about fifty men "passed up a creek about five miles above Tucson toward a village (San Xavier), where they had seen a large church from the hills they had passed over." The Mexican commander reported that the Americans had taken advantage of him, in that they had entered the town on Sunday, while he and his command and most of the inhabitants were absent at San Xavier, attending mass.

The Pima villages were reached four days later. By Cooke the Indians were called "friendly, guileless and singularly innocent and cheerful people."

In view of the prosperity of the Pima and Maricopa, Colonel Cooke suggested that this would be a good place for the exiled Saints to locate, and a proposal to this effect was favorably received by the Indians. It is possible that his suggestion had something to do with the colonizing by the Mormons of the upper part of the nearby Salt River Valley in later years.

About January 1, 1847, to lighten the load of the half-starved mules, a barge was made by placing two wagon bodies on dry cottonwood logs and on this 2500 pounds of provisions and corn were launched on the Gila River. The improvised boat found too many sandbars, and most of its cargo had to be jettisoned, lost in a time when rations had been reduced to a few ounces a day per man. January 9 the Colorado River was reached, and the command and its impedimenta were ferried over on the same raft contrivance that had proven ineffective on the Gila.

Colonel Cooke, in his narrative concerning the practicability of the route he had taken, said: "Undoubtedly the fine bottomland of the Colorado, if not of the Gila, will soon be settled; then all difficulty will be removed."

The Battalion had still more woe in its passage across the desert of Southern California, where wells often had to be dug for water and where rations were at a minimum, until Warner's ranch was reached, where each man was

14

given five pounds of beef a day, constituting almost the sole article of subsistence. Tyler, the Battalion historian, insists that five pounds is really a small allowance for a healthy laboring man, because "when taken alone it is not nearly equal to mush and milk," and he referred to an issuance to each of Fremont's men of ten pounds per day of fat beef.

Congratulation on Its Achievement

At the Mission of San Diego, January 30, 1847, the proud Battalion Commander issued the following memorable order:

The Lieutenant-Colonel commanding congratulates the Battalion on their safe arrival on the shore of the Pacific Ocean, and the conclusion of their march of over 2000 miles.

History may be searched in vain for an equal march of infantry. Half of it has been through a wilderness, where nothing but savages and wild beasts are found, or deserts where, for want of water, there is no living creature. There, with almost hopeless labor we have dug wells, which the future traveler will enjoy. Without a guide who had traversed them, we have ventured into trackless tablelands where water was not found for several marches. With crowbar and pick, and ax in hand, we worked our way over mountains, which seemed to defy aught save the wild goat, and hewed a pass through a chasm of living rock more narrow than our wagons. To bring these first wagons to the Pacific, we have preserved the strength of our mules by herding them over large tracts, which you have laboriously guarded without loss. The garrisons of four presidios of Sonora concentrated within the walls of Tucson, gave us no pause. We drove them out with our artillery, but our intercourse with the citizens was unmarked by a single act of injustice. Thus, marching, half-naked and half-fed, and living upon wild animals, we have discovered and made a road of great value to our country.

Arrived at the first settlements of California, after a single day's rest, you cheerfully turned off from the route to this point of promised repose, to enter upon a campaign and meet, as we supposed, the approach of an enemy; and this, too, without even salt to season your sole subsistence of fresh meat.

Lieutenants A. J. Smith and George Stoneman of the First Dragoons have shared and given invaluable aid in all these labors.

Thus, volunteers, you have exhibited some high and essential

15

qualities of veterans. But much remains undone. Soon you will turn your attention to the drill, to system and order, to forms also, which are all necessary to the soldier.

Mapping the Way Through Arizona

The only map of the route of the Mormon Battalion is one made by Colonel Cooke. Outlined on a map of Arizona, it is printed elsewhere in this work, insofar as it affects this State. The Colonel's map is hardly satisfactory, for only at a few points does he designate locations known today and his topography covers only the district within his vision as he marched.

Judging from present information of the lay of the land, it is evident that LeRoux did not guide the Mormon Battalion on the easiest route. Possibly this was due to the fact that it was necessary to find water for each daily camp. The Rio Grande was left at a point 258 miles south of Santa Fe, not far from Mesilla. Thence the journey was generally toward the southwest, over a very rough country nearly all the way to the historic old rancho of San Bernardino, now on the international line about 25 miles east of the present city of Douglas. The rancho had been abandoned long before, because of the depredating Apaches. It was stated by Cooke that before it had been deserted, on it were 80,000 cattle, ranging as far as the Gila to the northward. The hacienda was enclosed by a wall, with two regular bastions, and there was a spring fifteen feet in diameter.

The departure from San Bernardino was on December 4, 1846, the day's march to a camp in a pass eight miles to the westward, near a rocky basin of water and beneath a peak which Nature apparently had painted green, yellow and brown. This camp was noted as less than twenty miles from Fronteras, Mexico, and near a Coyotero trail into Mexico.

On the 5th was a march of fourteen miles, to a large spring. This must have been almost south of Douglas or Agua Prieta (Blackwater).

16

On the 6th the Battalion cut its way twelve miles through mesquite to a water hole in a fine grove of oak and walnut. It is suggested by Geo. H. Kelly that this was in Anavacachi Pass, twelve miles southwest of Douglas.

On December 8 seventeen miles were made northwest, to a dry camp, with a view of the valley of the San Pedro. On the 9th, either ten or sixteen miles, for the narrative is indefinite, the San Pedro was crossed and there was camp six miles lower down on the western side. There is notation that the river was followed for 65 miles, one of the camps being at what was called the Canyon San Pedro, undoubtedly at The Narrows, just above Charleston.

December 14 there was a turn westward and at a distance of nine miles was found a direct trail to Tucson. The day's march was twenty miles, probably terminating at about Pantano, in the Cienega Wash, though this is only indicated by the map or description.

On the 15th was a twelve-mile march to a dry camp and on the 16th, after a sixteen-mile march, camp was made a half mile west of the pueblo of Tucson.

From Tucson to the Pima villages on the Gila River, a distance of about 73 miles, the way was across the desert, practically on the present line of the Southern Pacific railroad. Sixty-two miles were covered in 51 hours. At the Gila there was junction with General Kearny's route.

From the Pima villages westward there is mention of a dry "jornada" (journey) of about forty miles, caused by a great bend of the Gila River. Thus is indicated that the route was by way of Estrella Pass, south of the Sierra Estrella, on the present railroad line, and not by the alternative route, just south of and along the river and north of the mountains. Thereafter the marches averaged only ten miles a day, through much sand, as far as the Colorado, which was reached January 8, 1847.

The Battalion's route across Arizona at only one point cut a spot of future Mormon settlement. This was in the

17

San Pedro Valley, where the march of a couple of days was through a fertile section that was occupied in 1878 by a community of the faith from Lehi. This community, now known as St. David, is referred to elsewhere, at length.

Manufactures of the Arizona Indians

Colonel Cooke told that the Maricopas, near the junction of the Gila and the Salt, had piled on their house arbors "cotton in the pod for drying." As he passed in the latter days of the year, it is probable he saw merely the bolls that had been left unopened after frost had come, and that this was not the ordinary method for handling cotton. That considerable cotton was grown is evidenced by the fact that a part of Cooke's company purchased cotton blankets. Historian Tyler states that when he reached Salt Lake the most material feature of his clothing equipment was a Pima blanket, from this proceeding an inference that the Indians made cotton goods of lasting and wearing quality. In the northern part of Arizona, the Hopi also raised cotton and made cloth and blankets, down to the time of the coming of the white man, with his gaudy calicoes that undoubtedly were given prompt preference in the color-loving aboriginal eye.

Cooke's Story of the March

"The Conquest of New Mexico and California" is the title of an excellent and entertaining volume written in 1878 by Lieut.-Col. P. St. George Cooke, commander of the Battalion. It embraces much concerning the political features found or developed in both Territories and deals somewhat with the Kearny expedition and with the Doniphan campaign into Mexico that moved from Socorro two months after the Battalion started westward from the Rio Grande. Despite his eloquent acknowledgment of good service in the San Diego order, he had little to say in his narrative concerning the personnel of his command. In addition to the estimate of the command printed on a preceding page, he wrote, "The Battalion have never been drilled and though obedient, have little discipline; they exhibit great heedlessness and ignorance and some obstinacy." The ignorance undoubtedly was of military matters, for the men had rather better than the usual schooling of the rough period. At several points his diary gave such details as, "The men arrived completely worn down; they staggered as they marched, as they did yesterday. A great many of the men are wholly without shoes and use every expedient, such as rawhide moccasins and sandals and even wrapping the feet in pieces of woolen and cotton cloth."

It is evident that to the Colonel's West Point ideas of discipline the conduct of his command was a source of irritation that eventually was overcome when he found he could depend upon the individuals as well as upon the companies. Several stories are told of his encounters in repartee with his soldiers, in which he did not always have the upper hand, despite his rank. Brusque in manner, he yet had a saving sense of humor that had to be drawn upon to carry off situations that would have been intolerable in his own command of dragoons.

Tyler's Record of the Expedition

The best of the narratives concerning the march of the Battalion is in a book printed in 1881 by Daniel Tyler, an amplification of a remarkable diary kept by him while a member of the organization. This book has an exceptionally important introduction, written by John Taylor, President of the Mormon Church, detailing at length the circumstances that led to the western migration of his people. He is especially graphic in his description of the riots of the summer of 1844, culminating in the assassination of Prophet Joseph Smith and his brother Hyrum at Carthage, Illinois, on June 27th. Taylor was with the Prophet at the time and was badly wounded. There also is an interesting introductory chapter, written by Col. Thos. L. Kane, not a Mormon, dramatically dwelling upon the circumstances of the exodus from Nauvoo and the later dedication there of the beautiful temple, abandoned immediately thereafter. He wrote also of the Mormon camps that were then working westward, describing the high spirit and even cheerfulness in which the people were accepting exile from a grade of civilization that had made them prefer the wilds. Colonel Kane helped in the organization of the Battalion, in bringing influence to bear upon the President and in carrying to Fort Leavenworth the orders under which the then Colonel Kearny proceeded.

Henry Standage's Personal Journal

One of the treasures of the Arizona Historian's office is a copy of a journal of about 12,000 words kept by Henry Standage, covering his service as a member of the Mormon Battalion from July 19, 1846, to July 19, 1847. The writer in his later years was a resident of Mesa, his home in Alma Ward. His manuscript descended to his grandsons, Orrin and Clarence Standage.

Standage writes from the standpoint of the private soldier, with the soldier's usual little growl over conditions that affect his comfort; yet, throughout the narrative, there is evidence of strong integrity of purpose, of religious feeling and of sturdiness befitting a good soldier.

There is pathos in the very start, how he departed from the Camp of Israel, near Council Bluffs, leaving his wife and mother in tears. He had been convinced by T. B. Platt of the necessity of obedience to the call of the President of the United States to enlist in the federal service. The narrative contradicts in no way the more extensive chronicle by Tyler. There is description of troubles that early beset the inexperienced soldiers, who appear to have been illy prepared to withstand the inclemency of the weather. There was sage dissertation concerning the efforts of an army surgeon to use calomel, though the men preferred the exercise of faith. Buffalo was declared the best meat he had ever eaten.

On November 1 satisfaction was expressed concerning

the resignation of Geo. P. Dykes as adjutant and over substitution to the place of Philemon C. Merrill. When the sick were sent to Pueblo, November 10, Standage fervently wrote, "This does in reality make solemn times for us, so many divisions taking place. May the God of Heaven protect us all."

San Bernardino, in Sonora, was reached December 2, being found in ruins, "though all around us a pleasant valley with good water and grass." Appreciation was expressed over the flavor of "a kind of root, baked, which the Spaniards called mas kurl" (mescal). Many of the cattle had Spanish brands on their hips, it being explained, "Indians had been so troublesome in times past that the Spaniards had to abandon the towns and vineyards, and cross the Cordillera Mountains, leaving their large flocks of cattle in the valley, thus making plenty of food for the Apalchas."

In San Pedro valley were found "good horse feed and fish in abundance (salmon trout), large herds of wild cattle and plenty of antelope and some bear." The San Pedro River was especially noted as having "mill privileges in abundance." Here it was that Lieutenant Stoneman, accidentally shot himself in the hand. Two old deserted towns were passed.

Standage tells that the Spanish soldiers had gone from Tucson when the Battalion arrived, but that, "we were kindly treated by the people, who brought flour, meal, tobacco and quinces to the camp for sale, and many of them gave such things to the soldiers. We camped about a half mile from the town. The Colonel suffered no private property to be touched, neither was it in the heart of any man to my knowledge to do so."

Considering the strength of the Spanish garrison, Standage was led to exclaim that, "the Lord God of Israel would save his people, inasmuch as he knoweth the causes of our being here in the United States." Possibly it was unfair to

21

say that no one but the Lord knew why the soldiers were there, and Tucson then was not in the United States.

The journey to the Gila River was a hard one, but the chronicler was compensated by seeing "the long looked-for country of California," which it was not. The Pimas were found very friendly, bringing food, which they readily exchanged for such things as old shirts. Standage especially was impressed by the eating of a watermelon, for the day was Christmas. January 10, 1847, at the crossing of the Colorado, he was detailed to the gathering of mesquite beans, "a kind of sweet seed that grows on a tree resembling the honey locust, the mules and men being very fond of this. The brethren use this in various ways, some grinding it and mixing it in bread with the flour, others making pudding, while some roast it or eat it raw." "January 27, at 1 o'clock, we came in sight of the ocean, the great Pacific, which was a great sight to some, having never seen any portion of the briny deep before."

California Towns and Soldier Experiences

At San Diego, which was reached by Standage and a small detachment January 30, provisions were found very scarce, while prices were exorbitant. Sugar cost 50 cents a pound, so the soldier regaled himself with one-quarter of a pound and gathered some mustard greens to eke out his diet. For 26 days he had eaten almost nothing but beef. He purchased a little wheat from the Indians and ground it in a hand mill, to make some cakes, which were a treat.

Late in April, at Los Angeles, there was a move to another camping ground, "as the Missouri volunteers (Error, New York volunteers—Author) had threatened to come down upon us. A few days later we were called up at night in order to load and fix bayonets, as Colonel Cooke had sent word that an attack might be expected from Colonel Fremont's men before day. They had been using all possible means to prejudice the Spaniards and Indians against us."

22

Los Angeles made poor impression upon the soldiers in the Battalion. The inhabitants were called "degraded" and it was declared that there were almost as many grog shops and gambling dens as private houses. Reference is made to the roofs of reeds, covered with pitch from tar springs nearby. Incidentally, these tar "springs" in a later century led to development of the oil industry, that now is paramount in much of California, and have been found to contain fossil remains of wonderful sort.

The Indians were said "to do all the labor, the Mexicans generally on horseback from morning till night. They are perhaps the greatest horsemen in the known world and very expert with lariat and lasso, but great gamblers."

Food assuredly was not dear, for cattle sold for $5 a head. Many cattle were killed merely for hides and tallow and for the making of soap.

About the most entertaining section of Standage's journal is that which chronicles his stay in Southern California, possibly because it gave him an opportunity to do something else beside tramping. There is much detail concerning re-enlistment, but there was general inclination to follow the advice of Father Pettegrew, who showed "the necessity of returning to the prophets of the Lord before going any further."

Just before the muster-out, the soldiers were given an opportunity to witness a real Spanish bull fight, called "a scene of cruelty, savoring strongly of barbarity and indolence, though General Pico, an old Mexican commander, went into the ring several times on horseback and fought the bulls with a short spear."

What with the hostility of the eastern volunteers, the downright enmity of Fremont's company and the alien habits of the Mexican population, the sober-minded members of the Battalion must have been compelled to keep their own society very largely while in the pueblo of Los Angeles, or, to give it its Spanish appellation, "El Pueblo

de Nuestra Senora la Reina de los Angeles de Porciuncula."
Still, some of them tried to join in the diversions of the
people of the country. On one occasion, according to Historian Eldridge, there was something of a quarrel between
Captain Hunt and Alcalde Carrillo, who had given offense
by observing that the American officer "danced like a
bear." The Alcalde apologized very courteously, saying
that bears were widely known as dancers, but the breach
was not healed.

Christopher Layton's Soldiering.

Another history of the Battalion especially interesting
from an Arizona standpoint, is contained in the life of
Christopher Layton, issued in 1911 and written by Layton's
daughter, Mrs. Selina Layton Phillips, from data supplied
by the Patriarch. The narrative is one of the best at hand
in the way of literary preparation, though with frank
statement that President Layton himself had all too little
education for the accomplishment of such a task.

Layton was a private soldier in Company C, under
Capt. James Brown. There is nothing of especial novelty in
the narrative, nor does there seem anything of prophecy
when the Battalion passed through the Valley of the San
Pedro in December, 1846, through a district to which
Layton was to return, in 1883, as leader of a Mormon
colony.

Layton was one of the number that remained in California after the discharge of the Battalion, eventually
rejoining the Saints, at Salt Lake, by way of his native
land, England.

In B. H. Roberts' very interesting little work on the
Mormon Battalion is told this story of the later patriarch
of the Gila settlement:

While Colonel Cooke was overseeing the ferrying of the Battalion
across the Colorado River, Christopher Layton rode up to the river
on a mule, to let it drink. Colonel Cooke said to him, "Young man, I
want you to ride across the river and carry a message for me to Cap-

24

MORMON BATTALION OFFICERS

1—P. St. George Cooke, Lieut. Col. Commanding
2—Lieut. George P. Dykes, Adjutant, succeeded by
3—Lieut. Philemon C. Merrill, Adjutant

BATTALION MEMBERS AT GOLD DISCOVERY

Above—Henry W. Bigler   Azariah Smith
Below—Wm. J. Johnston   **James S. Brown**

BATTALION MEMBERS WHO RETURNED TO ARIZONA

1—Sergt. Nathaniel V. Jones
2—Wm. C. McClellan
3—Sanford Porter
4—Lot Smith
5—John Hunt

6—Wilson D. Pace
7—Samuel Lewis
8—Wesley Adair
9—Lieut. James Pace
10—Christopher Layton

tain Hunt." It being natural for the men to obey the Colonel's order, he (Layton) tried to ride into the river, but he had gone but a few steps before his mule was going in all over. So Brother Layton stopped. The Colonel hallooed out, "Go on, young man; go on, young man." But Brother Layton, on a moment's reflection, was satisfied that, if he attempted it, both he and his mule would stand a good chance to be drowned. The Colonel himself was satisfied of the same. So Brother Layton turned his mule and rode off, saying, as he came out, "Colonel, I'll see you in hell before I will drown myself and mule in that river." The Colonel looked at him a moment, and said to the bystanders, "What is that man's name?" "Christopher Layton, sir." "Well, he is a saucy fellow."

That the Mormon Battalion did not always rigidly obey orders is shown in another story detailed by Roberts:

While the Battalion was at Santa Fe, Colonel Cooke ordered Lot Smith to guard a Mexican corral, and, having a company of United States cavalry camped by, he told Lot if the men came to steal the poles to bayonet them. The men came and surrounded the corral, and while Lot was guarding one side, they would hitch to a pole on the other end off with it. When the Colonel saw the poles were gone, he asked Lot why he did not obey orders and bayonet the thieves. Lot replied, "If you expect me to bayonet United States troops for taking a pole on the enemy's ground to make a fire of, you mistake your man." Lot expected to be punished, and he was placed under guard; but nothing further was done about it.

Western Dash of the Kearny Dragoons

Of collateral interest is the record of the Kearny expedition. The Colonel, raised to General at Santa Fe, left that point September 25, 1846, with 300 dragoons, under Col. E. V. Sumner. The historians of the party were Lieut. W. H. Emory of the Corps of Topographical Engineers (later in charge of the Boundary Survey) and Capt. A. R. Johnston, the latter killed at San Pascual. Kearny was piloted by the noted Kit Carson, who was turned back as he was traveling eastward with dispatches from Fremont. The Gila route was taken, though there had to be a detour at the box canyon above the mouth of the San Pedro. Emory and Johnston wrote much of the friendly Pima. The former made prophecy, since sustained, concerning the development of the Salt and other river valleys, and the working of great copper deposits noted by him on the Gila, at Mineral Creek. The Colorado was crossed November 24. On December 6 the small command, weary with its march and illy provisioned, was attacked at San Pascual by Gen. Andres Pico. Two days of fighting found the Americans in sad plight, with eighteen killed and thirteen wounded. The enemy had been severely handled, but still barred the way to the nearby seacoast. Guide Kit Carson and Naval Lieutenant E. F. Beale managed to slip through to San Diego, there to summon help. It came to the beleaguered Americans December 10, a party of 180 well-armed sailors and marines, sent by Commodore Stockton, falling upon the rear of the Mexican host, which dispersed. The following day, Kearny entered San Diego, thence proceeding northward to help in the final overthrow of Mexican authority within Alta California.

Chapter Three

The Battalion's Muster-Out

Heading Eastward Toward "Home"

Muster-out of the Battalion was at Los Angeles, July 16, 1847, just a year after enlistment, eight days before Brigham Young reached Great Salt Lake. The joyous ceremonial was rather marred by the fact that the muster-out officer was none other than Lieutenant Smith. There was an attempt to keep the entire Battalion in the service, both Kearny and Colonel Mason urging reenlistment. At the same time was an impolitic speech by Colonel Stevenson of the New York Volunteers. He said: "Your patriotism and obedience to your officers have done much toward removing the prejudices of the Government and the community at large, and I am satisfied that another year's service would place you on a level with other communities." This speech hardly helped in inclining the men toward extension of a service in which it was felt all that had been required had been delivered. Stevenson, a politician rather than a soldier, seemed to have a theory that the Mormons were seeking reenlistment of a second battalion or regiment, that California might be peopled by themselves. There was opposition to reenlistment among the elders, especially voiced by "Father" Pettegrew and by members Hyde and Tyler. Even promise that independent command would be given to Captain Hunt did not prove effective. Only one company was formed of men who were willing to remain in California for a while longer. In this new company were Henry G. Boyle, Henry Brizzee, Lot Smith and George Steele, all later residents of Arizona.

27

Most of the soldiers of the Battalion made haste in preparation to rejoin the main body of the people of their faith. Assuredly they had little knowledge of what was happening in the Rocky Mountains. On the 20th of July, four days before the Mormon arrival in the Salt Lake Valley, most of the men had been organized to travel "home" after what Tyler called "both the ancient and the modern Israelitish custom, in companies of hundreds, fifties and tens." The leaders were Andrew Lytle and James Pace, with Sergeants Hyde, Tyler and Reddick N. Allred as captains of fifties.

The first intention to travel via Cajon Pass was abandoned, and the companies took the northern route, via Sutter's Fort on the Sacramento River, to follow Fremont's trail across the Sierras. On the Sacramento they received the first news of their brethren since leaving Fort Leavenworth, a year before. They learned that the Saints were settling the Great Salt Lake Valley, and there also was news of the Brannan party at San Francisco.

With full assent from the leaders, some of the brethren remained in the vicinity of Sutter's Fort, where work was plenty, and probably half of those who went on across the mountains returned on receipt of advices that came to them at Donner Lake, at the hands of Capt. James Brown, of the Pueblo detachment. The Church authorities instructed all who had insufficient means to remain in California and labor and to bring their earnings with them in the spring. Tyler, with his party, arrived in Salt Lake Valley October 16, to find his relatives living in a fort, which had all rooms opening into an enclosure, with portholes for defense cut in the outer walls.

The new company, with additional enlistment of six months, was placed under Capt. Daniel C. Davis, who had been in command of Company E. The company was marched to San Diego, arriving August 2. A detachment under Lieut. Ruel Barrus garrisoned San Luis Rey. In

San Diego the men appeared to have had little military duty. They were allowed to work as mechanics, repaired wagons, did blacksmithing and erected a bakery. They became very popular with the townspeople, who wanted to retain them as permanent residents. It was noted that the Mormons had conquered prejudice and had effected a kind of industrial revolution in languid Alta California.

The enlistment term expired in January, but it was March, 1848, before the men were paid off and discharged. Most of the 78 members of the company went northward, but one party of 22, led by Henry G. Boyle, taking a wagon and 135 mules, started to Salt Lake by way of the Mojave desert, reaching its destination June 5. This would appear to have been a very important journey, the party probably being first with wagons to travel what later became known as the Mormon road.

Following the very practical customs of their people, the members of the Battalion picked up in California a large quantity of seeds and grains for replanting in Utah, welcomed in establishing the marvelous agricultural community there developed. Lieut. James Pace brought in the club-head wheat, which proved especially suited to inter-mountain climatic conditions. From Pueblo other members brought the Taos wheat, which also proved valuable. Daniel Tyler brought the California pea.

Although the Author has seen little mention of it, the Battalion membership took to Utah much valuable information concerning methods of irrigation, gained at Pueblo, in the Rio Grande Valley and in California. While most of the emigrants were of the farming class, their experience had been wholly in the Mississippi Valley or farther east, where the rains alone were depended upon to furnish the moisture necessary for crops.

With the Pueblo Detachment

Capt. James Brown would have led his band from Pueblo as soon as the snows had melted in the passes, but held back on receipt of information that the main body of Saints still was on the plains. As it was, he and his charge arrived at Salt Lake, July 29, 1847, five days after the advent of Brigham Young. Brown remained only a few days, setting out early in August for California, there to receive the pay of his command. The main body had been paid off at Los Angeles, July 15. On his westward way, Brown led a small company over the Carson route. In the Sierras, September 6, he met the first returning detachment of Battalion soldiers. To them he delivered letters from the First Presidency telling of the scarcity of food in the Salt Lake Valley. Sam Brannan, leader at San Francisco, had passed, going westward, only the day before, giving a gloomy account of the new home of the Saints. So about half the Battalion men turned back to Sutter's Fort, presumably with Brown. Brown returned from Los Angeles with the pay of his men, money sorely needed.

The Pueblo detachment arrived in Salt Lake with about fifty individuals from Mississippi added to the 150 men and women who had been separated from the main body of the Battalion in New Mexico. Forty-six of the Battalion men accompanied President Young when he started back, August 8, for Winter Quarters, on the west side of the Missouri, five miles above Omaha, to help in piloting over the plains the main body of Saints.

Captain Brown, according to a Brigham Young manuscript, was absent in California three months and seven days, returning late in November, 1847, bringing back with him the pay due the Pueblo contingent. Several stories were given concerning the amount. One was that it was about $5000, mainly in gold, and another that the amount was $10,000 in Mexican doubloons.

The Pueblo detachment had been paid last in Santa Fe in May, 1846. The muster-out rolls were taken by Brown to Paymaster Rich of Colonel Mason's command in California. Pay included July 29, 1847, thirteen days after expiration of the term of enlistment.

A part of the money, apparently considered as community property, was used early in 1848 in the purchase of a tract of land, about twenty miles square, at the mouth of Weber Canyon. The sum of $1950, cash, was paid to one Goodyear, who claimed to own a Mexican grant, but who afterward proved to have only a squatter right. The present city of Ogden is on this same tract.

California Comments on the Battalion

Very generally there has come down evidence that the men of the Battalion were of very decent sort. Colonel Mason, commanding the California military department, in June, 1847, made report to the Adjutant General of the Army:

Of the service of this Battalion, of their patience, subordination and general good conduct you have already heard; and I take great pleasure in adding that as a body of men they have religiously respected the rights and feelings of these conquered people, and not a syllable of complaint has reached my ears of a single insult offered or outrage done by a Mormon volunteer. So high an opinion did I entertain of the Battalion and of their especial fitness for the duties now performed by the garrisons in this country that I made strenuous efforts to engage their services for another year.

With reference to the Mormon Battalion, Father Engelhardt, in his "Missions and Missionaries of California," wrote:

It is not likely that these Mormons, independent of United States and military regulations, would have wantonly destroyed any part of the church property or church fixtures during their several months' stay at San Luis Rey. Whatever some of the moral tenets held by them in those days, the Mormons, to all appearances, were a God-fearing body, who, ... manifested some respect for the religious convictions and feelings of other men, notably of the Catholics. It is, therefore, highly improbable that they . . . raved against . . . religious emblems found in the missions of California. On the contrary, they appear to have let everything alone, even made repairs, and minded their own duties to their Creator, in that they practiced their religion openly whithersoever they went . . . .

Colonel Cooke for a while was in command of the southern half of Alta California, incidentally coming into a part of the row created when Fremont laid claim upon the governorship of the Territory. In this his men were affected to a degree, for Fremont's father-in-law and patron, Senator Benton, was believed one of the bitterest foes of the Mormon people.

Cooke resigned as lieutenant-colonel of volunteers, effective May 13, 1847, he thus leaving the Battalion before the date of its discharge. He accompanied General Kearny on an 83-day ride eastward, returning to Fort Leavenworth August 22. With them was Fremont, arrested, charged with mutiny in refusing to acknowledge the authority of Kearny in California. He was found guilty, but a sentence of dismissal from the army was remitted by President Polk. Fremont immediately resigned from the service.

Cooke, in 1857-8, led the cavalry of Gen. Albert Sidney Johnston's expedition to Utah and there is a memorandum that, when his regiment marched through the streets of Salt Lake City, the Colonel rode with uncovered head, "out of respect to the brave men of the Mormon Battalion he had commanded in their march to the Pacific." In the Civil War he was a brigadier-general, with brevet of major-general in 1865.

Lieut. A. J. Smith, whose disciplinary ideas may have been too severe for a command that started with such small idea of discipline, nevertheless proved a brave and skillful officer. He rose in 1864 to be major-general of volunteers and was brevetted major-general of regulars for distinguished service in command of the Sixteenth army corps, under General Thomas, at the battle of Nashville.

Lieut. George Stoneman in 1854 commanded a dragoon escort for Lieut. J. G. Parke, who laid out a railroad route across Arizona, from the Pima villages through Tucson, much on the line of the present Southern Pacific. He was a captain, commanding Fort Brown, Texas, at the outbreak of the Civil War, in which he rose to the rank of major-general of volunteers, with fame in the Virginia campaign as chief of cavalry of the Army of the Potomac, in which he later was a division and corps commander. In 1870 and 1871 he commanded the military department of Arizona, during the time of the Old Fort Grant massacre, and his name is still borne by the Stoneman Grade, above Silver King, a trail built by him to better command the Indian-infested mountains beyond. He was Democratic Governor of California from 1883 to 1887. A son, Geo. J. Stoneman, for years resided in Phoenix.

Lieut. Edw. F. Beale, who helped save the Kearny expedition near San Diego was a member of a party that had been sent from San Diego to meet the dragoons. The following March, he and Carson carried dispatches east, taking the Gila route. In August, 1848, again in California, he was made the naval messenger to advise Washington of the discovery of gold in California. In 1857 he made a remarkable survey of the 35th parallel across Arizona, using camels, and he repeated the trip in 1859.

The camels had been brought from Syria. They carried three times a mule load and were declared ideal for pioneer transportation uses. But Beale was alone in their praise and the camels eventually were turned loose on the plains. He was minister to Austria in 1878.

Both adjutants of the Mormon Battalion later became permanent residents of Arizona. Geo. P. Dykes for years was a resident of Mesa, where he died in 1888, at the age of 83. Philemon C. Merrill, in 1881, was one of the custodians of the Utah stone, sent from Salt Lake, for insertion in the Washington Monument, in Washington. He and his family constituted the larger part of the D. W. Jones party that founded Lehi in March, 1877, and it was he, who, soon thereafter, led in the settlement of St.

David in the San Pedro Valley, on the route of the Mormon Battalion march. He died at San Jose, in the Gila Valley, September 15, 1904.

Pauline Weaver, the principal guide, was a Frenchman, who had been in the Southwest at least since 1832, when he visited the Pima villages and Casa Grande. In 1862, while trapping, he was one of the discoverers of the La Paz gold diggings. The following year he was with the Peeples party that found gold on Rich Hill, in central Arizona. Thereafter he was an army scout. He died at Camp Verde in 1866.

Antoine LeRoux, the other guide named, was with the Whipple expedition across northern Arizona in 1853. His name is borne by LeRoux Springs, northwest of Flagstaff, and by LeRoux Wash, near Holbrook.

Passing of the Battalion Membership

No member of the Mormon Battalion now is living. The last to pass was Harley Mowrey, private Co. C, who died in his home in Vernal, Utah, October 21, 1920, at the age of 98. He was one of the men sent from New Mexico to Pueblo and who arrived at Salt Lake a few days after the Pioneers. On the way to Salt Lake he married the widow of another Battalion member, Martha Jane Sharp, who survives, as well as seven children, 41 grandchildren, 94 great-grandchildren and thirty of the latest generation. Mowrey and wife were members of the San Bernardino colony.

A Memorial of Noble Conception

On the Capitol grounds at Salt Lake soon is to arise a noble memorial of the service of the Mormon Battalion. The legislature of Utah has voted toward the purpose $100,000, contingent upon the contribution of a similar sum at large. A State Monument Commission has been created, headed by B. H. Roberts, and this organization has been extended to all parts of Utah, Idaho and Arizona.

In the 1921 session of the Arizona Legislature was voted

a contribution to the Battalion Monument Fund of $2500, this with expression of State pride in the achievement that meant so much to the Southwest and Pacific Coast.

From nineteen designs submitted have been selected the plans of G. P. Riswold. A condensed description of the monument is contained in a report of the Commission:

The base is in triangular form, with concave sides and rounded corners. A bronze figure of a Battalion man is mounted upon the front corner. Flanking him on two sides of the triangle are: cut in high relief, on the left, the scene of the enlistment of the Battalion under the flag of the United States of America; on the right a scene of the march, where the men are assisting in pulling the wagons of their train up and over a precipitous ascent, while still others are ahead, widening a cut to permit the passage of the wagons between the outjutting rocks. The background is a representation of mountains of the character through which the Battalion and its train passed on its journey to the Pacific.

Just below the peak, in the center and in front of it, is chiseled a beautiful head and upper part of a woman, symbolizing the "Spirit of the West." She personifies the impulsive power and motive force that sustained these Battalion men, and led them, as a vanguard of civilization, across the trackless plains and through the difficult defiles and passes of the mountains. The idea of the sculptor in the "Spirit of the West" is a magnificent conception and should dominate the whole monument.

The bronze figure of the Battalion man is dignified, strong and reverential. He excellently typifies that band of pioneer soldiers which broke a way through the rugged mountains and over trackless wastes.

Hovering over and above him, the beautiful female figure, with an air of solicitous care, guards him in his reverie. Her face stands out in full relief, the hair and diaphanous drapery waft back, mingling with the clouds, while the figure fades into dim outline in the massive peaks and mountains, seeming to pervade the air and the soil with her very soul.

Battalion Men Who Became Arizonans

Of the Battalion members, 33 are known to have become later residents of Arizona, with addition of one of the women who had accompanied the Battalion to Santa Fe and who had wintered at Pueblo. There is gratification over the fact that it has been found possible to secure photographs of nearly all the 33. Reproduction of these photographs accompanies this chapter. When this work was begun, only about ten Battalion members could be located as having been resident in this State. Some of those who came back to Arizona were notable in their day, for all of them now have made the last march of humanity.

Jas. S. Brown, who helped find gold in California, was an early Indian missionary on the Muddy and in northeastern Arizona. Edward Bunker founded Bunkerville, a Virgin River settlement, and later died on the San Pedro, at St. David. Geo. P. Dykes, who was the first adjutant of the Battalion, did service for his Church in 1849 and 1850 in Great Britain and Denmark. Philemon C. Merrill, who succeeded Dykes as adjutant, was one of the most prominent of the pioneers of the San Pedro and Gila valleys. There is special mention, elsewhere, of Christopher Layton. In the same district, at Thatcher, lived and died Lieut. James Pace. Henry Standage was one of the first settlers of Alma Ward, near Mesa. Lot Smith, one of the vanguard in missionary work in northeastern Arizona and a leader in the settlement of the Little Colorado Valley, was slain by one of the Indians to whose service he had dedicated himself. Henry W. Brizzee was a leading pioneer of Mesa. Henry G. Boyle became the first president of the Southern States mission of his church, and was so impressed with the view he had of Arizona, in Battalion days, that, early in 1877, he sent into eastern Arizona a party of Arkansas immigrants. Adair, in southern Navajo County, was named after a Battalion member.

A complete list of Arizona Battalion members follows:

Wesley Adair, Co. C.—Showlow.
Rufus C. Allen, Co. A.—Las Vegas.
Reuben W. Allred, Co. A.—Pima.
Mrs. Elzada Ford Allred—Accompanied husband.
Henry G. Boyle, Co. C.—Pima.
Henry W. Brizzee, Co. D.—Mesa.

THE MORMON BATTALION MONUMENT

Proposed to be erected at a cost of $200,000 on the Utah State Capitol
Grounds.

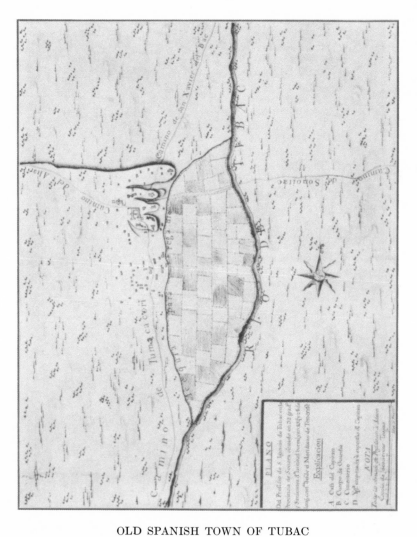

OLD SPANISH TOWN OF TUBAC

Map made 1754. Where a Mormon Colony located in the fall of 1851;
42 miles south of Tucson.

James S. Brown, Co. D.—Moen Copie.
Edward Bunker, Co. E.—St. David.
George P. Dykes, Co. D.—Mesa.
Wm. A. Follett, Co. E.—Near Showlow.
Schuyler Hulett, Co. A.—Phoenix.
John Hunt—Snowflake—Accompanied his father, Capt.
    Jefferson Hunt.
Marshall (Martial) Hunt, Co. A.—Snowflake.
Wm. J. Johnston, Co. C.—Mesa.
Nathaniel V. Jones, Co. D.—Las Vegas.
Hyrum Judd, Co. E.—Sunset and Pima.
Zadok Judd, Co. E.—Fredonia.
Christopher Layton, Co. C.—Thatcher.
Samuel Lewis, Co. C.—Thatcher.
Wm. B. Maxwell, Co. D.—Springerville.
Wm. C. McClellan, Co. E.—Sunset.
Philemon C. Merrill, Co. B.—Pima.
James Pace, Co. E.—Thatcher.
Wilson D. Pace, Co. E.—Thatcher.
Sanford Porter, Co. E.—Sunset.
Wm. C. Prous (Prows), Co. B.—Mesa.
David Pulsipher, Co. C.—Concho.
Samuel H. Rogers, Co. B.—Snowflake.
Henry Standage, Co. E.—Mesa.
George E. Steele, Co. A.—Mesa.
John Steele, Co. D.—Moen Copie.
Lot Smith, Co. E.—Sunset and Tuba.
Samuel Thompson, Co. C.—Mesa.

Chapter Four

California's Mormon Pilgrims

The Brooklyn Party at San Francisco

The members of the Mormon Battalion were far from being the first of their faith to tread the golden sands of California. Somehow, in the divine ordering of things mundane, the Mormons generally were very near the van of Anglo-Saxon settlement of the States west of the Rockies. Thus it happened that on July 29, 1846, only three weeks after the American naval occupation of the harbor, there anchored inside the Golden Gate the good ship Brooklyn, that had brought from New York 238 passengers, mainly Saints, the first American contribution of material size to the population of the embarcadero of Yerba Buena, where now is the lower business section of the stately city of San Francisco.

The Brooklyn, of 450 tons burden, had sailed from New York February 4, 1846, the date happening to be the same as that on which began the exodus from Nauvoo westward. The voyage was an authorized expedition, counseled by President Brigham Young and his advisers in the early winter. At one time it was expected that thousands would take the water route to the west shore, on their way to the Promised Land. Elder Samuel Brannan was in charge of the first company, which mainly consisted of American farmer folk from the eastern and middle-western States. The ship had been chartered for $1200 a month and port charges. Fare had been set at $50 for all above fourteen years and half-fare for children above five. Addition was made of $25 for provisions. The passengers embraced

38

seventy men, 68 women and about 100 children. There was a freight of farming implements and tools, seeds, a printing press, many school books, etc.

The voyage appears to have been even a pleasant one, though with a few notations of sickness, deaths and births and of trials that set a small number of the passengers aside from the Church. Around Cape Horn and as far as the Robinson Crusoe island of Juan Fernandez, off the Chilian coast, the seas were calm. Thereafter were two storms of serious sort, but without phase of disaster to the pilgrims. The next stop was at Honolulu, on the Hawaiian Islands, thence the course being fair for the Golden Gate.

When Captain Richardson dropped his anchors in the cove of Yerba Buena it appears to have been the first time that the emigrants appreciated they had arrived at anything save a colony of old Mexico. But when a naval officer boarded the ship and advised the passengers they were in the United States, "there arose a hearty cheer," though Brannan has been quoted as hardly pleased over the sight of the Stars and Stripes.

Beginnings of a Great City

As written by Augusta Joyce Cocheron, one of the emigrants:

They crowded upon the deck, women and children, questioning husbands and fathers, and studied the picture before them—they would never see it just the same again—as the foggy curtains furled towards the azure ceiling. How it imprinted itself upon their minds! A long sandy beach strewn with hides and skeletons of slaughtered cattle, a few scrubby oaks, farther back low sand hills rising behind each other as a background to a few old shanties that leaned away from the wind, an old adobe barracks, a few donkeys plodding dejectedly along beneath towering bundles of wood, a few loungers stretched lazily upon the beach as though nothing could astonish them; and between the picture and the emigrants still loomed up here and there, at the first sight more distinctly, the black vessels—whaling ships and sloops of war—that was all, and that was Yerba Buena, now San Francisco, the landing place for the pilgrims of faith.

In John P. Young's "Journalism in California" is recited:

39

It is not without significance that the awakening of Yerba Buena did not occur till the advent of the printing press. From the day when Leese built his store in 1836 till the arrival of the Mormon colony on July 31, 1846, the village retained all the peculiarities of a poverty-stricken settlement of the Spanish-American type. From that time forward changes began to occur indicative of advancement and it is impossible to disassociate them from the fact that a part of the Brooklyn's cargo was a press and a font of type, and that the 238 colonists aboard that vessel and others who found their way to the little town, brought with them books—more, one careful writer tells us, than could be found at the time in all the rest of the Territory put together.

Brannan and his California Star had a part in the very naming of San Francisco. This occurred January 30, 1847, rather hurried by discovery of the fact that a rival settlement on the upper bay proposed to take the name. So there was formal announcement in the Star that, from that date forward, there would be abandonment of the name Yerba Buena, as local and appertaining only to the cove, and adoption of the name of San Francisco. This announcement was signed by the Alcalde, Lieut. Washington A. Bartlett, who had been detached by Capt. J. B. Montgomery from the man-of-war Portsmouth on September 15, 1846, and who rejoined his ship the following February.

One of the Brooklyn's passengers in later years became a leader in the settlement of Mesa, Arizona. He was Geo. W. Sirrine, a millwright, whose history has been preserved by a son, Warren L. Sirrine of Mesa. The elder Sirrine was married on the ship, of which and its voyage he left many interesting tales, one being of a drift to the southward on beating around Cape Horn, till icebergs loomed and the men had to be detailed to the task of beating the rigging with clubs to rid it of ice. When danger threatened there was resort to prayer, but work soon followed as the passengers bore a hand with the crew.

Sirrine, who had had police experience in the East, was of large assistance to Brannan in San Francisco, where the rougher element for a time seized control, taking property at will and shooting down all who might disagree with their sway. It was he who arrested Jack Powers, leader of the outlaws, in a meeting that was being addressed by Brannan, and who helped in the provision of evidence under which the naval authorities eliminated over fifty of the desperados, some of them shipping on the war vessels in port. Some of the Mormons still had a part of their passage money unpaid and these promptly proceeded to find employment to satisfy their debt. The pilgrims' loyalty appears to have been of the highest. They had purchased arms in Honolulu and had had some drill on the passage thence. At least on one occasion, they rallied in San Francisco when alarm sounded that hostile Mexicans might attack.

According to Eldridge, historian of San Francisco:

The landing of the Mormons more than doubled the population of Yerba Buena. They camped for a time on the beach and the vacant lots, then some went to the Marin forests to work as lumbermen, some were housed in the old Mission buildings and others in Richardson's Casa Grande (big house) on Dupont Street. They were honest and industrious people and all sought work wherever they could find it.

Brannan's Hope of Pacific Empire

A party of twenty pioneers was sent over to the San Joaquin Valley, to found the settlement of New Hope, or Stanislaus City, on the lower Stanislaus River, but the greater number for a while remained on the bay, making San Francisco, according to Bancroft, "for a time very largely a Mormon town. All bear witness to the orderly and moral conduct of the Saints, both on land and sea. They were honest and industrious citizens, even if clannish and peculiar." There was some complaint against Brannan, charged with working the Church membership for his own personal benefit.

New Hope had development that comprised a log house, a sawmill and the cultivation of eighty acres of land. It was abandoned in the fall, after word had been received that the main body of the Saints, traveling overland, would settle in the valley of the Great Salt Lake. Brannan pushed with vigor his idea that the proper location would be in California. He started eastward to present this argument and met the western migration at Green River in July, and unsuccessfully argued with Brigham Young, returning with the vanguard as far as Salt Lake. His return to San Francisco was in September, on his way there being encounter with several parties from the Mormon Battalion, to them Brannan communicating rather gloomy ideas concerning the new site of Zion.

It is one of the many remarkable evidences of the strength of the Mormon religious spirit that only 45 adults of the Brooklyn party, with their children, remained in California, even after the discovery of gold. The others made their way across the Sierra Nevadas and the deserts, to join their people in the intermountain valley. A few were cut off from the Church. These included Brannan, who gathered large wealth, but who died, poor, in Mexico, in 1889.

There might be speculation over what would have been the fate of the Mormon Church had Brannan's idea prevailed and the tide of the Nauvoo exodus continued to California. Probably the individual pilgrims thereby might have amassed worldly wealth. Possibly there might have been established in the California valleys even richer Mormon settlements than those that now dot the map of the intermountain region. But that such a course would have been relatively disruptive of the basic plans of the leaders there can be no doubt, and it is also without doubt that under a condition of greater material wealth there would have been diminished spiritual interest.

Possibly even better was the grasp upon the people shown in Utah at the time of the passage of the California emigrants, in trains of hypnotized groups all crazed by lust for the gold assumed to be in California for the gathering. The Mormons sold them provisions and helped them on their way, yet added few to their numbers.

In after years, President Lorenzo Snow, referring to

the Brannan effort, stated his belief that it would have been nothing short of disastrous to the Church had the people gone to California before they had become grounded in the faith. They needed just the experiences they had had in the valley of Salt Lake, where home-making was the predominant thought and where wealth later came on a more permanent basis.

Present at the Discovery of Gold

By a remarkable freak of fortune, about forty of the members of the Mormon Battalion discharged at Los Angeles, were on hand at the time of the discovery of gold in California. Divided into companies, they had made their way northward, expecting to pass the Sierras before the coming of snow. They found work at Sutter's Fort and nearby in the building of a sawmill and a grist-mill and six of them (out of nine employees) actually participated in the historic picking up of chunks of gold from the tail-race they had dug under the direction of J. W. Marshall. Sutter in after years wrote: "The Mormons did not leave my mill unfinished, but they got the gold fever like everybody else." They mined especially on what, to this day, is known as Mormon Island, on the American River, and undoubtedly the wealth they later took across the mountains did much toward laying a substantial foundation for the Zion established in the wilderness.

Henry W. Bigler, of the gold discovery party, kept a careful journal of his California experiences, a journal from which Bancroft makes many excerpts. An odd error is in the indexing of the Bancroft volumes on California, Henry W. Bigler being confused with John Bigler. The latter was governor of California in 1852-55. A truckling California legislature unsuccessfully tried to fasten his name upon Lake Tahoe. But the Mormon pioneer turned his back upon the golden sands after only a few months of digging, and later, for years, was connected with the Mormon temple at St. George, Utah.

43

January 24, 1898, four of the six returned to San Francisco, guests of the State of California in its celebration of the fiftieth anniversary of the discovery of gold. They were Henry W. Bigler, Jas. S. Brown, Wm. J. Johnston and Azariah Smith. A group photograph, then taken, is reproduced in this volume. The others of the Mormon gold discoverers, Alexander Stephens and James Barger, had died before that date.

Looking Toward Southern California

All through the Church administration led by Brigham Young there was evidence of well-defined intention to spread the Church influence southward into Mexico and, possibly tracking back the steps of the Nephites and Lamanites, to work even into South America. There seemed an attraction in the enormous agricultural possibilities of Southern California. The long-headed Church President, figuring the commercial and agricultural advantages that lay in the Southwest, practically paved the way for the connection that since has come by rail with Los Angeles. It naturally resulted that the old Spanish trail that had been traversed by Dominguez and Escalante in 1776 was extended on down the Virgin River toward the southwest and soon became known as the Mormon Road. Over this road there was much travel. It was taken by emigrants bound from the East for California and proved the safest at all seasons of the year. It was used by the Mormons in restocking their herds and in securing supplies and for a while there was belief that the Colorado River could be utilized as a means of connecting steamboat transportation with the wagons that should haul from Callville, 350 miles from Salt Lake.

In 1851, nearly four years after the settlement at Salt Lake, President Young made suggestion that a company be organized, of possibly a score of families, to settle below Cajon Pass and cultivate the grape, olive, sugar cane and cotton and to found a station on a proposed Pacific mail route. There was expectation that the settlement later would be a gathering place for the Saints who might come from the islands of the Pacific, and even from Europe. The idea proved immensely popular, the suggestion· having come after a typical Salt Lake winter, and the pilgrimage embraced about 500 individuals. President Young, at the time of their leaving, March 24, said he "was sick at the sight of so many Saints running to California, chiefly after the gods of this earth" and he expressed himself unable to address them. Arrival at San Bernardino was in June.

The Author has been fortunate in securing personal testimony from a member of this migration, Collins R. Hakes, who later was President of the Maricopa Stake at Mesa, and, later, head of the Bluewater settlement in New Mexico. The hegira was led by Amasa M. Lyman and Chas. C. Rich, prominent Mormon pioneers.

A short distance below Cajon Pass, Lyman and Rich in September purchased the Lugo ranch of nine square leagues, including an abandoned mission. They agreed to pay $77,500 in deferred payments, though the total sum rose eventually to $140,000. Even at that, this must be accounted a very reasonable price for nearly thirty square miles of land in the present wonderful valley of San Bernardino.

Forced From the Southland

With those of the Carson Valley, the California brethren mainly returned to Utah, late in 1857, or early in 1858, at the time of the Johnston invasion. Mr. Hakes gave additional details. On September 11, 1857, occurred the Mountain Meadows massacre in the southwest corner of Utah. This outrage, by a band of outlaws, emphatically discountenanced by the Church authorities and repugnant to Church doctrines, which denounce useless shedding of blood, was promptly charged, on the Pacific and, indeed, all over the Union, as something for which the Mormon organization itself was responsible. So it happened that, in

45

December, 1857, J. Riley Morse, of the colony, rode southward post haste from Sacramento with the news that 200 mountain vigilantes were on their way to run the Mormons out of California. Not wishing to fight and not wishing to subject their families to abuse, about 400 of the San Bernardino settlers, within a few weeks, started for southern Utah, leaving only about twenty families. The news of this departure went to the Californians and they returned to their homes without completing their projected purpose. Many Church and coast references tell of the "recall" of the San Bernardino settlers, but Hakes' story appears ample in furnishing a reason for the departure. Many of these San Bernardino pioneers later came into Arizona. Those who remained prospered, and many of the families still are represented by descendants now in the Californian city. The settlement is believed to have been the first agricultural colony founded by persons of Anglo-Saxon descent in Southern California.

How Sirrine Saved the Gold

Geo. W. Sirrine, later of Mesa, had an important part in the details of the San Bernardino ranch purchase. Amasa M. Lyman and Chas. C. Rich went to San Francisco for the money needed for the first payment. They selected Sirrine to be their money carrier, entrusting him with $16,000, much of it in gold, the money presumably secured through Brannan. Sirrine took ship southward for San Pedro or Wilmington, carrying a carpenter chest in which the money was concealed in a pair of rubber boots, which he threw on the deck, with apparent carelessness, while his effects were searched by a couple of very rough characters. Delivery of the money was made without further incident of note. Sirrine helped survey the San Bernardino townsite, built a grist mill and operated it, logged at Bear Lake and freighted on the Mormon road. Charles Crismon, a skillful miller, also a central Arizona pioneer, for a while was associated with him. Crismon also built a sawmill in nearby mountains. Sirrine spent his San Bernardino earnings, about $10,000, in attempted development of a seam of coal on Point Loma, near San Diego, sinking a shaft 183 feet deep. He left California in 1858, taking with him to Salt Lake a wagonload of honey. In a biography of Charles Crismon, Jr., is found a claim that the elder Crismon took the first bees to Utah, from San Bernardino, in 1863. This may have added importance in view of the fact that Utah now is known as the Beehive State.

Chapter Five

The State of Deseret

A Vast Intermountain Commonwealth

Probably unknown to a majority of Arizonans is the fact that the area of this State once was included within the State of Deseret, the domain the early Mormons laid out for themselves in the western wilds. The State of Deseret was a natural sort of entity, with a governor, with courts, peace officers and a militia. It was a great dream, yet a dream that had being and substance for a material stretch of time. Undoubtedly its conception was with Brigham Young, whose prophetic vision pictured the day when, under Mormon auspices, there would be development of the entire enormous basin of the Colorado River, with seaports on the Pacific. The name was not based upon the word "desert." It is a Book of Mormon designation for "honey bee."

This State of Deseret was a strictly Mormon institution, headed by the Church authorities and with the bishops of all the wards ex-officio magistrates. At the same time, there should be understanding that in nowise was it antagonistic to the government of the United States. It was a grand plan, under which there was hope that, with a population at the time of about 15,000, there might be admission of the intermountain region into the union of States.

The movement for the new State started with a call issued in 1849, addressed to all citizens of that portion of California lying east of the Sierra Nevada Mountains. There was a convention in March, probably attended by

48

very few outside the Church, despite the broadness of the plan. In the preamble of the constitution adopted there was recitation that Congress had failed to provide any civil government, so necessary for the peace, security and prosperity of society, that "all political power is inherent in the people, and governments instituted for their protection, security and benefit should emanate from the same." Therefore, there was recommendation of a constitution until the Congress should provide other government and admit the new State into the Union. There was expression of gratitude to the Supreme Being for blessings enjoyed and submission to the national government freely was acknowledged.

Boundary Lines Established

Deseret was to have boundaries as follows:

Commencing at the 33d parallel of north latitude, where it crosses the 108th deg. of longitude west of Greenwich; thence running south and west to the boundary of Mexico; thence west to and down the main channel of the Gila River (or the northern line of Mexico), and on the northern boundary of Lower California to the Pacific Ocean; thence along the coast northwesterly to 118 degrees, 30 minutes of west longitude; thence north to where said line intersects the dividing ridge of the Sierra Nevada Mountains; thence north along the summit of the Sierra Nevada Mountains to the dividing range of mountains that separate the waters flowing into the Columbia from the waters running into the Great Basin; thence easterly along the dividing range of mountains that separate said waters flowing into the Columbia River on the north, from the waters flowing into the Great Basin on the south, to the summit of the Wind River chain of mountains; thence southeast and south by the dividing range of mountains that separate the waters flowing into the Gulf of Mexico from the waters flowing into the Gulf of California, to the place of beginning, as set forth in a map drawn by Charles Preuss, and published by order of the Senate of the United States in 1848.

This description needs some explanation. The point of beginning, as set forth, was at the headwaters of the Gila River near the Mexican line, which then, and until the Gadsden Purchase in 1854, followed down the Gila River to the

49

Colorado. At that time the boundary between Upper and Lower California had been established to the point below San Diego, which thus became included within the territory claimed. Here, naturally, there was inclusion of practically all Southern California to a point near Santa Barbara. Thence the line ran northward and inland to the summit of the Sierra Nevadas, not far from Mt. Whitney. It followed the Sierra Nevadas to the northwestward, well within the present California line, up into northwestern Nevada, thence eastward through southern Idaho and Wyoming to about South Pass, where the eastern line was taken up southward, along the summit of the Rockies to the point of beginning. So, there was general inclusion of that part of California lying east of the Sierras, of all southern California, all Nevada and Utah, the southern portions of Oregon and Idaho, southwestern Wyoming, western Colorado, not reaching as far as Denver, western New Mexico and all Arizona north of the Gila.

There can be no doubt that the region embraced, probably too large for a State under modern conditions, at that time was as logical a division as could have been made, considering the semi-arid climatic conditions, natural boundaries, generally by great mountain ranges, a single watershed, that of the Colorado River, and, in addition to all these, the highway outlet to the Pacific Ocean, to the southwest, through a country where the mountains broke away, along the course of the Colorado, even then demonstrated the most feasible route from Great Salt Lake City to the ocean.

Segregation of the Western Territories

At no time was there more than assumption by this central Salt Lake government of authority over any part of the area of the State of Deseret, save within the central Utah district, where the settlers, less than two years established, were striving to carve out homes in what was to be the nucleus of this commonwealth of wondrous proportions.

50

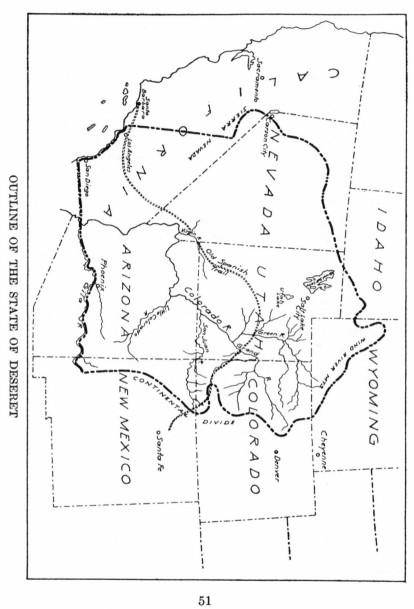

OUTLINE OF THE STATE OF DESERET

There was nothing very unusual about the constitution. It was along the ordinary line of such documents, though the justices of the Supreme Court at first were chosen by the Legislature. Brigham Young was the first Governor, Willard Richards was Secretary and Heber C. Kimball Chief Justice.

The first Legislature met July 2, 1849, at Great Salt Lake City and supported an application to Congress for the organization of a territorial government. The boundaries of the Territory of Deseret were somewhat changed from the original. The northern line was to be the southern line of Oregon and to the east there was to be inclusion of most of the present State of Colorado. Another memorial, soon thereafter, asked admission as a full State and still another plan, later proposed, was that Deseret and California be admitted as a single State, with power to separate thereafter. This suggestion was not well received in California and had short life.

September 9, 1850, President Millard Fillmore signed a bill creating the Territory of Utah, to be bounded on the west by California, on the north by Oregon, on the east by the summit of the Rocky Mountains and on the south by the 37th parallel of north latitude. South of this parallel there had been recognition of New Mexico, which included the present Arizona. Thus was denial of the dream of an empire state that should embrace the entire intermountain region.

Chapter Six

Early Roads and Travelers

Old Spanish Trail Through Utah

There can be little more than speculation concerning the extent of the use of the old Spanish Trail, through southern Utah, by the Spaniards. It is known, however, that considerable travel passed over it between Santa Fe and the California missions and settlements. In winter there was the disadvantage of snow in the Rockies and in summer were the aridity and heat of the Mohave desert. In Utah was danger from the Utes and farther westward from the Paiutes, but expeditions went well armed and exercised incessant watchfulness.

The much more direct route across Arizona on the 35th parallel was used by few Spaniards, though assuredly easier than that northward around the Canyon of the Colorado River. This direct route was traversed in 1598 by Juan de Onate, New Mexico's first Spanish governor, and, in 1776, Father Garces went from the Colorado eastward to the Hopi villages. There was travel over what became known as the "Road of the Bishop" from Santa Fe to the Zuni and Hopi towns, but not beyond. Possibly the preference for the San Juan-Virgin route lay in the fact that it had practicable river fords.

This old Spanish Trail from Santa Fe to Los Angeles, undoubtedly was over a succession of aboriginal highways. The first Europeans to follow it were the Franciscan friars Escalante and Dominguez, in 1776. They took a route running northwest from Taos, New Mexico, through the San Juan country into Utah as far as Utah Lake, not

53

reaching Great Salt Lake, and thence to the southwest through the Sevier Valley to the upper waters of the Virgin hoping to work through to California. They had an intelligent idea concerning the extent of the Grand Canyon of the Colorado and knew there could be no crossing for several hundred miles. After traveling down the Santa Clara and Virgin to about where the Arizona line now is, they turned eastward again, probably because of lack of supplies and fear of the desert. Their travel eastward was not far from the 37th parallel on either side and their Indian guides finally led them, by way of the mouth of the Paria, to the Ute ford of the Colorado, now known as the Crossing of the Fathers. Thence, crossing the river November 8, 1776, they made their way to the Hopi villages and back to the Rio Grande, finishing one of the most notable exploring trips ever known in the west. It is interesting to consider how, nearly a century later, the "Pathfinder," John C. Fremont, thought himself on a new line of discovery when he took much the same road westward through the passes of the Rockies.

This Spanish Trail is outlined on a fur-trade map in the Bancroft Library, covering the period from 1807 to 1843. No road is marked across the present area of Arizona. The Spanish Trail seems to have been considered as the western extension of the Santa Fe Trail.

The famous old traveler, Jedediah Smith, in 1826 and 1827, journeyed by the Sevier and Virgin River route to the Colorado River, though he appears to have made his own way, paralleling the aboriginal highway. In August of 1827, a number of his party were killed by Mohave Indians on the Colorado River.

Creation of the Mormon Road

The discovery of gold in California gave very great added importance to this southern Utah route. When the Washoe passes were closed by snow, California travel by the plains route necessarily was diverted, either around by

54

Oregon or southward through the Virgin River section. The latter route appears to have been safe enough in winter, save for occasional attacks by Indians, who were bent more upon plunder than upon murder. Occasionally, parties sought a shorter cut to the westward and suffered disaster in the sands of the Amargosa desert or of Death Valley. Sometimes such men as Jacob Hamblin were detailed to act as guides, but this seemed to be more needed with respect to dealings with the Indians than to show the road, as the highway was a plain one through to San Bernardino and San Gabriel. Of summers, undoubtedly the travel was much lessened, as the goldseekers chose the much more direct and better-watered routes passing either north or south of Lake Tahoe, by Donner Lake and Emigrant Gap or by the Placerville grade.

The western end of the southern Utah-Nevada trail, after the establishment of the San Bernardino colony, soon became known as the Mormon road, a name preserved.

Mail service was known over the old Spanish or Mormon Trail, down the Virgin and to Los Angeles, at different times between 1850 and 1861. This service seems to have been as an alternative when the passes of the Sierra Nevadas were closed. The best evidence at hand concerning this route is contained within a claim made by one Chorpending, for compensation from the United States for mules and equipment stolen by Indians in 1854-1856. John Hunt, later of Snowflake, carried mail on the route in 1856 and 1857. There must be assumption that stage stations were maintained on the Muddy and at Vegas.

With the Lyman and Rich expedition, in 1851, one of the wagons bore Apostle Parley P. Pratt who, accompanied by Rufus C. Allen, was starting upon a mission to the southwest coast of South America. On May 13, there was note of encampment at "a large spring, usually called Las Vegas," after having traveled 200 miles through worthless desert and between mountains of naked rock.

55

Mormon Settlement at Tubac

To Commissioner John R. Bartlett, of the International Boundary Survey, the Author is indebted for a memorandum covering what clearly was the first Mormon settlement within the present confines of Arizona. It was at the old Spanish pueblo of Tubac, in the Santa Cruz valley, about forty miles south of Tucson. Both places then (in July, 1852), still were in Mexico, the time being two years before perfecting the Gadsden Purchase.

Tubac, according to the Commissioner, was "a collection of dilapidated buildings and huts, about half tenantless, and an equally ruinous church." He called it "a God-forsaken place," but gave some interesting history. After a century and a half of occupation, usually with a population of about 400, it had been abandoned a year before the Commissioner's arrival, but had been repopulated by possibly 100 individuals. There was irrigation from the Santa Cruz, but of uncertain sort, and it was this very uncertainty that lost to Arizona a community of settlers of industry surely rare in that locality. Bartlett's narrative recites:

> The preceding fall (of 1851), after the place has been again occupied, a party of Mormons, in passing through on their way to California, was induced to stop there by the representations of the Mexican comandante. He offered them lands in the rich valley, where acequias (irrigation ditches) were already dug, if they would remain and cultivate it; assuring them that they would find a ready market for all the corn, wheat and vegetables they could raise, from the troops and from passing emigrants. The offer was so good and the prospects were so flattering that they consented to remain. They, therefore, set to work, plowed and sowed their lands, in which they expended all their means, anticipating an abundant harvest. But the spring and summer came without rain: the river dried up; their fields could not be irrigated; and their labor, time and money was lost. They abandoned the place, and, though reduced to the greatest extremities, succeeded in reaching Santa Isabel in California, where we fell in with them.

The Santa Isabel meeting referred to had taken place in the previous May, 1852. Santa Isabel was an old visita of

San Diego Mission, about forty miles northeast of San Diego and on the road from that port to Fort Yuma. In the Commissioner's party, eastbound, was the noted scout, Antoine LeRoux, who had been one of the guides of the Mormon Battalion westward, in 1846. Bartlett wrote:

LeRoux had been sent to the settlement at San Bernardino, to purchase a vehicle from newly-arrived Mormon immigrants and to return with it to Santa Isabel. When the wagon came . . . . . . it was driven by its owner, named Smithson. After paying him, I invited him to remain with us over night, as he had had a fatiguing day's journey. We were very much amused during the evening in listening to the history of our Mormon friend, who also enlightened us with a lecture on the peculiar doctrines of his sect. He seemed a harmless, though zealous man, ardent in his religious belief and was, I should think, a fair specimen of his fraternity. His people had lately purchased the extensive haciendas and buildings at San Bernardino, covering several miles square, for $70,000, one-half of which amount they had paid in cash. This is one of the richest agricultural districts in the State and is said to have been a great bargain.

Bartlett's narrative, while interesting, does not inform concerning the identity of the Mormons at Tubac. Including Smithson, doubtless they were swallowed within the San Bernardino settlement. Just where the Tubac settlers came from is not clear. There seems probability that they were from one of the southern States, started directly for San Bernardino, instead of via Salt Lake, in the same manner that an Arkansas expedition went directly to the Little Colorado settlements in later years.

Tubac dates back to about 1752. Possibly not pertinent to the subject of this work, yet valuable, is a map of Tubac, herewith reproduced, drawn about 1760 by Jose de Urrutia. This map lately was found in the British Museum at London by Godfrey Sykes, of the Desert Laboratory at Tucson. From him receipt of a copy is acknowledged, with appreciation. The plat includes the irrigated area below the presidio.

A Texan Settlement of the Faith

The Commissioner traveled broadly and chronicled

much and the Author is indebted to his memoirs for several items of early Mormon settlement in the Southwest.

One of the earliest details given by Bartlett concerns his arrival, October 14, 1850, at the village of Zodiac, in the valley of the Piedernales River, near Fredericksburg, about seventy miles northwest of San Antonio, Texas. Zodiac he found a village of 150 souls, headed by Elder Wight, locally known as "Colonel," who acted as host. That the settlement, even in such early times, was typically Mormon, is shown by the following extract from Bartlett's diary:

Everywhere around us in this Zodiacal settlement we saw abundant signs of prosperity. Whatever may be their theological errors, in secular matters they present an example of industry and thrift which the people of the State might advantageously imitate. They have a tract of land which they have cultivated for about three years and which has yielded profitable crops. The well-built houses, perfect fences and tidy dooryards give the place a homelike air such as we had not seen before in Texas. The dinner was a regular old-fashioned New England farmer's meal, comprising an abundance of everything, served with faultless neatness. The entire charge for the dinner for twelve persons and corn for as many animals was $3. . . . The colonel said he was the first settler in the valley of the Piedernales and for many miles around. In his colony were people of all trades. He told me his crop of corn this year would amount to 7000 bushels, for which he expected to realize $1.25 a bushel.

Chapter Seven

Missionary Pioneering

Hamblin, "Leatherstocking of the Southwest"

In Southern Arizona the first pioneering was done by devoted Franciscans and Jesuits, their chiefest concern the souls of the gentile Indians. In similar wise, the pioneering of northern Arizona had its initiation in a hope of the Mormon Church for conversion of the Indians of the canyons and plains. In neither case was there the desired degree of success, but each period has brought to us many stories of heroism and self-sacrifice on the part of the missionaries. In the days when the American colonists were shaking off the English yoke, our Southwest was having exploration by the martyred Friar Garces. Three-quarters of a century later, the trail that had been taken by the priest to the Hopi villages was used by a Mormon missionary, Jacob Hamblin, sometimes called the "Leatherstocking of the Southwest," more of a trail-blazer than a preacher, a scout of the frontier directly commissioned under authority of his Church, serene in his faith and confident that his footsteps were being guided from on high.

The Author has found himself unable to write the history of northernmost Arizona without continual mingling of the name and the personal deeds of Jacob Hamblin. Apparently Hamblin had had no special training for the work he was to do so well. It seemed to "merely happen" that he was in southwestern Utah, as early as 1854, when his Church was looking toward expansion to the southward.

Hamblin's first essay into the Arizona country was in the troublous fall and winter of 1857, a year when he and his family were living in the south end of Mountain Meadows, Utah. He happened to be in Salt Lake when the famous Arkansas emigrant train passed through his district. Brigham Young sent a messenger southward with instructions to let the wagon train (an especially troublesome one) pass as quietly as possible, but these instructions were not received and Hamblin learned on the way home, of the massacre. The information came personally from John D. Lee, the assassin-in-chief. In Hamblin's autobiography is written, "The deplorable affair caused a sensation of horror and deep regret throughout the entire community, by whom it was unqualifiedly condemned."

Thereafter, Hamblin and his associates rode hard after other emigrants who were to be attacked by Indians, and found a company on the Muddy, surrounded by Paiutes preparing to attack and destroy them. As a compromise, the Indians were given the loose horses and cattle, which later were recovered, and the Mormons remained with the company to assist in its defense.

Aboriginal Diversions

Late in the autumn of 1857, a company came through on the way to California, bringing a letter from President Young, directing Hamblin to act as guide to California. On his way to join the train, Hamblin found a naked man in the hands of the Paiutes, who were preparing "to have a good time with him," that is, "they intended to take him to their camp and torture him." He saved the man's life and secured the return of his clothing. As the caravan neared the Muddy, news came of another Indian attack. Hamblin rode ahead and joined the Indians. He later wrote, "I called them together and sat down and smoked a little tobacco with them, which I had brought along for that purpose." Apparently there was a good deal of native diplomacy in the negotiations. There were some promises of blankets and shirts and finally there was agreement to let the travelers proceed.

60

JACOB HAMBLIN
"Apostle to the Lamanites"

CHURCH PRESIDENTS

Brigham Young—above
Wilford Woodruff—below

Lorenzo Snow—above
Joseph Smith, the Prophet—center
Heber J. Grant—below

John Taylor—above
Joseph F. Smith—below

Incidentally, they were met by Ira Hatch and Dudley Leavitt, on their return from a mission to the Mohave Indians. The Mohaves, careless of the Gospel privileges afforded, held a council over the Mormon missionaries and decided that they should die. Hatch thereupon knelt down among the savages and "asked the Lord to soften their hearts, that they might not shed further blood." The prayer was repeated to the Mohaves by a Paiute interpreter. "The heart of the chief was softened" and before dawn the next morning he set the two men afoot on the desert and directed them to Las Vegas Springs, eighty miles distant. Their food on the journey was mesquite bread, "made by pounding the seeds of the mesquite fruits in the valley."

Hamblin at all times was very careful in his dealings with the Indians. At an early date he might have killed one of them, but his gun missed fire, a circumstance for which he later repeatedly praised the Lord. Probably his greatest influence came through his absolute fearlessness. He was firmly convinced that he was in the Lord's keeping and that his time would not come till his mission had been accomplished.

Without doubt, Hamblin's course was largely sustained by a letter received by him March 5, 1858, from President Brigham Young, in which he prophesied that "the day of Indian redemption draws nigh," and continued, "you should always be careful to impress upon them that they should not infringe upon the rights of others; and our brethren should be very careful not to infringe upon their rights, thus cultivating honor and good principles in their midst by example, as well as precept."

In the spring of 1857, Hamblin and Dudley Leavitt, at a point 35 miles west of Las Vegas, smelted some lead ore, Hamblin having some knowledge of the proper processes. The lead later was left on the desert. The wagons were needed to haul iron, remnants of old emigrant wagons that had been abandoned on the San Bernardino road.

61

Encounter with Federal Explorers

In the course of his missionary endeavor, in the spring of 1858, Hamblin took five men and went by way of Las Vegas Springs to the Colorado River, at the foot of the Cottonwood Hills, 170 miles from the Santa Clara, Utah, settlement. Upon this trip he had remarkable experiences. On the river he saw a small steamer. Men with animals were making their way upstream on the opposite side. Thales Haskell, sent to investigate, returned next morning with information that the steamer company was of military character and very hostile to the Mormons, that the expedition had been sent out by the Government to examine the river and learn if a force could not be taken through southern Utah in that direction, should it be needed, to subjugate the Mormons. Hamblin returned to Las Vegas Springs and thought the situation so grave that he counseled abandonment of the Mormon settlement then being made at that point.

This record is very interesting in view of contemporary history. Without doubt, the steamboat he saw was the little "Explorer," of the topographical exploration of the Colorado River in the winter of 1857-8. Commanding was Lieut. J. C. Ives of the army Topographical Corps, the same officer who had been in the engineering section of Whipple's railway survey along the 35th parallel. The craft was built in the east and put together at the mouth of the river. The journey upstream was at a low stage of water and there was continual trouble with snags and sandy bars. Finally, when Black Canyon had been reached, the "Explorer" ran upon a sunken rock, the boiler was torn loose, as well as the wheelhouse, and the river voyage had to be abandoned, though Ives and two men rowed up the stream as far as Vegas Wash.

The steamboat was floated back to Yuma, but Ives started eastward with a pack train, guided by the Mohave chief, Iritaba, taking the same route that had been pursued many years before by Friar Garces through the Hava Supai and Hopi country.

It is to be regretted that Hamblin did not go on board the "Explorer," where no doubt he would have received cordial welcome. Even at that time, Brigham Young undoubtedly would have been pleased to have helped in forwarding the opening of a route to the southwestern coast by way of the Colorado River.

Incidentally, the steamer had a trip that was valuable mainly in the excellent mapping that was done by Ives and his engineers. Captain Johnston and the steamer "Colorado" had been over the same stretch of river before the "Explorer" came and had served to ferry across the stream, about where Fort Mohave later stood, the famous camel party of Lieutenant Beale.

The Hopi and the Welsh Legend

There was serious consideration by the Church authorities of a declaration that the Moqui (Hopi) Indians of northern Arizona had a dialect that at least embraced many Welsh words. President Young had heard that a group of Welshmen, several hundred years before, had disappeared into the western wilds, so, with his usual quick inquiry into matters that interested him, he sent southward, led by Hamblin, in the autumn of 1858, a linguistic expedition, also including Durias Davis and Ammon M. Tenney. Davis was a Welshman, familiar with the language of his native land. Tenney, then only 15, knew a number of Indian dialects, as well as Spanish, the last learned in San Bernardino. They made diligent investigation and found nothing whatever to sustain the assertion. Not a word could they find that was similar in anywise to any European language.

It happens that the Hopi tongue is a composite, mainly a Shoshonean dialect, probably accumulated as the various clans of the present tribe gathered in northeastern Arizona, from the cactus country to the south, the San Juan country

63

to the northward and the Rio Grande valley to the eastward. But the Welsh legend was slow in dying.

This expedition of 1858, besides the two individuals noted, included Frederick and William Hamblin, Dudley and Thomas Leavitt, Samuel Knight, Ira Hatch, Andrew S. Gibbons (later an Arizona legislator), Benjamin Knell and a Paiute guide, Naraguts. The journey started at Hamblin's home in the Santa Clara settlement and was by way of the mouth of the Paria, where a good ferry point was found, but not used, and the Crossing of the Fathers on the Colorado, probably crossed by white men for the first time since Spanish days. The Hopi villages were found none too soon, for the men were very hungry. They had lost the mules that carried the provisions. The Hopi were found hospitable and furnished food until the runaway mules were brought in. There was some communication through the Ute language, after failure with the language of Wales. William Hamblin, Thomas Leavitt, Gibbons and Knell were left as missionaries and the rest of the dozen made a difficult return journey to their homes, a part of the way through snow.

The missionaries left with the Hopi returned the same winter. They had not been treated quite as badly as Father Garces, but there had been a division among the tribes, started by the priesthood. There was very good prophecy, however, by the Indians, to the effect that the Mormons would settle in the country to the southward and that their route of travel would be by way of the Little Colorado.

It might be well to insert, at this point, a condensation of the Welsh legend, though affecting, especially, the Zuni, a pueblo-dwelling tribe, living to the eastward of the Hopi and with little ethnologic connection. The following was written by Llewellyn Harris (himself of Welsh extraction), who was a Mormon missionary visitor to the Zuni in January, 1878, and is reprinted without endorsement:

They say that, before the conquest of Mexico by the Spaniards, the Zuni Indians lived in Mexico. Some of them still claim to be the descendants of Montezuma. At the time of the conquest they fled to Arizona and settled there. They were at one time a very powerful tribe, as the ruins all over that part of the country testify. They have always been considered a very industrious people. The fact that they have, at one time, been in a state of civilization far in advance of what they are at present, is established beyond a doubt. Before the Catholic religion was introduced to them, they worshipped the sun. At present they are nearly all Catholics. A few of them have been baptized into our Church by Brothers Ammon M. Tenney and R. H. Smith, and nearly all the tribe say they are going to be baptized.

They have a great many words in the language like the Welsh, and with the same meaning. Their tradition says that over 300 years before the conquest of Mexico by the Spaniards, some white men landed in Mexico and told the Indians that they had come from the regions beyond the sea to the east. They say that from these white men came the ancient kings of Mexico, from whom Montezuma descended.

These white men were known to the Indians of Mexico by the name of Cambaraga; and are still remembered so in the traditions of Zuni Indians. In time those white people became mixed with Indians, until scarcely a relic of them remained. A few traditions of the Mexican Indians and a few Welsh words among the Zunis, Navajos and Moquis are all that can be found of that people now.

I have the history of the ancient Britons, which speaks of Prince Madoc, who was the son of Owen Guynedd, King of Wales, having sailed from Wales in the year 1160, with three ships. He returned in the year 1163, saying he had found a beautiful country, across the western sea. He left Wales again in the year 1164, with fifteen ships and 3000 men. He was never again heard of.

Indians Await Their Prophets

President Young kept the Hopi in mind, for the following year (1859) he sent Hamblin on a second trip to the Indians, with a company that consisted of Marion J. Shelton, Thales Haskell, Taylor Crosby, Benjamin Knell, Ira Hatch and John Wm. Young. They reached the Hopi villages November 6, talked with the Indians three days and then left the work of possible conversion on the shoulders of Shelton and Haskell, who returned to the Santa Clara the next spring. The Indians were kind, but un-

65

believing, and "could make no move until the reappearance of the three prophets who led their fathers to that land and told them to remain on those rocks until they should come again and tell them what to do." Both ways of the journey were by the Ute ford.

Navajo Killing of Geo. A. Smith, Jr.

In the fall of 1860, Hamblin was directed to attempt to establish the faith in the Hopi towns. This time, from Santa Clara, he took Geo. A. Smith, Jr., son of an apostle of the Church, Thales Haskell, Jehiel McConnell, Ira Hatch, Isaac Riddle, Amos G. Thornton, Francis M. Hamblin, James Pearce and an Indian, Enos, with supplies for a year. Young Ammon Tenney was sent back. This proved a perilous adventure. Hamblin told he had had forebodings of evil. Failure attended an attempt to cross the Colorado at the Paria. For two days south of the Crossing of the Fathers, there was no water. The Navajo gathered around them and barred further progress. There was a halt, and bartering was started for goods that had been brought along to exchange for Indian blankets. At this point, Smith was shot. The deed was done with his own revolver, which had been passed to an Indian who asked to inspect it. The Indians readily admitted responsibility, stating that it was in reprisal for the killing of three Navajos by palefaces and they demanded two more victims before the Mormon company would be allowed to go in peace. The situation was a difficult one for Jacob, but he answered bravely, "I would not give a cent to live after I had given up two men to be murdered; I would rather die like a man than live like a dog." Jacob went out by himself and had a little session of prayer and then the party started northward, flanked by hostile Navajos, but accompanied by four old friendly tribesmen. Smith was taken along on a mule, with McConnell behind to hold him on. Thus it was that he died about sundown. His last words, when told that a stop could not be made, were, "Oh, well, go on then;

66

but I wish I could die in peace." The body was wrapped in a blanket and laid in a hollow by the side of the trail, for no stop could be made even to bury the dead.

About a week later, Santa Clara was reached by the worn and jaded party, sustained the last few days on a diet mainly of pinon nuts.

That winter, through the snow and ice, Hamblin led another party across the Colorado out upon the desert, to bring home the remains of their brother in the faith. The head and the larger bones were returned for burial at Salt Lake City. It was learned that the attacking Indians were from Fort Defiance and on this trip it was told that the Navajo considered their own action a grave mistake.

A Seeking of Baptism for Gain

That the Shivwits were susceptible to missionary argument was indicated about 1862, when James H. Pearce brought from Arizona into St. George a band of 300 Indians, believed to comprise the whole tribe. All were duly baptized into the Church, the ceremony performed by David H. Cannon. Then Erastus Snow distributed largess of clothing and food. Ten years later Pearce again was with the Indians, greeted in affectionate remembrance. But there was complaint from the Shivwits they "had not heard from the Lord since he left." Then followed fervent suggestions from the tribesmen that they be taken to St. George and be baptized again. They wanted more shirts. They also wanted Pearce to write to the Lord and to tell Him the Shivwits had been pretty good Indians.

The First Tour Around the Grand Canyon

Hamblin's adventures to the southward were far from complete. In the autumn of 1862 President Young directed another visit to the Hopi, recommending that the Colorado be crossed south of St. George, in the hope of finding a more feasible route. Hamblin had had disaster the previous spring, in which freshets had swept away his grist mill and

67

other improvements. Most of the houses and cultivated land of the Santa Clara settlement had disappeared. He was given a company of twenty men, detailed by Apostles Orson Pratt and Erastus Snow. A small boat was taken to the river by wagon. Hamblin's chronicle does not tell just where the crossing was made, but it is assumed that it was at the mouth of the Grand Wash. From the river crossing there were four days of very dry travel toward the southeast, with the San Francisco Mountains in the far distance. There is no reference in his diary to the finding of any roads, but it is probable that most of the journey was on aboriginal trails. Snow was found at the foot of the San Francisco Mountains and two days thereafter the Little Colorado was crossed and then were reached the Hopi, who "had been going through some religious ceremonies to induce the Great Spirit to send storms to water their country that they might raise abundance of food the coming season." This may have been the annual Snake Dance. The Hopi refused to send some of their chief men to Utah, their traditions forbidding, but finally three joined after the expedition had started. There had been left behind McConnell, Haskell, and Hatch to labor for a season, and as hostages for the return of the tribesmen.

This journey probably was the first that ever circled the Grand Canyon, for return was by the Ute Crossing, where fording was difficult and dangerous, for the water was deep and ice was running. The three Hopi were dismayed over their violation of tradition, but were induced to go on. Incidentally, food became so scarce that resort was had to the killing and cooking of crows.

The Indians were taken on to Salt Lake City and were shown many things that impressed them greatly. An unsuccessful attempt was made to learn whether they spoke Welsh. Hamblin wrote that the Indians said, "They had been told that their forefathers had the arts of reading, writing, making books, etc."

LIEUTENANT IVES' STEAMER ON THE COLORADO IN 1858

AMMON M. TENNEY
Pioneer Scout of the Southwest

Here it may be noted that the Grand Canyon was circumtoured in the fall of 1920 by Governor and Mrs. Campbell, but under very different circumstances. The vehicle was an automobile. Crossing of the Colorado was at the Searchlight ferry, about forty miles downstream from old Callville. On the first day 248 miles were covered, mainly on the old Mormon road, to Littlefield, through the Muddy section, now being revived. St. George and other pioneer southern Utah settlements were passed on the way to Kanab and Fredonia. The road to the mouth of the Paria and to Lee's Ferry appears to have been found very little less rough than when traveled by the Mormon ox teams, and the river crossing was attended by experiences with quicksand and other dangers, while the pull outward on the south side was up a steep and hazardous highway.

A Visit to the Hava-Supai Indians

Hamblin had about as many trips as Sindbad the Sailor and about as many adventures. Of course, he had to take the Hopi visitors home, and on this errand he started from St. George on March 18, 1863, with a party of six white men, including Gibbons, Haskell, Hatch and McConnell. They took the western route and found a better crossing, later called Pearce's Ferry. At this point they were overtaken by Lewis Greeley, a nephew of Horace Greeley of the New York Tribune, who had been sent on to the river by Erastus Snow.

A trail was taken to the left of the former route. This trail very clearly was the main thoroughfare used by the Wallapai into Cataract Canyon, which was so known at that time. Down the trail, into the abysmal "voladero" of Father Garces, they traveled a day and part of another, leading their horses most of the way. In many places they could not have turned their animals around had they wished to do so.

Cataract Canyon, the home of the Hava-Supai, is a veritable Yosemite, with craggy walls that rise nearly

69

3000 feet to the mesa above. Hamblin especially noted the boiling from the bottom of the canyon of a beautiful large spring, the same which today irrigates the lands of the well-disposed Indians. These Indians gave assistance to the party and told of an attack made a short time before by Apaches from the southeast, who had been met in a narrow pass where several of their number had been slain. Assuring the Hava-Supai they would send no enemies into their secret valley, Hamblin led his party to the eastward, up the Tope-Kobe trail to the plateau. This was reached April 7. Though along the Moqui trail at no point were they very far from the Grand Canyon, that gorge was not noted in Hamblin's narrative, for the brethren were not sight-seeing. A few days later they were in the Hopi towns, to which the three much-traveled Indians preceded them, in eagerness to see their people again.

Only two days were spent with the Indians and on April 15, taking Haskell, Hatch and McConnell, the party struck toward the southwest, to find the Beale road. On the 20th, Greeley discovered a pond of clear cold water several acres in extent in the crater of a volcanic peak. The San Francisco peaks were passed, left to the southward, and the Beale road was struck six miles west of LeRoux Springs, the later site of Fort Moroni, seven miles northwest of the present Flagstaff.

The Beale road was followed until the 28th. Thence, the men suffered thirst, for 56 hours being without water. Ten of their eighteen horses were stolen. This, it was explained, was due to the failure of the Hava-Supai to return Wallapai horses which the men had left in Cataract Canyon on the outward journey. St. George was reached May 13, 1863. The main result had been the exploration of a practicable, though difficult, route for wagons from St. George to the Little Colorado and to the Hopi towns.

Experiences with the Redskins

Ammon M. Tenney in Phoenix lately told the Author

that the Navajo were the only Indians who ever really fought the Mormons and the only tribe against which the Mormons were compelled to depart from their rule against the shedding of blood. It is not intended in this work to go into any history of the many encounters between the Utah Mormons and the Arizona Navajo, but there should be inclusion of a story told by Tenney of an experience in 1865 at a point eighteen miles west of Pipe Springs and six miles southwest of Canaan, Utah. There were three Americans from Toquerville, the elder Tenney, the narrator, and Enoch Dodge, the last known as one of the bravest of southern Utah pioneers. The three were surrounded by sixteen Navajos, and, with their backs to the wall, fought for an hour or more, finally abandoning their thirteen horses and running for better shelter. Dodge was shot through the knee cap, a wound that incapacitated him from the fight thereafter. The elder Tenney fell and broke his shoulder blade and was stunned, though he was not shot. This left the fight upon the younger Tenney, who managed to climb a twelve-foot rocky escarpment. He reached down with his rifle and dragged up his father and Dodge. The three opportunely found a little cave in which they secreted themselves until reasonably rested, hearing the Indians searching for them on the plateau above. Then, in the darkness, they made their way fifteen miles into Duncan's Retreat on the Virgin River in Utah. "There is one thing I will say for the Navajo," Tenney declared with fervor. "He is a sure-enough fighting man. The sixteen of them stood shoulder to shoulder, not taking cover, as almost any other southwestern Indian would have done."

Apparently, on each of the visits that had been made by Hamblin to the Hopi, he had made suggestion that the tribes leave their barren land and move to the northward, across the Colorado, where good lands might be allotted them, on which they might live in peace and plenty, where they might build cities and villages the same as other people, but, according to Hamblin's journal, "They again told us that they could not leave their present location until the three prophets should appear again."

This was written particularly in regard to a visit made to the villages in 1864, and in connection with a theft of horses by Navajos near Kanab. It was found inexpedient to go into the Navajo country, as Chief Spaneshanks, who had been relatively friendly, had been deposed by his band and had been succeeded by a son of very different inclination.

In autumn of the same year, Anson Call, Dr. Jas. M. Whitmore, A. M. Cannon and Hamblin and son visited Las Vegas Springs and the Colorado River, stopping a while with the Cottonwood Island Indians and the Mohave, and establishing Callville.

Killing of Whitmore and McIntire

January 8, 1866, Doctor Whitmore and his herder, Robert McIntire, were killed in Arizona, four miles north of Pipe Springs by a band of Paiede Paiutes and Navajos, that drove off horses, sheep and cattle. There was pursuit from St. George by Col. D. D. McArthur and company.

A tale of the pursuit comes from Anthony W. Ivins, a member of the company, then a mere boy who went out on a mule with a quilt for a saddle. The weather was bitterly cold. The bodies were found covered with snow, which was three feet deep. Each body had many arrow and bullet wounds. The men had been attacked while riding the range, only McIntire being armed. A detachment, under Captain James Andrus, found the murderous Indians in camp and, in a short engagement, killed nine of them.

The trail to the Hopi towns must have been well known to the Mormon scout when in October, 1869, again he was detailed to investigate the sources of raids on the Mormon borders. He had a fairly strong company of forty men, including twenty Paiutes. The crossing was at the mouth of the Paria. Apparently all that was accomplished on this trip was to learn that the Indians intended to make still another raid on the southern settlements. Hamblin wanted to go back by way of the Ute trail and the Crossing of the Fathers, but was overruled by his brethren, who preferred the Paria route. When they returned, it was to learn that the Navajos already had raided and had driven off more than 1200 head of animals, and that, if the Mormon company, on returning, had taken the Ute trail, the raiders would have been met and the animals possibly recovered. The winter was a hard one for the Mormons who watched the frontier, assisted by friendly Paiutes. The trouble weighed heavily upon Hamblin's mind and, in the spring of 1870, at Kanab, he offered himself to President Young as an ambassador to the Navajo, to prevent, if possible, further shedding of blood.

Chapter Eight

Hamblin Among the Indians

Visiting the Paiutes with Powell

It was in the summer of 1870 that Hamblin met Major
J. W. Powell, who had descended the Colorado the previous
year. Powell's ideas coincided very well with those of
Hamblin. He wanted to visit the Indians and prevent
repetition of such a calamity as that in which three of his
men had been killed near Mount Trumbull, southwest of
Kanab. So, in September, 1870, there was a gathering at
Mount Trumbull, with about fifteen Indians. What followed is presented in Powell's own language:

This evening, the Shivwits, for whom we have sent, come in, and
after supper we hold a long council. A blazing fire is built, and around
this we sit—the Indians living here, the Shivwits, Jacob Hamblin
and myself. This man, Hamblin, speaks their language well and
has a great influence over all the Indians in the region round about.
He is a silent, reserved man, and when he speaks it is in a slow, quiet
way that inspires great awe. His talk is so low that they must listen
attentively to hear, and they sit around him in deathlike silence.
When he finishes a measured sentence the chief repeats it and they
all give a solemn grunt. But, first, I fill my pipe, light it, and take a
few whiffs, then pass it to Hamblin; he smokes and gives it to the
man next, and so it goes around. When it has passed the chief, he
takes out his own pipe, fills and lights it, and passes it around after
mine. I can smoke my own pipe in turn, but when the Indian pipe
comes around, I am nonplussed. It has a large stem, which has
at some time been broken, and now there is a buckskin rag wound
around it and tied with sinew, so that the end of the stem is a huge
mouthful, exceedingly repulsive. To gain time, I refill it, then engage
in very earnest conversation, and, all unawares, I pass it to my neighbor
unlighted. I tell the Indians that I wish to spend some months in
their country during the coming year and that I would like them to
treat me as a friend. I do not wish to trade; do not want their lands.

74

Heretofore I have found it very difficult to make the natives understand my object, but the gravity of the Mormon missionary helps me much.

Then their chief replies: "Your talk is good and we believe what you say. We believe in Jacob, and look upon you as a father. When you are hungry, you may have our game. You may gather our sweet fruits. We will give you food when you come to our land. We will show you the springs and you may drink; the water is good. We will be friends and when you come we will be glad. We will tell the Indians who live on the other side of the great river that we have seen Kapurats (one-armed—the Indian name for Powell) and that he is the Indian's friend. We will tell them he is Jacob's friend."

The Indians told that the three men had been killed in the belief they were miners. They had come upon an Indian village, almost starved and exhausted with fatigue, had been supplied with food and put on their way to the settlements. On receipt of news that certain Indians had been killed by whites, the men were followed, ambushed and slain with many arrows. Powell observes that that night he slept in peace, "although these murderers of my men were sleeping not 500 yards away." Hamblin improved the time in trying to make the Indians understand the idea of an overruling Providence and to appreciate that God was not pleased with the shedding of blood. He admitted, "These teachings did not appear to have much influence at the time, but afterwards they yielded much good fruit."

Wm. R. Hawkins, cook for this first Powell expedition, died a few years ago in Mesa, Arizona. Willis W. Bass, a noted Grand Canyon guide, lately published an interesting booklet carrying some side lights on the Powell explorations. In it is declared, on Hawkins' authority, that the three men who climbed the cliffs, to meet death above, left the party after a quarrel with Powell, the dispute starting in the latter's demand for payment for a watch that had been ruined while in possession of one of the trio. Powell is charged with having ordered the man to leave his party if he would not agree to pay for the watch.

A Great Conference with the Navajo

One of the greatest of Hamblin's southern visitations was in the autumn of 1870, when he served as a guide for Major Powell eastward, by way of the Hopi villages and of Fort Defiance. Powell's invitation was the more readily accepted as this appeared to be an opening for the much-desired peace talk with the Navajo. In the expedition were Ammon M. Tenney, Ashton Nebecker, Nathan Terry and Elijah Potter of the brethren, three of Powell's party and a Kaibab Indian.

According to Tenney, in the previous year, the Navajo had stolen $1,000,000 worth of cattle, horses and sheep in southern Utah. Tenney, in a personal interview with the Author in 1920, told that the great council then called, was tremendously dramatic. About a dozen Americans were present, including Powell and Captain Bennett. Tenney estimated that about 8000 Indians were on the council ground at Fort Defiance. This number would have included the entire tribe. It was found that the gathering was distinctly hostile. Powell and Hamblin led in the talking. The former had no authority whatever, but gave the Indians to understand that he was a commissioner on behalf of the whites and that serious chastisement would come to them in a visit of troops if there should be continuation of the evil conditions complained of by the Mormons. Undoubtedly this talk had a strong effect upon the Indians, who in Civil War days had been punished harshly for similar depredations upon the pueblos of New Mexico and who may have remembered when Col. Kit Carson descended upon the Navajo, chopped down their fruit trees, and laid waste their farms, later most of the tribe being taken into exile in New Mexico.

Dellenbaugh and Hamblin wrote much concerning this great council. Powell introduced Hamblin as a representative of the Mormons, whom he highly complimented as industrious and peaceful people. Hamblin told of the evils

76

of a war in which many men had been lost, including twenty or thirty Navajos, and informed the Indians that the young men of Utah wanted to come over to the Navajo country and kill, but "had been told to stay at home until other means of obtaining peace had been tried and had failed." He referred to the evils that come from the necessity of guarding stock where neither white nor Indian could trust sheep out of sight. He then painted the beauties of peace, in which "horses and sheep would become fat and in which one could sleep in peace and awake and find his property safe." Low-voiced, but clearly, the message concluded:

What shall I tell my people, the Mormons, when I return home? That we may live in peace, live as friends, and trade with one another? Or shall we look for you to come prowling around our weak settlements, like wolves in the night? I hope we may live in peace in time to come. I have now gray hairs on my head, and from my boyhood I have been on the frontiers doing all I could to preserve peace between white men and Indians I despise this killing, this shedding of blood. I hope you will stop this and come and visit and trade with our people. We would like to hear what you have got to say before we go home.

Barbenceta, the principal chief, slowly approached as Jacob ended and, putting his arms around him, said, "My friend and brother, I will do all that I can to bring about what you have advised. We will not give all our answer now. Many of the Navajos are here. We will talk to them tonight and will see you on your way home." The chief addressed his people from a little eminence. The Americans understood little or nothing of what he was saying, but it was agreed that it was a great oration. The Indians hung upon every word and responded to every gesture and occasionally, in unison, there would come from the crowd a harsh "Huh, Huh," in approval of their chieftain's advice and admonition.

A number of days were spent at Fort Defiance in attempting to arrive at an understanding with the Navajo. Hamblin wrote, "through Ammon M. Tenney being able to converse in Spanish, we accomplished much good."

On the way home, in a Hopi village, were met Barbenceta and also a number of chiefs who had not been at Fort Defiance. The talk was very agreeable, the Navajos saying, "We hope that we may be able to eat at one table, warm by one fire, smoke one pipe, and sleep in one blanket."

An Official Record of the Council

Determination of the time of the council has come to the Arizona Historian's office, within a few days of the closing of the manuscript of this work, the data supplied from the office of the Church Historian at Salt Lake City. In it is a copy of a final report, dated November 5, 1870, and signed by Frank F. Bennett, Captain United States Army, agent for the Navajo Indians at Fort Defiance. The report is as follows:

To Whom It May Concern:

This is to certify that Capt. Jacob Hamblin of Kanab, Kane Co., Southern Utah, came to this agency with Prof. John W. Powell and party on the 1st day of November, 1870, and expressed a desire to have a talk with myself and the principal men of the Navajo Indians in regard to depredations which the Navajos are alleged to have committed in southern Utah.

I immediately informed the chiefs that I wished them to talk the matter over among themselves and meet Captain Hamblin and myself in a council at the agency in four days. This was done and we, today, have had a long talk. The best of feeling existed. And the chiefs and good men of the Navajo Indians pledge themselves that no more Navajos will be allowed to go into Utah; and that they will not, under any circumstances, allow any more depredations to be committed by their people. That if they hear of any party forming for the purpose of making a raid, that they will immediately go to the place and stop them, using force if necessary. They express themselves as extremely anxious to be on the most friendly terms with the Mormons and that they may have a binding and lasting peace.

I assure the people of Utah that nothing shall be left undone by me to assist these people in their wishes and I am positive that they are in earnest and mean what they say.

I am confident that this visit of Captain Hamblin and the talk we have had will be the means of accomplishing great good.

Together with this Bennett letter is one addressed by

Jacob Hamblin to Erastus Snow, dated November 21, 1870, and reciting in detail the circumstances of the great council, concluded November 5, 1870. Most of the debate was between Hamblin and Chief Barbenceta, with occasional observations by Powell concerning the might of the American Nation and the absolute necessity for cessation of thievery. Hamblin told how the young men and the middle-aged of his people had gathered to make war upon the Navajo, "determined to cross the river and follow the trail of the stolen stock and lay waste the country, but our white chief, Brigham Young, was a man of peace and stopped his people from raiding and wanted us to ask peace. This is my business here." He told that, five years before, the Navajos were led by three principal men of the Paiutes and at that time seven Paiutes were killed near the place where the white man was killed. These were not the right Indians, not the Paiutes who had done the mischief. Barbenceta talked at great length. To a degree he blamed the Paiutes, but could not promise that no more raids would be made, but he told the agent he would endeavor to stop all future depredations and would return stolen stock, if found.

Navajos to Keep South of the River

There finally was agreement that Navajos should go north of the river only for horse trading, or upon necessary errands, and that when they did go, they would be made safe and welcome, this additionally secure, if they were to go first to Hamblin.

The Hopi and the Navajo, at that time, and probably for many years before, were unfriendly. There was a tale how the Hopi had attacked 35 Navajos, disarmed them, and then had thrown them off a high cliff between two of their towns. Hamblin went to the place indicated and found a number of skeletons and remains of blankets and understood that the deed had been done the year before. The

Navajo had plundered the Hopi for generations and the latter had retaliated.

Hamblin's diary gives the great Navajo council as in 1871. There also is much confusion of dates in several records of the time. But the year appears to be definitely established through the fact that Powell was in Salt Lake in October and November of 1871. It is a curious fact, also, that Powell, in his own narrative of the 1870 trip, makes no reference to Hamblin's presence with him south of the river or even to the dramatic circumstances of the great council, set by Hamblin and Dellenbaugh on November 2. Powell's diary places him at Fort Defiance October 31, 1870, and at a point near Fort Wingate November 2.

Tuba's Visit to the White Men

It was on the return from the grand council with the Navajo, in November, 1870, that Hamblin took to Utah, Tuba, a leading man of the Oraibi Hopi and his wife, Pulaskaninki.

In Hamblin's journal is a charming little account of how Tuba crossed the prohibited river. Tuba told Hamblin, "I have worshipped the Father of us all in the way you believe to be right. Now I wish you would do as the Hopi think is right before we cross." So the two knelt, Hamblin accepting in his right hand some of the contents of Tuba's medicine bag and Tuba prayed "for pity upon his Mormon friends, that none might drown, and for the preservation of all the animals we had, as all were needed, and for the preservation of food and clothing, that hunger nor cold might be known on the trail." They arose and scattered the ingredients from the medicine bag into the air, upon the men and into the waters of the river. Hamblin wrote, "To me the whole ceremony seemed humble and reverential. I feel the Father had regard for such petitions." There was added prayer by Tuba when the expedition safely landed on the opposite shore, at the mouth of the Paria.

Tuba had a remarkable trip. He was especially interest-

80

ed in the spinning mill at Washington, for he had made blankets, and his wife, with handmill experience, thought of labor lost when she looked at the work of a flour mill. At St. George they saw President Young, who gave them clothing.

Tuba was taken back home to Oraibi in safety in September, 1871, and his return was celebrated by feasting.

Of date December 24, 1870, in the files of the Deseret News is found a telegram from George A. Smith, who was with President Brigham Young and party in Utah's Dixie, at St. George. He wired:

Jacob Hamblin, accompanied by Tooby, a Moqui magistrate of Oraibi village, and wife, who are on a visit to this place to get information in regard to agriculture and manufactures, came here lately. Tooby, being himself a skillful spinner, examined the factory and grist mill at Washington. Upon seeing 360 spindles in operation, he said he had no heart to spin with his fingers any more.

On the trip southward in 1871, on which Hamblin returned Tuba and his wife to their home, he served as guide as far as the Ute ford for a party that was bearing provisions for the second Powell expedition. He arrived at the ford September 25, but remained only a day, then going on to Moen Copie, Oraibi and Fort Defiance, where he seems to have had some business to conclude with the chiefs. In his journal is told that he divided time at a Sunday meeting with a Methodist preacher. Returning, with three companions and nine Navajos, Hamblin reached the Paria October 28, taken across by the Powell party, though Powell had gone on from Ute ford to Salt Lake, there to get his family. The expedition had reached the ford October 6, and had dropped down the river to the Paria, where arrival was on the 22d. Hamblin went on to Salt Lake.

The Sacred Stone of the Hopi

The trust placed in Mormon visitors to the Hopi was shown by exhibition to them of a sacred stone. On one of the visits of Andrew S. Gibbons, accompanied by his sons,

Wm. H. and Richard, the three were guests of old Chief Tuba in Oraibi. Tuba told of this sacred stone and led his friends down into an underground kiva, from which Tuba's son was despatched into a more remote chamber. He returned bringing the stone. Apparently it was of very fine-grained marble, about 15x18 inches in diameter and a few inches in thickness. Its surface was entirely covered with hieroglyphic markings, concerning which there was no attempt at translation at the time, though there were etched upon it clouds and stars. The Indians appeared to have no translation and only knew that it was very sacred. Tuba said that at one time the stone incautiously was exhibited to an army officer, who attempted to seize it, but the Indians saved the relic and hid it more securely.

The only official record available to this office, bearing upon the stone, is found in the preface of Ethnological Report No. 4, as follows:

Mr. G. K. Gilbert furnished some data relating to the sacred stone kept by the Indians of the village of Oraibi, on the Moki mesas. This stone was seen by Messrs. John W. Young and Andrew S. Gibbons, and the notes were made by Mr. Gilbert from those furnished him by Young. Few white men have had access to this sacred record, and but few Indians have enjoyed the privilege. The stone is a red-clouded marble, entirely different from anything found in the region.

In the Land of the Navajo

In 1871, 1872 and 1873 Hamblin did much exploration. He located a settlement on the Paria River, started a ranch in Rock House Valley and laid out a practicable route from Lee's Ferry to the Little Colorado.

Actual use of the Lee's Ferry road by wagons was in the spring of 1873 by a party headed by Lorenzo W. Roundy, who crossed the Colorado at Lee's Ferry, passing on to Navajo Springs, seven miles beyond, and thence about ten miles to Bitter Springs and then on to Moen Copie. The last he described as a place "a good deal like St. George, having many springs breaking out from the hills, land limited, partly impregnated with salts." He passed by a Moqui village and thence on to the overland mail route. The Little Colorado was described as "not quite the size of the Virgin River, water a little brackish, but better than that of the Virgin." In May of the same year, Hamblin piloted, as far as Moen Copie, the first ten wagons of the Haight expedition that failed in an attempt to found a settlement on the Little Colorado.

Just as the Chiricahua Apaches to the southward found good pickings in Mexico, so the Navajo early recognized as a storehouse of good things, for looting, the Mormon settlements along the southern border of Utah. A degree of understanding was reached by the Mormons with the Ute. There was more or less trouble in the earlier days with the Paiute farther westward, this tribe having a number of subdivisions that had to be successively pacified by moral or forcible suasion. But it was with the Navajo that trouble existed in the largest measure.

Hamblin was absolutely sure of the identity of the American Indians with the Lamanites of the Book of Mormon. He regarded the Indians at all times as brethren who had strayed from the righteous path and who might be brought back by the exercise of piety and patience. Very much like a Spanish friar of old, he cheerfully dedicated himself to this particular purpose, willing to accept even martyrdom if such an end were to serve the great purpose. Undoubtedly this attitude was the basis of his extraordinary fortitude and of the calmness with which he faced difficult situations. There is admission by him, however, that at one time he was very near indeed to death, this in the winter of 1873-74. It is noted that nearly all of Hamblin's trips in the wild lands of Arizona were at the direction of the Church authorities, for whom he acted as trail finder, road marker, interpreter, missionary and messenger of peace to the aborigines.

So it happened that it was upon Hamblin that Brigham

Young placed dependence in a very serious situation that came through the killing of three Navajos, on the east fork of the Sevier River, a considerable distance into south-central Utah. Four Navajos had come northward to trade with the Ute. Caught by snow, they occupied a cabin belonging to a non-Mormon named McCarty, incidentally killing one of his calves. McCarty, Frank Starr and a number of associates descended upon the Indians, of whom one, badly wounded, escaped across the river, taking tidings to his tribesmen that the murder had been by Mormons. The Indian was not subtle enough to distinguish between sects, and so there was a call for bloody reprisals, directed against the southern Mormon settlements. The Indian Agent at Defiance sent an investigating party that included J. Lorenzo Hubbell.

Hamblin's Greatest Experience

In January, 1874, Hamblin left Kanab alone, on a mission that was intended to pacify thousands of savage Indians. Possibly since St. Patrick invaded Erin, no bolder episode had been known in history. He was overtaken by his son with a note from Levi Stewart, advising return, but steadfastly kept on, declaring, "I have been appointed to a mission by the highest authority of God on earth. My life is of small moment compared with the lives of the Saints and the interests of the kingdom of God. I determined to trust in the Lord and go on." At Moen Copie Wash he was joined by J. E. Smith and brother, not Mormons, but men filled with a spirit of adventure, for they were well informed concerning the prospective Navajo uprising. At a point a day's ride to the eastward of Tuba's home on Moen Copie Wash, the three arrived at a Navajo village, from which messengers were sent out summoning a council.

The next noon, about February 1, the council started, in a lodge twenty feet long by twelve feet wide, constructed of logs, leaning to the center and covered with dirt. There was only one entrance. Hamblin and the Smiths were at the farther end. Between them and the door were 24 Navajos. In the second day's council came the critical time. Hamblin knew no Navajo and there had to be resort to a Paiute interpreter, a captive, terrified by fear that he too might be sacrificed if his interpretation proved unpleasant. His digest of a fierce Navajo discussion of an hour was that the Indians had concluded all Hamblin had said concerning the killing of the three men was a lie, that he was suspected of being a party to the killing, and, with the exception of three of the older Indians, all present had voted for Hamblin's death. They had distinguished the Smiths as "Americans," but they were to witness the torture of Hamblin and then be sent back to the Colorado on foot. The Navajos referred especially to Hamblin's counsel that the tribe cross the river and trade with the Mormons. Thus they had lost three good young men, who lay on the northern land for the wolves to eat. The fourth was produced to show his wounds and tell how he had traveled for thirteen days, cold and hungry and without a blanket. There was suggestion that Hamblin's death might be upon a bed of coals that smoked in the middle of the lodge.

The Smiths tightened their grasps upon their revolvers. In a letter written by one of them was stated:

Had we shown a symptom of fear, we were lost; but we sat perfectly quiet, and kept a wary eye on the foe. It was a thrilling scene. The erect, proud, athletic form of the young chief as he stood pointing his finger at the kneeling figure before him; the circle of crouching forms; their dusky and painted faces animated by every passion that hatred and ferocity could inspire, and their glittering eyes fixed with one malignant impulse upon us; the whole partially illuminated by the fitful gleam of the firelight (for by this time it was dark), formed a picture not easy to be forgotten.

Hamblin behaved with admirable coolness. Not a muscle in his face quivered, not a feature changed as he communicated to us, in his usual tone of voice, what we then fully believed to be the death warrant of us all. When the interpreter ceased, he, in the same easy tone and collected manner, commenced his reply. He reminded the Indians of his long acquaintance with their tribe, of the many negotiations he had conducted between his people and theirs, and his many dealings with them in years gone by, and challenged them to prove that he had ever deceived them, ever had spoken with a forked tongue. He drew a map of the country on the ground, and showed them the improbability of his having been a participant in the affray.

In the end, the three were released after a discussion in the stifling lodge that had lasted for eleven hours, "with every nerve strained to its utmost tension and momentarily expecting a conflict which must be to the death."

The Indians had demanded 350 head of cattle as recompense, a settlement that Hamblin refused to make, but which he stated he would put before the Church authorities. Twenty-five days later, according to agreement, he met a delegation of Indians at Moabi. Later he took Chief Hastele, a well-disposed Navajo, and a party of Indians to the spot where the young men had been killed, and there demonstrated, to the satisfaction of the Indians, the falsity of the accusation that Mormons had been responsible.

In April, 1874, understanding that the missionaries south of the river were in grave danger, a party of 35 men from Kanab and Long Valley, led by John R. Young, was dispatched southward. At Moen Copie was found a gathering of about forty. It appeared the reinforcement was just in time, as a Navajo attack on the post had been planned. Hamblin persisted in braving all danger and set out with Ammon M. Tenney and a few others for Fort Defiance, but found it unnecessary to go beyond Oraibi.

The Utah affair, after agency investigation, was brought up again at Fort Defiance, August 21, with Hamblin and Tenney present, and settled in a way that left Hamblin full of thanksgiving.

In 1875, Hamblin located a road from St. George to the Colorado River, by way of Grand Wash.

The Old Scout's Later Years

In May, 1876, Hamblin served as guide for Daniel H.

Wells, Erastus Snow and a number of other leading men of Utah on their way to visit the new Arizona settlements. The Colorado was at flood and the passage at Lee's Ferry, May 28, was a dangerous one. The ferryboat bow was drawn under water by the surges and the boat swept clear of three wagons, with the attendant men and their luggage. One man was lost, Lorenzo W. Roundy, believed to have been taken with a cramp. His body never was found. L. John Nuttall and Hamblin swam to safety on the same oar. Lorenzo Hatch, Warren Johnson and another clung to a wagon from which they were taken off by a skiff just as they were going over the rapids.

In the same year, in December, Hamblin was assigned by President Young to lay out a wagon route from Pearce's Ferry, south of St. George, to Sunset on the Little Colorado. The Colorado was crossed at a point five miles above the old crossing. The animals were made to swim and the luggage was conveyed in a hastily constructed skiff. The route was a desert one, about on the same line as that to be used by the proposed Arizona-Utah highway between Grand Wash and the present Santa Fe railroad station of Antares. Returning, Hamblin went as far south as Fort Verde, where Post Trader W. S. Head advanced, without money, provisions enough to last until the party arrived at the Colorado, south of St. George.

An interview at St. George with President Young succeeding this trip was the last known by Hamblin with the Church head, for the President died the following August. In that interview, December 15, 1876, Hamblin formally was ordained as "Apostle to the Lamanites."

In the spring of 1877, Hamblin journeyed again into Arizona by the Lee's Ferry route to the Hopi towns, trying to find an escaping criminal. On this trip, the Hopi implored him to pray for rain, as their crops were dying. Possibly through his appeal to grace, rain fell very soon thereafter, assuring the Indians a crop of corn, squashes and beans. There was little rain elsewhere. When Hamblin returned to his own home, he found his crops burned from drouth.

The estimation in which the Indians held the old scout may have indication in a story told lately in the Historian's office by Jacob Hamblin Jr. It follows:

One day my father sent me to trade a horse with an old Navajo Indian chief. I was a little fellow and I went on horseback, leading the horse to be traded. The old chief came out and lifted me down from my horse. I told him my father wanted me to trade the horse for some blankets. He brought out a number of handsome blankets, but, as my father had told me to be sure and make a good trade, I shook my head and said I would have to have more. He then brought out two buffalo robes and quite a number of other blankets and finally, when I thought I had done very well, I took the roll on my horse, and started for home. When I gave the blankets to my father, he unrolled them, looked at them, and then began to separate them. He put blanket after blanket into a roll and then did them up and told me to get on my horse and take them back and tell the chief he had sent me too many. When I got back, the old chief took them and smiled. He said, "I knew you would come back; I knew Jacob would not keep so many; you know Jacob is our father, as well as your father."

In 1878 Hamblin moved to Arizona and was made a counselor to President Lot Smith. He was appointed in 1879 to preside over the Saints in Round Valley, the present Springerville, living at Fort Milligan, about one mile west of the present Eagar.

He died of malarial fever, August 31, 1886, at Pleasanton, in Williams Valley, New Mexico, where a settlement of Saints had been made in October, 1882.

Hamblin's remains were removed from Pleasanton before 1889, to Alpine, Arizona, where was erected a shaft bearing this very appropriate inscription:

In memory of
JACOB V. HAMBLIN,
Born April 2, 1819,
Died August 31, 1886.
Peacemaker in the Camp of the Lamanites.

Chapter Nine

Crossing the Mighty Colorado

Early Use of "El Vado de Los Padres"

The story of the Colorado is most pertinent in a work such as this, for the river and its Grand Canyon formed a barrier that must be passed if the southward extension of Zion were to become an accomplished fact. Much of detail has been given elsewhere concerning the means of passage used by the exploring, missionary and settlement expeditions that had so much to do with Arizona's development. In this chapter there will be elaboration only to the extent of consideration of the ferries and fords that were used.

The highest of the possible points for the crossing of the Colorado in Arizona, is on the very Utah line, in latitude 37. It is the famous "Vado de los Padres," the Crossing of the Fathers, also known as the Ute ford. The first historic reference concerning it is in the journal of the famous Escalante-Dominguez priestly expedition of. 1776. The party returning from its trip northward as far as Utah Lake, reached the river, at the mouth of the Paria, about November 1. The stream was found too deep, so there was a scaling of hills to the Ute ford, which was reached November 8.

This ford is approached from the northward by natural steps down the precipices, traveled by horses with some difficulty. On the southern side, egress is by way of a long canyon that has few difficulties of passage. The ford, which is illustrated in the frontispiece of this work, reproduced from an official drawing of the Wheeler expedition, may be used more than half the year. In springtime the stream

89

is deep when the melted snows of the Rockies are drained by the spring freshet. Usually, the Mormon expeditions southward started well after the summer season, when the crossing could be made without particular danger.

The Ute ford could hardly be made possible for wagon transportation, so there was early effort to find a route for a through road. As early as November, 1858, with some such idea in view, Jacob Hamblin was at the mouth of the Paria, 35 miles southwest of the Ute ford, but was compelled, then and also in November, 1859, to pursue his journey on, over the hills, to the ford.

Ferrying at the Paria Mouth

The first crossing of the river, at the mouth of the Paria, was made by a portion of a party, headed by Hamblin, in the fall of 1860. A raft was constructed, on which a few were taken across, but, after one animal had been drowned and there had been apparent demonstration that the dangers were too great, and that there was lack of a southern outlet, the party made its way up the river to the ford.

The first successful crossing at the Paria was in March, 1864, by Hamblin, on a raft. The following year there was a Mormon settlement at or near the Paria mouth. August 4, 1869, the first of the Powell expeditions reached the mouth of the Paria, this on the trip that ended at the mouth of the Virgin.

In September, 1869, Hamblin crossed by means of a raft. That the route had been definitely determined upon was indicated by the establishment, January 31, 1870, of a Paria fort, with guards. In the fall of that year President Brigham Young visited the Paria, as is shown in a letter written by W. T. Stewart, this after the President had seen the mouth of the Virgin and otherwise had shown his interest in a southern outlet for Utah. In this same year, according to Dellenbaugh, Major Powell built a rough scow, in order to reach the Moqui towns. This was the crossing in October, when Jacob Hamblin guided Powell to the Moqui villages and Fort Defiance.

In his expedition of 1871, Powell left the river at the Ute ford and went to Salt Lake. A few days later, October 22, his men, with a couple of boats, reached the Paria for a lengthy stay, surveying on the Kaibab plateau, in the vicinity of Kanab. It was written that the boat "Emma Dean" was hidden across the river. By that time ferry service had been established, for on October 28, 1871, Jacob Hamblin and companions, on their way home from the south, were rowed across.

John D. Lee on the Colorado

It is remarkable, in the march of history, how there will cling to a spot a name that, probably, should not have been attached and that should be forgotten. This happens to be the case with Lee's Ferry, a designation now commonly accepted for the mouth of the Paria, though it commemorates the Mountain Meadows massacre, through the name of the leading culprit in that awful frontier tragedy. Yet John Doyle Lee was at the river only a few years of all the years of the ferry's long period of use. The name seems to have been started within that time, firmly fixed in the chronicles of the Powell expedition, in the books of the expeditions later and of Dellenbaugh.

John D. Lee located at the mouth of the Paria early in 1872 and named it "Lonely Dell," by Dellenbaugh considered a most appropriate designation. Lee built a log cabin and acquired some ferry rights that had been possessed by the Church.

An interesting detail of the ferry is given by J. H. Beadle, in his "Western Wilds." He told of reaching the ferry from the south June 28, 1872. The attention of a ferryman could not be attracted, so there was use of a boat that was found hidden in the sand and brush. This was the "Emma Dean," left by Powell. The ferryman materialized two days later, calling himself "Major Doyle,"

91

but his real identity was developed soon thereafter. Beadle gives about a chapter to his interview with Lee, whom he called "a born fanatic." Beadle, who had written much against the Church, also had given a false name, but his identity was discovered by Mrs. Lee through clothing marks. Beadle quoted "Mrs. Doyle" as saying that her husband had been with the Mormon Battalion. This was hardly exact, though it does appear that Lee, October 19, 1846, was in Santa Fe with Howard Egan, the couple returning to Council Bluffs with pay checks the Battalion members were sending back toward the support of their families. The two messengers had overtaken the Battalion at the Arkansas crossing. But Beadle slept safely in Lee's house, which he left on Independence Day, departing by way of Jacob's Pools.

July 13, another of Powell's boats was brought down the river. Just a month later, Powell arrived at Lonely Dell from Kanab. August 17, he started down the river again from the Paria, leaving the "Nellie Powell" to the ferryman. This trip was of short duration, for the river was left, finally, at Kanab Wash.

In May, 1873, came the first of the real southern Mormon migration. This was when H. D. Haight and his party crossed the river at the Paria, on a trip that extended only about to Grand Falls, but which was notable from the fact that it laid out the first Mormon wagon road south of the river, down to and along the Little Colorado.

October 15, 1873, was launched at the ferry, by John L. Blythe, a much larger boat than had been known before, made of timber brought from a remote point near the Utah line. That same winter Hamblin located a new road from the Paria mouth to the San Francisco Mountains.

In June of 1874, an Indian trading post was established at the ferry and there was erection of what was called a "strong fort."

In the fall of 1874, Lee departed from the river, this

for the purpose of securing provisions in the southern settlements of Utah. Several travelers noted in their journals that Lee wanted nothing but provisions in exchange for ferry tolls. It was on this trip he was captured by United States marshals in southern Utah, thereafter to be tried, convicted and legally executed by shooting (March 23, 1877), on the spot where his crime had been committed.

Lee's Canyon Residence Was Brief

Much of romance is attached to Lee's residence on the Colorado. The writer has heard many tales how Lee worked rich gold deposits nearby, how he explored the river and its canyons and how, for a time, he was in seclusion among the Hava-Supai Indians in the remote Cataract Canyon, to which, there was assumption, he had brought the fruit seeds from which sprang the Indian orchards. This would appear to be mainly assumption, for Lee made his living by casual ferrying, and had to be on hand when the casual traveler called for his services. Many of the old tales are plausible, and have had acceptance in previous writings of the Author, but it now appears that Lee's residence on the Canyon was only as above stated. J. Lorenzo Hubbell states that Lee was at Moen Copie for a while before going to take charge of the ferry.

In the summer of 1877, Ephriam K. Hanks was advised by President Brigham Young to buy the ferry, but this plan fell through on the death of the President. The ferry, later, was bought from Emma Lee by Warren M. Johnson, as Church agent, he paying 100 cows, which were contributed by the people of southern Utah and northern Arizona settlements, they receiving tithing credits therefor.

About ten years ago, Lee's Ferry was visited by Miss Sharlot M. Hall, Arizona Territorial Historian. She wrote entertainingly of her trip, by wagon, northwest into the Arizona Strip, much of her diary published in 1912 in the Arizona Magazine. The Lee log cabin showed that some of its logs originally had been used in some sort of raft or rude ferryboat. There also was found in the yard a boat, said to have been one of those of the Powell expedition. This may have been the "Nellie Powell."

Of the Lee occupancy, Miss Hall tells a little story that gives insight into the trials of the women of the frontier:

When Lee's wife stayed here alone, as she did much of the time, the Navajo Indians often crossed here and they were not always friendly. A party of them came one night and built their campfire in the yard and Mrs. Lee understood enough of their talk to know she was in danger. Brave woman as she was, she knew she must overawe them, and she took her little children and went out and spread a bed near the fire in the midst of the hostile camp and stayed there till morning. When the Navajos rode away they called her a brave woman and said she should be safe in the future.

The first real ferryboat was that built by John L. Blythe, on October 15, 1873, a barge 20x40 feet, one that would hold two wagons, loads and teams. It was in this boat that the Jas. S. Brown party crossed in 1875, and a much larger migration to the Little Colorado in the spring of 1876.

In 1877, there was consideration of the use of the Paria road, as a means for hauling freight into Arizona, at least as far as Prescott, which was estimated by R. J. Hinton as 448 miles distant from the terminus, at that time, of the Utah Southern Railroad. Via St. George and Grand Wash, the haul was set at 391 miles, though the Paria route seemed to be preferred. It should be remembered that at that time the nearest railroad was west of Yuma, a desert journey from Prescott of about 350 miles.

Crossing the Colorado on the Ice

The Paria crossing had served as route of most of the Mormon migration south. The ferry has been passed occasionally by river explorers, particularly by the Stanton expedition, which reached that point on Christmas Day, 1889, in the course of a trip down the Colorado that extended as far as salt water. The ferryboat was not needed at one stage of the history of Lee's Ferry. The story comes in the journals of several members of a missionary party. Anthony W. Ivins (now a member of the Church First Presidency) and Erastus B. Snow reached the river January 16, 1878, about the same time as did John W. Young and a number of prospective settlers bound for the Little Colorado. The Snow narrative of the experience follows:

The Colorado River, the Little Colorado and all the springs and watering places were frozen over. Many of the springs and tanks were entirely frozen up, so that we were compelled to melt snow and ice for our teams. We (that is J. W. Young and I), crossed our team and wagon on the ice over the Colorado. I assure you it was quite a novelty to me, to cross such a stream of water on ice; many other heavily loaded wagons did the same, some with 2500 pounds on. One party did a very foolish trick, which resulted in the loss of an ox; they attempted to cross three head of large cattle all yoked and chained together, and one of the wheelers stepped on a chain that was dragging behind, tripped and fell, pulling his mate with him, thereby bringing such a heft on the ice that it broke through, letting the whole into the water; but the ice being sufficiently strong they could stand on it and pull them out one at a time. One got under the ice and was drowned, the live one swimming some length of time holding the dead one up by the yoke.

Concerning the same trip, Mr. Ivins has written the Arizona Historian that, "the river was frozen from shore to shore, but, above and below for a short distance, the river was open and running rapidly." Great care was taken in crossing, the wagons with their loads usually pulled over by hand and the horses taken over singly. Thus the ice was cracked. Mr. Ivins recites the episode of the oxen and then tells that a herd of cattle was taken across by throwing each animal, tying its legs and dragging it across. One man could drag a grown cow over the smooth ice. Mr. Ivins tells that he remained at the river several days, crossing on the ice 32 times. On the 22d the missionaries and settlers all were at Navajo Springs, ready

95

to continue the journey. It is believed that the Colorado has not been frozen over since that time.

There now is prospect that the Paria route between Utah and Arizona will be much bettered by construction of a road that avoids Paria Creek and attains the summit of the mesa, to the northward, within a comparatively short distance. At a point six miles below the ferry, the County of Coconino, with national aid, is preparing for construction of a suspension bridge, with a 400-foot span. Upon its completion, Lee's Ferry will pass, save for its place in history.

Crossings Below the Grand Canyon

Below Lee's Ferry comes the Grand Canyon of the Colorado, cut a full mile deep for about 200 miles, in a winding channel, with only occasional spots where trails are feasible to the river's edge. A suspension bridge is being erected by the United States Forest Service below El Tovar, with a trail northward up Bright Angel Canyon. A feasible trail exists from the mouth of Kanab Wash to the northward. To the southward there is possibility of approach to the river by wagon at Diamond Creek, but the first real crossing lies immediately below the great Canyon at Grand Wash, a point where there was ferrying, in 1862, by Hamblin and a party who brought a boat from Kanab. Return on this expedition was via the Ute ford. Hamblin, with Lewis Greeley, crossed again at the Grand Wash in April, 1863, and there is record of a later trip of indefinite date, made by him on the river from Grand Wash to Callville, in company with Crosby and Miller. Several of the Hamblin expeditions crossed at Grand Wash in the years thereafter, but it appears that it was not until December, 1876, that a regular ferry there was established, this by Harrison Pearce. The place bears the name of Pearce's Ferry unto this day, though the maps give it as "Pierce." A son of Harrison Pearce, and former assistant in the operation of the ferry, James Pearce, was the first settler of Taylor on Silver Creek, Arizona, where he still resides.

The next ferry was at the mouth of the Virgin, where there were boats for crossing at necessity, including the time when President Brigham Young and party visited the locality, in March, 1870. When the settlers on the Muddy and the Virgin balloted upon the proposition of abandoning the country, Daniel Bonelli and wife were the only ones who voted the negative. When the Saints left southern Nevada, Bonelli and wife moved to a point about six miles below the mouth of the Virgin, and there established a ferry that still is owned by a son of the founder. This is the same noted on government maps as Stone's Ferry, though there has been a change of a few miles in location. About midway between the Virgin and Grand Wash, about 1881, was established the Mike Scanlon ferry. Downstream, early-day ferries were operated at the El Dorado canyon crossing and on the Searchlight road, at Cottonwood Island. W. H. Hardy ferried at Hardyville. About the later site of Fort Mohave, Capt. Geo. A. Johnston, January 23, 1858, in a sternwheel steamer, ferried the famous Beale camel expedition across the river.

Settlements North of the Canyon

Moccasin Springs, a few miles south of the Utah line and eighteen miles by road southwest of Kanab, has had no large population at any time, save that about 100 Indians were in the vicinity in 1900. The place got its name from moccasin tracks in the sand. The site was occupied some time before 1864 by Wm. B. Maxwell, but was vacated in 1866 on account of Indian troubles. In the spring of 1870, Levi Stewart and others stopped there for a while, with a considerable company, breaking land, but moved on to found Kanab, north of the line. This same company also made some improvements around Pipe Springs. About a year later, a company under Lewis Allen, mainly from the Muddy, located temporarily at Pipe Springs and Moccasin. To some extent there was a claim upon the two localities by the United Order or certain of its members. The place for years was mainly a missionary settlement, but it was told that "even when the brethren would plow and plant for them, the Indians were actually too lazy to attend to the growing crops."

That the climate of Moccasin favors growth of sturdy manhood is indicated by the history of one of its families, that of Jonathan Heaton. At hand is a photograph taken in 1905, of Heaton and his fifteen sons. Two of the sons died in accidents within the past two years, but the others all grew to manhood, and all were registered for the draft in the late war. With the photograph is a record that, of the whole family, not one individual has tasted tea, coffee, tobacco or liquor of any kind.

Arizona's First Telegraph Station

Pipe Springs is situate three miles south of Moccasin Springs and eight miles south of the Utah line. It was settled as early as 1863 by Dr. Jas. M. Whitmore, who owned the place when he was killed by the Indians January 8, 1866. President Brigham Young purchased the claims of the Whitmore estate and in 1870 there established headquarters of a Church herd, in charge of Anson P. Winsor. Later was organized the Winsor Castle Stock Growing Company, in which the Church and President Young held controlling interest. It is notable that one of the directors was Alexander F. Macdonald, later President of Maricopa Stake. At the spring, late in 1870, was erected a sizable stone building, usually known as Winsor Castle, a safe refuge from savages, or others, with portholes in the walls. In 1879 the company had consolidation with the Canaan Co-operative Stock Company. The name, Pipe Springs, had its origin, according to A. W. Ivins, in a halt made there by Jacob Hamblin and others. William Hamblin claimed he could shoot the bottom out of Dudley Leavitt's pipe at 25 yards, without breaking the bowl. This he proceeded to do.

Pipe Springs was a station of the Deseret Telegraph,

extended in 1871 from Rockville to Kanab. While the latter points are in Utah, the wires were strung southward around a mountainous country along the St. George-Kanab road. This would indicate location of the first telegraph line within Arizona, as the first in the south, a military line from Fort Yuma to Maricopa Wells, Phoenix, Prescott and Tucson, was not built till 1873.

Arizona's Northernmost Village

Fredonia is important especially as the northernmost settlement of Arizona, being only three miles south of the 37th parallel that divides Utah and this State. It lies on the east bank of Kanab Creek, and is the center of a small tract of farming land, apparently ample for the needs of the few settlers, who have their principal support from stock raising. The first settlement was from Kanab in the spring of 1885, by Thomas Frain Dobson, who located his family in a log house two miles below the present Fredonia townsite. The following year the townsite was surveyed and there was occupation by Henry J. Hortt and a number of others.

The name was suggested by Erastus Snow, who visited the settlement in its earliest days, naturally coming from the fact that many of the residents were from Utah, seeking freedom from the enforcement of federal laws.

Fredonia is in Coconino County, Arizona, with county seat at Flagstaff, 145 miles distant in air line, but across the Grand Canyon. The easiest method of communication with the county seat is by way of Utah and Nevada, a distance of over 1000 miles.

Fredonia was described by Miss Sharlot M. Hall, as "the greenest, cleanest, quaintest village of about thirty families, with a nice schoolhouse and a church and a picturesque charm not often found, and this most northerly Arizona town is almost one of the prettiest. The fields of alfalfa and grain lie outside of the town along a level valley and are dotted over with haystacks, showing that crops have been good." Reference is made to the fact that some of the families were descended from the settlers of the Muddy Valley. There had been the usual trouble in the building of irrigating canals and the washing away of headgates by floods that came down Kanab Creek. Miss Hall continued, "I am constantly impressed with the courage and persistence of the Mormon colony; they have good, comfortable houses here that have been built with the hardest labor amidst floods and drouth and all sorts of discouragement. It is one of the most beautiful valleys I have seen in Arizona and has a fine climate the year round; but these first settlers deserve a special place in history by the way they have turned the wilderness into good farms and homes."

Concerning the highway to Fredonia, Miss Hall observes, "The Mormon colonists who traveled this road certainly had grit when they started, and grit enough more to last the rest of their lives on the road."

For years efforts have been made by Utah to secure from Arizona the land lying north of the Colorado River, on the ground that, topographically, it really belongs to the northern division, and that its people are directly connected by birth and religion with the people of Utah. As a partial offset, they have offered that part of Utah that lies south of the San Juan River, thus to be created a northern Arizona boundary wholly along water courses. The suggestion, repeatedly put before Arizona Legislatures, invariably has met with hostile reception, especially based upon the desire to keep the whole of the Grand Canyon within Arizona. Indeed, in later years, the great 200-mile gorge of the Colorado more generally is referred to as the Grand Canyon of Arizona, this in order to avoid confusion with any scenic attributes of the State of Colorado.

PIPE SPRINGS OR WINSOR CASTLE

The sign on the upper porch is of the first telegraph line in Arizona, built in 1870

MOCCASIN SPRINGS ON ROAD TO THE PARIA

IN THE KAIBAB FOREST NEAR THE HOME OF THE
SHIVWITS INDIANS

Chapter Ten

Arizona's Pioneer Northwest

History of the Southern Nevada Point

Assuredly within the purview of this work is the settlement of what now is the southern point of Nevada, a part of the original area of New Mexico and, hence, included within the Territory of Arizona when created in 1863. This embraced the district south of latitude 37, westward to the California line, west and north of the Colorado River. The main stream of the district is the Virgin, with a drainage area of 11,000 square miles, Muddy River and Santa Clara Creek being its main tributaries. It is a torrential stream, subject to sudden floods and carrying much silt. A section of its valley in the northwestern corner of the present Arizona, near Littlefield, is to be dammed in the near future for the benefit of small farms that have been cultivated for many years and for carrying out irrigation plans of much larger scope.

Especial interest attaches to this district through the fact that its area once was embraced within the now almost forgotten Arizona County of Pah-ute or was part of the present Arizona county of Mohave.

In the Bancroft Library at Berkeley, much information concerning the Nevada point was found in a series of pioneer maps. Of very early designation were old Las Vegas Springs and Beaver Dams, the latter now known as Littlefield. South of the 37th parallel, on a map of 1873, are found Cane Springs, Grapevine Springs and West Point, with Las Vegas (Sp., The Meadows) and Cottonwood as stations on the Mormon road, which divided to the westward at the last-named point.

The main road to Callville appears to have been down the Virgin for a short distance from St. Thomas, and then to have led over the hills to the westward. From Callville, a road connected with the main highway at Las Vegas.

A map of California, made by W. M. Eddy in 1853, has some interesting variations of the northwestern New Mexico nomenclature. The Muddy is set down as El Rio Atascoso (Sp., "Boggy") and Vegas Wash as Ojo del Gaetan (galleta grass?). Nearby was Agua Escorbada, where scurvy grass probably was found. There also was Hernandez Spring. There was an outline of the Potosi mining district. North of Las Vegas on a California map of 1864, was placed the "Old Mormon Fort." Reference by the reader is asked to the description of the Old Spanish Trail, which was followed partially by the line of the later Mormon road.

On a late map of the section that was lost by Arizona to Nevada, today are noted only the settlements of Bunkerville, Moapa, Logan, St. Joseph, Mesquite, Overton and St. Thomas. There is a ferry at Rioville, at the mouth of the Virgin, and another is at Grand Wash. The name of Las Vegas is borne by a railroad station on the Salt Lake and Los Angeles line, a few miles from the Springs. There are the mining camps of Pahrump, Manse, Keystone, El Dorado and Newberry. The westernmost part of the triangle, at an elevation of about 3000 feet, is occupied by the great Amargosa desert, which descends abruptly on the California side into the sink of Death Valley to below sea level. There has been no development of large value in this strip. Its interest to Arizona is merely historical.

Today, few Arizonans know that Pah-ute County once existed as an Arizona subdivision, or that Nevada took a part of Arizona, or that later, Nevada was given full sixty miles expansion eastward of her boundary line, at the expense of both Arizona and Utah. The natural

102

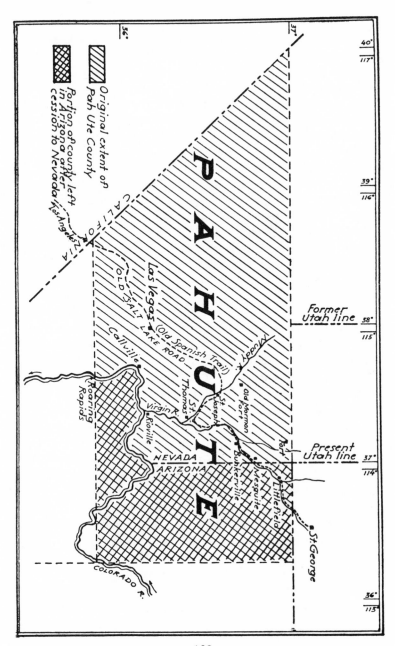

103

boundary line in that section between Nevada and Arizona would have been the Virgin River.

The information contained in this chapter has been gathered from diverse sources, but largely from the records of the Church Historian at Salt Lake, wherein, practically, is the only history of the Mormon settlements of the southwestern section of what was and is known as "Utah's Dixie."

The southern Nevada point had some value in a mineral way. As early as 1857, Mormons worked the Potosi silver mines, eighteen miles southwest of Las Vegas. Little data is at hand concerning their value. In Bancroft is found this sober chronicle: "Believing the mines to be lead, Brigham Young sent miners to work them, in anticipation of war with the United States, but the product was found too hard for bullets and the mines were abandoned."

The Congressional Act of May, 1866, giving Nevada all that part of Arizona lying between the Colorado River and California, from about longitude 114, took from Arizona 31,850 square miles. This followed the extension of Nevada eastward for one degree of longitude. Annexed was appropriation of $17,000 for surveys.

Missionaries of the Desert

In the record of the Whipple expedition of 1853-4, is found evidence of Mormon influence already material in the Southwest. Whipple thought highly of the agricultural possibilities of the valley of the Colorado River, above the mouth of Bill Williams' Fork and wrote, "The Mormons made a great mistake in not occupying the valley of the Colorado." This Whipple expedition made a painful journey from the Colorado across the Mohave desert and, on March 13, 1854, struck what even then was known as the Mormon Road. The next day Whipple met a party of Mormons en route to Salt Lake. He told them of the murder of one of his Mexican herders by the Paiutes, but the travelers expressed no fear. They said they were at peace with the Indians, a statement over which Whipple expressed surprise.

About the earliest American occupation of the southern Nevada point available in the records upon which this office has worked, appears to have been the detail by Brigham Young in 1854 of a party of thirty young men "to go to Las Vegas, build a fort there to protect immigrants and the United States mail from the Indians, and to teach the latter how to raise corn, wheat, potatoes, squash and melons."

The missionary party arrived at Las Vegas June 14, 1855. Four days later was started construction of an adobe fort on the California road, on an eminence overlooking the valley. This fort, 150 feet square, had walls, upon a stone foundation, fourteen feet high, with bastions on the southeast and northwest corners. Gates were not procured until the following year. Houses were built against the inside of the wall and lots were drawn to decide just where each of the brethren should erect his dwelling. There was a garden plot, just below, on the creek, and small farms were provided nearby. Inside the fort was a schoolhouse, in which meetings also were held, this indicating that families soon followed the pioneer missionaries. It is told that "the gospel was preached and that many Indians were converted and baptized."

One of these missionaries was Benjamin Cluff, who in later years became a prominent member of the Gila Valley settlements in Arizona. In his biography is found notation that the Las Vegas missionaries worked in lead mines, assumed to have been those in the Potosi section. Some of this lead undoubtedly went back to Utah but, happily, was not used at the time of the 1858 invasion.

Another notable member was Wm. C. A. Smoot who died in Salt Lake City in the spring of 1920, and who was one of the original Pioneers who reached Salt Lake July

24, 1847. Having been the last of the first pioneer company to enter the valley, it was quite in keeping that he was the last of the company to leave the valley for the celestial shores.

Here there might be notation that of the venerated Salt Lake Pioneers, the following-named later had residence in Arizona: Edmund Ellsworth, Charles Shumway, Edson Whipple, Francis M. Pomeroy, Conrad Klineman, Andrew S. Gibbons and Joseph Matthews.

Of the Pioneers of especial distinction, the following-named were later visitors to Arizona: Brigham Young, Wilford Woodruff, Geo. A. Smith, Erastus Snow, Amasa M. Lyman and Lorenzo D. Young.

Missionaries John Steele and Wm. A. Follett were former Battalion members.

Rufus C. Allen, who was Private No. 1 of the First Company of the Mormon Battalion, returned from Chile to become a missionary in the Las Vegas section and in the Virgin River country. One of Allen's daughters, Mrs. Rachael Berry of St. Johns, represented Apache County in the House of Representatives of Arizona's Second State Legislature, in 1915.

Diplomatic Dealings with the Redskins

With the exception of the missionaries and the travelers between Utah and San Bernardino, the white man had little place in the southern point of Nevada in the early days. At hand, however, is a tale of the adventures of Ira Hatch, who was sent into the lonely, barren desert in the hope that something of missionary value might be done with the Indians. These Indians, Paiutes, were described as "always ready to attack the weak and defenseless traveler, including any opportunity to prey upon the animals of the watchful and strong." Nevertheless missionaries from southern Utah attempted Christianization. Whatever their degree of success, and though often in serious danger, they made the redskins understand that,

106

personally, they were friendly. This missionary effort, it was hoped, would serve to make safer the through road.

Elder Hatch, in January, 1858, was sent alone into the Muddy Valley, 100 miles from the nearest settlement, Santa Clara. He was among the savages for two weeks, camped in a broken-down wagon left by one of the Crismons. His main trouble was in saving food from the Indians, who descended upon him like locusts and manifested their friendliness by stealing everything they could carry away. Hatch held the fort, however, translating and serving as guide for travelers, and occasionally having to threaten with his pistol redskins who menaced him with their bows and arrows.

After a fortnight, Jacob Hamblin sent him a companion, Thales Haskell, another noted pioneer, and together the two spent the balance of the winter in the lonely outpost. There was an interesting diversion in the passage of Col. Thos. L. Kane, the statesman who had done so much for the Mormon people at the time of exodus from Nauvoo and who later served so effectively as a mediator between Deseret and the national government. Kane, with a party, was on his way from California to Salt Lake. He had an idea of creating a haven of refuge for beleagured travelers in a cave about sixty miles northeast of Overton. In this cave he had placed bottles of medicine, which he wished the Indians to understand was good only for white men. This refuge he called the "Travelers' Home." It had been known as "Dr. Osborn's Cave."

A number of the Indians were gathered and a treaty was concluded. At this meeting there developed the unusual condition that Hatch had spent so much time with the Indians that his English was very imperfect and broken, while Colonel Kane's language was of cultured sort, unfamiliar and almost unintelligible to Hatch. So a third person (Amasa M. Lyman) had to interpret between Kane and Hatch and the latter then interpreted to the Indians,

107

the return message going the same route back to the Colonel. Inasmuch as the treaty had been upon the basis of certain trade articles that were to have been furnished by the Utah Indian agent, and were not furnished, the contract was not completed. Ammon M. Tenney, a mere lad, spent several months in Las Vegas at that time. Hatch and Haskell returned to their homes in Utah in March, 1858.

Near Approaches to Indian Warfare

Continual trouble was known with the Indians, though, after a few years, was written, "many of the Indians are being taught to labor and are learning better things than to rob and murder."

When the first agricultural settlers came, they were visited by To-ish-obe, principal chief of the Muddy Indians, and a party of other redskins, who transmitted information that had been sent them to the effect that President Erastus Snow had planned to poison the Muddy and kill off all the Indians. The chief was disabused of the idea.

The same chief appears to have been decent enough. In February, 1866, there is record how he had declared outlaws two Indians who had stolen horses and cattle. One of these Indians, Co-quap, was taken prisoner and was killed at St. Thomas. About the same time, Indians on the Muddy, above Simonsville (a grist mill site), stole wheat from about thirty acres and left for the mountains, threatening the Muddy settlers. Within a month, 32 head of horses, mules and cattle were driven off by Indians, from St. Joseph and Simonsville. An expedition of 25 men started after the marauders, but failed to recapture the stock.

Andrew S. Gibbons (who had come in 1864), sought To-ish-obe on the upper Muddy, to interpret and make peace, if possible. In June at St. Joseph was a conference between Erastus Snow and a group of the leading Indians, representing the Santa Clara, Muddy, Colorado and other bands, in all seven chiefs and 64 of their men. The conference was an agreeable one and it was felt that some good had been done.

There was more trouble with the Indians in February, 1868, when the tribesmen on the upper Muddy, where a new settlement had been formed, came to the camp in anger, with blackened faces, armed with bows and arrows, to demand pay for grain lands that had been occupied by the whites. Gibbons acted as peacemaker, but told, "the fact that the brethren were all well armed appeared to pacify the Indians more than any arguments." The farmers formed in battle line, with Helaman Pratt as captain, Gibbons in front, interpreting.

The Indians of the region, mainly Paiutes, were a never-ending source of irritation and of potential danger to the settlers. They had grown fields of a few acres along the Muddy and hence resented the coming of the settlers who might include the aboriginal farms within their holdings. In accordance with the traditional policy of the Church, however, conciliation was used wherever possible, though the settlers sometimes, when goaded to the last extremity, had to exhibit firearms and make a show of force.

In 1868, Joseph W. Young wrote, "These Indians were considered about the worst specimens of the race. They lived almost in a state of nudity and were among the worst thieves on the continent. But through the kind, though determined, course pursued towards them by our brethren who have been among them, they are greatly changed for the better, and I believe I may safely say that they are the best workers of all the tribes. They are, nevertheless, Indians, and much wisdom is required to get along with them pleasantly. Brother Andrew Gibbons is worthy of honorable mention, because of the good influence that he maintains over these rude men."

In November, 1870, the Indians were reported "very hostile and saucy." The Chemehuevis and Mohaves were at war. A band of the former, about 100 or more, came into the Muddy Valley. In December a band of Wallapai came for a friendly visit.

Utilization of the Colorado River

The Colorado River drains nearly all the lands of present Mormon settlement, mainly lying betwixt the Rockies and the Sierras. The Colorado, within the United States is reckoned as only inferior to the Mississippi-Missouri and Columbia, with an annual flow sufficient to supply for irrigation needs about 20,000,000 acre feet of water. It has a drainage area of 244,000 square miles and a length of 1700 miles. It is of torrential character, very big indeed in the late spring and early summer and very low most of the remainder of the year. In years, not far distant, there will be storage dams at many points, to hold back the springtime floods from the melting of the snows of the Rockies, and from the river's flow will be generated electric power for the turning of the wheels of the Southwest. All this is in plans made by the League of the Southwest, a body now headed by Governor Campbell of Arizona. But these things are of the future, and it is the past we especially are considering.

Several attempts were made during and prior to the Civil War to make of the Colorado a highway through which Utah, southern Nevada and northern Arizona might have better transportation. The scheme was not a wild one by any means, though handicapped by the difficulties of both the maximum and minimum flows.

Inspector General J. F. Rusling had recommended that military supplies for the forces in Utah be brought in by way of the Colorado River.

Fort Yuma was visited late in 1854 by Lieut. N. Michler, of the Topographical Engineers, who wrote:

The belief is entertained and strongly advocated that the Colorado will be the means of supplying the Mormon territory, instead of the great extent of land transportation now used for that purpose.

110

Its headwaters approach the large settlements of Utah and may one day become the means of bearing away the products of those pioneers of the far West. With this idea prominent in the minds of speculators, a city on paper, bearing the name of "Colorado City," had already been surveyed, the streets and blocks marked out and many of them sold. It is situated on the east bank, opposite Fort Yuma.

From 1858 to about 1882, even after the Santa Fe railroad had reached Needles, there was much traffic on the Colorado. Supplies went by river to the mines, which sent downstream occasional shipments of ore. Military supplies went by water to Fort Mohave or to Ehrenberg, the latter point a depot for Whipple Barracks and other posts. Salt came down stream from the Virgin River mines, for use mainly in the amalgamation processes of the small stamp mills of the period.

Steamboats on the Shallow Stream

Traffic on the river had been established as early as December, 1852. Capt. Geo. A. Johnston, an early steamboat pilot, ferried the Beale party, in January, 1858, near where Fort Mohave later was established. Johnston made several trips far up the river with the Jesup and with a newer steamer, the Colorado. He is understood to have gone even farther than Lieut. J. C. Ives, of the Topographical Corps, in the little steamer Explorer. This sternwheeler made the trip in January, 1858, and was passed by Johnston on his way downstream. The river was at low stage and the Explorer butted into snags and muddy banks continually. Finally there was disaster when Black Canyon was reached, when the boat ran upon a sunken rock. Ives rowed as far up as Vegas Wash.

In 1866, the Arizona Legislature, at Prescott, by resolution thanked "Admiral" Robert Rogers, commander of the steamer Esmeralda, and Capt. William Gilmore, for the successful accomplishment of the navigation of the Colorado River to Callville, "effected by the indomitable energy of the enterprising Pacific and Colorado Navigation Co.," a concern managed by Thos. E. Trueworthy, an experienced steamboat man from the Sacramento River of California. Both Arizona and Nevada Legislatures petitioned Congress to improve the stream.

Captain Johnston later formed the Colorado Steam Navigation Company and, more or less, controlled the river traffic for years. There were other noted Captains, including C. V. Meeden, Isaac Polhamus, A. D. Johnson, William Poole, S. Thorn, J. H. Godfrey and J. A. Mellen.

Captain Mellen told that sometimes schooner barges were used in the lower canyons, where the wind was either upstream or downstream. When it was downstream, the upward-bound craft moored until the breeze changed to astern.

The deck hands were Cocopah or Yuma Indians, amphibious, always ready to plunge overboard to help in lightening their craft over any of the numerous sand bars. Mellen told of lying 52 days in one bar and of often being held up for a week. There was no possible mapping of the river channel, for the bars changed from week to week. Even in the earliest times, steamboats were never molested by the Indians. They seemed in awe of the puffing, snorting craft that threw showers of sparks from the smokestacks. Not infrequently, a steamer had to tie up for a few days at a point where fuel conveniently could be cut from the cottonwood or mesquite thickets.

In June, the river is at flood, with danger always present in floating trees and driftwood, muddy torrents coming from the melting snows of the Rocky Mountains. In the autumn the river falls, until in places there are mere trickles around the muddy banks. Navigation, perforce, had to be suspended. These were the conditions under which it was proposed to make of the Colorado the great trade artery of the inter-mountain region.

The Colorado now absolutely has lost all possibilities for commerce. Pioneer conditions are about the same as far southward as the Laguna dam. This structure, built to divert water for the Yuma and Imperial valleys, absolutely bars the river channel for navigation. Above it and below it now are only ferries and a few power boats. The great Imperial canal system, at a point below Yuma, for much of the year drains the river flow. Where good-sized steamers once plied from tidewater, at the head of the Gulf of California, now, for months at a time, is only a dry sand wash. To this extent the advance of civilization has obliterated a river that ranks, in geography at least, among the greatest streams of the United States.

Establishing a River Port

Callville, established on the Colorado by Anson Call in December, 1864, for a while was the southernmost outpost of Mormon settlement. Call himself was a pioneer of most vigorous sort. November 24, 1851, he was one of the founders of Fillmore, Millard County, 150 miles south of Salt Lake, a settlement for a while the capital of the Territory of Utah, created during the administration of President Millard Fillmore in 1850. In the following year he built Call's Fort in Box Elder County, in the extreme northern part of Utah.

In a compilation made by Andrew Jenson is found definite statement that the settlement made by Anson Call on the Colorado was "as agent for the Trustee in Trust (the President) of the Church in December, 1864, according to a plan which was conceived of at that time to bring the Church immigration from Europe to Utah via Panama, the Gulf of California and up the river to this landing." In conjunction with this, a number of leading merchants of Salt Lake City combined to build a warehouse on the Colorado, with a view to bringing goods in by the river route. This company also constituted Anson Call its agent. November 1, Call was directed to take a suitable company, locate a road to the Colorado, explore the river, find a suitable place for a warehouse, build it and form a settlement at or near the landing. All these things he accomplished. At St. George he employed Jacob Hamblin and son, Angus M. Cannon and Dr. Jas. M. Whitmore.

The journal of travel tells of leaving the mouth of the Muddy, continuing down the Virgin twelve miles, thence up what was named Echo Wash, twelve miles, and thence twenty miles, generally southwestward, to the Colorado, a mile below the narrows, above the mouth of Black Canyon, where, on December 2, was found a black rocky point, considered a suitable spot for the erection of a warehouse, above high-water mark. This later was named Callville.

With the exception of a small bottom around the warehouse site, the country was considered most barren and uninviting. Two and a half miles down the river was the mouth of Las Vegas Wash, up which Call and party traveled to old Fort Vegas, where a half-dozen men were found established. In the company's journeyings, El Dorado Canyon was found occupied by miners and there were some adventurers on Cottonwood Island, a tract of bottom land nearby. The expedition was ferried across the Colorado to Hardy's Landing, 337 miles above Yuma. Hardy had a rather extensive establishment, with a store, warehouse, hotel, blacksmith shop, carpenter shop and several dwelling houses. Possibly notable was the launching at that time of the barge "Arizona," fifty feet long and ten feet wide, sharp at both ends and flat-bottomed.

By river there was a visit to Fort Mohave. This, garrisoned by forty soldiers of the California Column, was of log and willow houses, the latter wattled and daubed with mud. There was reference by Call to the Colorado River mesquito, described as "very large."

Returning to Call's Landing, there were measured off forty lots, each 100 feet square, and a start was made by leaving Thomas Davids and Lyman Hamblin, on December 18, to dig the foundation of the warehouse.

This expedition made a preliminary survey of the Mud-

114

dy and declared settlement upon the stream entirely feasible.

Wm. H. Hardy of Hardyville, or Hardy's Landing, was not at home when Anson Call visited in December, but returned soon thereafter and, January 2, 1865, started northward with his new barge, propelled by poles and oars and a sail. A distance of 150 miles by river was made in twelve days. Though later some jealousy was expressed over the activities at Callville, Hardy proffered all possible assistance and expressed belief that from July to November steamers could ply from the mouth of the Colorado to Call's Landing. The warehouse was built, but appears to have been little used. Capt. Geo. A. Johnston had submitted the Church authorities formal proposals to ship direct from New York to the mouth of the river, in barques of about 600 tons burden, preferably arriving at the river mouth in the fall. The cost of freight from New York to the river mouth was set at $16 a ton, and the cost to El Dorado Canyon at $65, but, figuring currency at 50 cents, the freight was estimated to cost $7.16 per 100 pounds in currency.

In March, 1865, Capt. Thos. E. Trueworthy, told of opposition at Hardy's Landing to the establishment of Callville. He had started for Call's Landing with 100 tons of freight, including 35,000 feet of lumber, to find that Call had returned to Utah. Trueworthy left his boat and cargo below Callville and went on to Salt Lake. He stated the trip from the mouth to Call's Landing would take a boat a month, there being difficulty in passing rapids and in finding wood for fuel.

Historian B. H. Roberts states:

There was shipment of some goods from that point, though at first there were some disappointments and dissatisfaction among the Salt Lake merchants who patronized the route. Two steamboats, the Esmeralda and Nina Tilden made the trip somewhat regularly from the mouth of the Colorado to Call's Landing, connecting with steamships plying between the mouth of the Colorado and San Francisco. The owners of the river boats carried a standing advertisement in the Salt Lake Telegraph, thus seeking trade, up to December 1, 1866. Doubtless the certainty of the early completion of the transcontinental railroad from the Missouri River to the Pacific Ocean stopped the development of this southwest route for immigration and freight, via Utah's southern settlements and the Colorado River.

The port of Callville had only a short life. In June, 1869, the Deseret News printed an article that Callville then had been abandoned. This was in connection with the escape of three horsethieves from St. George. These men wrenched four large doors from the Callville warehouse for the construction of a raft, upon which they committed themselves to the river at flood time, leaving horses and impedimenta behind. Whether they escaped has not been chronicled.

As late as 1892, the walls of the old storehouse still were standing, the only remaining evidences of a scheme of broad ambition designed to furnish a new supply route for a region comprising at least one-fourth of the national expanse.

PRESIDENT BRIGHAM YOUNG AND PARTY AT THE MOUTH OF THE VIRGIN, MARCH 17, 1870

Others in the party are: Amelia Young, Geo. A. Smith, Bathsheba W. Smith, John Taylor, Erastus Snow, Minerva Snow, Jos. W., Lorenzo D. and Brigham Young, Jr., B. S. and Albert C. Young, A. S. Gibbons, Jno. W. Young, Nathaniel V. Jones, John Squires, Joseph Assay, Van Etta, Levi Stewart

Photo by C. R. Savage

BAPTISM OF SEVERAL HUNDRED SHIVWITS INDIANS BY
DAVID H. CANNON AT ST. GEORGE

Chapter Eleven

𝕴𝖓 𝖙𝖍𝖊 𝖁𝖎𝖗𝖌𝖎𝖓 𝖆𝖓𝖉 𝕸𝖚𝖉𝖉𝖞 𝖁𝖆𝖑𝖑𝖊𝖞𝖘

First Agriculture in Northern Arizona

There can be no doubt that the first agricultural settlement in northern Arizona was by a Mormon party, led by Henry W. Miller, which made location at Beaver Dams, on the north bank of the Virgin River on the earlier Mormon road to California. On a tract of land lying six miles below the point where the river emerges from a box canyon, land was cleared in the fall of 1864, crops were put in "and then the enterprise was dedicated to the Lord," according to a report by the leader at Salt Lake. An item in the Deseret News tells that Miller was "called" in the fall of 1863 to go to the Virgin.

Early in 1865, another report told, "affairs in the settlement are progressing very satisfactorily. A large number of fruit trees and grapevines have been set out. Corn, wheat and other vegetation are growing thriftily and the settlers are very industriously prosecuting their several useful vocations, with good prospects of success."

There was notation of some trouble because beavers were numerous and persisted in damming irrigation ditches. In 1867 a river flood destroyed much of the results of the colonists' labors and there was abandonment of the location. Between 1875 and 1878 settlers began to come again and a thriving community now is in existence at that point, known as Littlefield. It is to benefit in large degree by plans approved by the Arizona Water Commissioner, for damming of the canyon for storage of water to irrigate land of the Virgin Valley toward the southwest. Littlefield is the extreme northwestern settlement of the present Arizona, five miles south of the Utah line and three miles east of the Nevada line.

In the same fall conference of 1864 that sent Anson Call on his pioneering expedition, there was designation of a large number (183, according to Christopher Layton) of missionaries, to proceed, with their families, to the Muddy and lower Virgin, thereon to establish colonies that might serve as stations in the great movement toward the Pacific. Undoubtedly, full information was at hand concerning the country and its possibilities, for the colonists began to arrive January 8, 1865, before there could have been formulation of Call's report. Thos. S. Smith was in charge of the migration, and after him was named St. Thomas, one of the settlements. May 28, Andrew S. Gibbons settled at St. Thomas, sent as Indian interpreter. Joseph Warren Foote led in a new settlement at St. Joseph.

Villages of Pioneer Days

In what was known as the Muddy section, comprising the valleys of the lower Virgin River and its main lower tributary, the Muddy, were seven settlements of Mormon origin, during the time when the locality was included in the area of Arizona. These settlements were Beaver Dams on the Virgin, St. Thomas, on the Muddy, about two and a half miles from its junction with the Virgin, Overton, on the same side of the Muddy Valley, about eight miles northwest of St. Thomas, St. Joseph, which lay on the opposite side of the stream, five miles to the northward, West Point (now Logan), on the west bank, possibly fifteen miles west of St. Joseph, and Mill Point and Simonsville between St. Joseph and Overton. To these was addition of the port of Callville. Nearly westward from the last-named point was Las Vegas Springs, distant about twenty miles, a camping point on the road between San Bernardino and Salt Lake, and permanent residence of missionaries. In later days were established Junction City, otherwise Rioville, at the mouth of the Virgin, Bunkerville on the east bank of the

Virgin, three miles west of the later Arizona line, and Mesquite, which lay east across the river.

The valley of the Virgin offered very limited opportunities for settlement, as the stream, an alkaline one, usually ran between deep cliffs. The Muddy, however, despite its name, was a clear stream of slight fall, with a lower valley two miles wide, continuing, upstream, northwesterly for eighteen miles. A number of swamps had to be drained by the first residents. These people constructed a canal, nine miles long, on the southwest side and were preparing to dig a similar canal on the opposite side when there was abandonment.

St. Thomas has been described as a beautiful village, its streets outlined by rows of tall cottonwoods that still survive. There were 85 city lots of one acre each, about the same number of vineyard lots, two and a half acres each, and of farm lots of five acres.

St. Joseph mainly comprised a fort on a high bluff, from which the town had been laid out on a level bench west and northward. It included a flour mill, owned by James Leithead. In August, 1868, the fort was almost destroyed by fire, which burned up nineteen rooms and most of their contents, the meetinghouse and a cotton gin also being included in the destruction. There was a stiff gale and most of the men were absent.

Every settlement along the Virgin and Muddy was organized into a communal system, the United Order. Of this there will be found more detail in Chapter Twelve of this work.

At St. Joseph, June 10, 1869, was organized a cooperative mercantile institution for the Muddy settlement, with Joseph W. Young at its head, R. J. Cutler as secretary and James Leithead as business agent.

There were the usual casualties of the desert country. In June, James Davidson, wife and son died of thirst on the road from the Muddy settlements to St. George, their

119

journey delayed on the desert by the breaking of a wagon wheel.

On a visit made by Erastus Snow and company in the summer of 1869, the Muddy settlements subscribed heavily toward the purchase of stock in a cotton factory at St. George, and toward extension of the Deseret telegraph line. In the record of this company's journey it is told that the Virgin River was crossed 37 times before arrival at St. Thomas.

The condition of the brethren late in 1870 was set forth by James Leithead as something like destitution. He wrote that, "many are nearly naked for want of clothing. We can sell nothing we have for money, and the cotton, what little there is, appears to be of little help in that direction. There are many articles we are more in need of than the cloth, such as boots and shoes and tools of various kinds to work with."

Brigham Young Makes Inspection

President Brigham Young was a visitor to the Muddy settlements in March of 1870. Ammon M. Tenney states that the President was disappointed, for he found conditions unfavorable for agriculture or commercial development. The journey southward was by way of St. George, Utah, a point frequently visited by the Presidency. The return journey was northward, by the desert route. In the party were John Taylor, later President of the Church, Erastus Snow, Geo. A. Smith, Brigham Young, Jr., Andrew S. Gibbons and other notables. In the fall (September 10), was authorized the founding of Kanab. From St. George the President followed the rough road through Arizona to the Paria, personally visiting and selecting the site of Kanab. Very opportunely, from D. K. Udall, lately was received a photograph of the Young party (herewith reproduced), taken March 17 on a mesa overlooking the Colorado at the mouth of the Virgin. Here may be noted that every president of the Mormon Church, with the exception of Joseph Smith, the founder, and Lorenzo Snow has set foot on Arizona soil.

Nevada Assumes Jurisdiction

The beginning of the end of the early Muddy settlements came in a letter from the Church Presidency, dated December 14, 1870, addressed to James Leithead, in charge. It referred to the Nevada survey, placing the settlements within the jurisdiction of that State, the onerous taxes, license and stamp duties imposed, the isolation from the market, the high rate at which property is assessed in Nevada, the unscrupulous character of many officials, all as combining to render conditions upon the Muddy matters of grave consideration, even though the country occupied might be desirable. The settlers, it was said, had done a noble work, making and sustaining their outposts of Zion against many difficulties, amid exposure and toil. It was advised that the settlers petition the Nevada Legislature for an abatement of back taxes and for a new county, but, "if the majority of the Saints in council determine that it is better to leave the State, whose burdens and laws are so oppressive, let it be so done." There was suggestion that if the authorities of Lincoln County, Nevada, chose to enforce tax collections, it might be well to forestall the seizure of property, to remove it out of the jurisdiction of the State.

The Nevada Point Abandoned

December 20, 1870, the people of the Muddy met with John W. Young of Salt Lake and resolved to abandon the location and to look for new homes. The only opposing votes were those of Daniel Bonelli and wife. Bonelli later was a ferryman on the Colorado and his son now is a prominent resident of Mohave County. Among those who voted to move were a number who later were residents of the Little Colorado settlements of Arizona.

In accordance with the suggestion from Salt Lake, the

Nevada Legislature was petitioned for relief. It was told that seven years before had been established St. Joseph and St. Thomas. Thereafter Congress had taken one degree of longitude from Utah and Arizona and attached this land to Nevada. Taxes had been paid in Utah and Arizona. For two years the authorities of Lincoln County, Nevada, had attempted to assess the back taxes. To the Nevada authorities was presented statement of a number of facts, that $100,000 had been expended on water projects, that the settlers had been compelled to feed the Indian population, outnumbering their own, and that they had been so remote from markets that produce could not be converted into cash. It was asked that a new county, that of Las Vegas, be organized, taking in the southern point of Nevada. Attached to the petition were 111 names of citizens of St. Joseph, Overton and St. Thomas.

A similar petition was sent to Congress. There was detail how lumber had to be hauled 150 miles at a cost of $200 per 1000 feet. There had been constructed 150 dwellings. Orchards and vineyards had been planted and 500 acres of cotton fields had been cleared. In all 3000 acres were cultivated. Nevada had imposed a tax of 3 per cent upon all taxable property and $4 poll tax per individual, all payable in gold, something impossible. It therefore was asked that Congress cede back to Utah and Arizona both portions of country detached from them and attached to Nevada.

At that time, the State gave the Muddy-Virgin settlement a population of 600. St. Joseph had 193, St. Thomas about 150, West Point 138 and Overton 119. In other settlements around, namely Spring Valley, Eagle Valley, Rye Valley, Rose Valley, Panaca and Clover, were 658, possibly two score of them not being of the Church. Thus was shown a gross population of 1250.

Most of the settlers on the Muddy left early in 1871, the exodus starting February 1. On returning to Utah, very largely to Long Valley, they left behind their homes, irrigating canals, orchards and farms. The crops, including 8000 bushels of wheat, were left to be harvested by an individual who failed to comply with his part of the contract and who later tore down most of the remaining houses.

Political Organization Within Arizona

Including practically all the Mormons then resident within the new Territory of Arizona, the first Arizona county to be created by additional legislative enactment, following the Howell Code, was that of Pah-ute, in December, 1865, by the first act approved in the Second Arizona Territorial Legislative Assembly. The boundaries of the county were described as: Commencing at a point on the Colorado River known as Roaring Rapids; thence due east to the line of 113 deg. 20 min. west longitude; thence north along said line of longitude, to its point of intersection with the 37th parallel of north latitude; thence west, along said parallel of latitude, to a point where the boundary line between the State of California and the Territory of Arizona strikes said 37th parallel of latitude; thence southeasterly along said boundary line, to a point due west from said Roaring Rapids; thence due east to said Roaring Rapids and point of beginning. Callville was created the seat of justice and the governor was authorized to appoint the necessary county officers.

The new subdivision was taken entirely from Mohave County, which retained the southernmost part of the Nevada point. It may be noted that its boundaries were entirely arbitrary and not natural and the greater part of the new county's area lay in what now is Nevada. October 1, 1867, the county seat was moved to St. Thomas. November 5, 1866, a protest was sent in an Arizona memorial to Congress against the setting off to the State of Nevada of that part of the Territory west of the Colorado. The grant of this tract to Nevada under the terms of a congressional act approved May 5, 1866, had been conditioned

123

on similar acceptance by the Legislature of Nevada. This was done January 18, 1867.

Without effect, the Arizona Legislature twice petitioned Congress to rescind its action, alleging, "it is the unanimous wish of the inhabitants of Pah-ute and Mohave Counties and indeed of all the constituents of your memorialists that the territory in question should remain with Arizona; for the convenient transaction of official and other business, and on every account they greatly desire it." But Congress proved obdurate and Nevada refused to give up the strip and the County of Pah-ute, deprived of most of her area, finally was wiped out by the Arizona Legislature in 1871. At one time there was claim that St. George and a very wide strip of southern Utah really belonged to Arizona.

Pah-ute's Political Vicissitudes

In the Second Legislature, at Prescott, in 1865, at the time of the creation of Pah-ute County, northwest Arizona, or Mohave County, was represented in the Council by W. H. Hardy of Hardyville and in the House by Octavius D. Gass of Callville. In the Third Legislature, which met at Prescott, October 3, 1866, Pah-ute was represented in the Council by Gass, who was honored by election as president of the body, in which he also served as translator and interpreter. He was described as a very able man, though rough of speech. He explored many miles of the lower Grand Canyon. He was not a Mormon, but evidently was held in high esteem by his constituents, who elected him to office in Arizona as long as they had part in its politics. Royal J. Cutler of Mill Point represented the county in the House of Representatives.

In the Fourth Legislature, which met at Prescott, September 4, 1867, Gass, who had moved to Las Vegas, was returned to the Council where again he was chosen president, and Cutler, who had moved to St. Joseph, again was in the House. On the record of the Legislature's proceedings, Gass is styled "ranchero" and Cutler "farmer."

124

Though most of the area of Pah-ute County already had been wiped out by congressional enactment and given to Nevada, Gass again was in the Legislature in 1868, in the fifth session, which met in Tucson, December 10. The House member was Andrew S. Gibbons of St. Thomas, a senior member of a family that since has had much to do with the development of northeastern Arizona. A very interesting feature in connection with this final service in the Legislature, was the fact that Gass and Gibbons floated down the Colorado River to Yuma and thence took conveyance to Tucson. They were in a fourteen-foot boat that had been built at St. Thomas by James Leithead. Gibbons' son, William H. (now resident at St. Johns), hauled the craft to Callville, twenty miles, and there sped the legislators.

At the outset, there was necessity for the voyageurs to pass through the rapids of Black Canyon, an exciting experience, not unmixed with danger. Gibbons knew something of boating and so was at the oars. Gass, seated astern, firmly grabbed the gunwales, shut his eyes and trusted himself in the rapids to providence and his stout companion, with at least one fervent admonition, "For God's sake, Andy, keep her pointed down stream." The passage was made in safety, though both men were soaked by the dashing spray.

The start was made November 1. By day all possible progress was made, the boat being kept in midstream and away from bushes, for fear of ambush by Indians. At night a place for camp would be selected in a secluded spot and a fire would be lighted only when safety seemed assured.

There was some delay in securing transportation eastward from Fort Yuma. Indians had been active along the stage route and had just waylaid a coach and killed its driver. Thus it came that the members from Pah-ute were six days late in their taking seats in the territorial assembly.

At the close of the legislative session, Gibbons journeyed

home on horseback, for much of the way through districts infested by wild Indians of several tribes, a trip of at least 500 miles. Gass went to California before returning home. Such a return journey is not mentioned, however, in an interesting record, furnished the Author by A. V., Richard and Wm. H. Gibbons, sons of the pioneer.

Royal J. Cutler, on April 3, 1869, came again into official notice as clerk of the Probate and County Court of Rio Virgen County, which had been created out of the western part of Washington County, Utah, by the Utah Legislature. The first session of the court was at St. Joseph, with Joseph W. Young as magistrate. This county organization is not understood, even under the hypothesis that Utah claimed a sixty-mile strip of Nevada, for St. Joseph, on the Muddy, lies a considerable distance south of the extension of the southern Utah line, the 37th parallel.

A tax was levied of one-half of 1 per cent, this later increased to three-quarters of 1 per cent. Direct taxes in 1869 had been received of $156.19, and the amount transferred from Pah-ute County was $24.10, a total of $180.29, which hardly could be considered an onerous levy or fat treasury for the support of a political subdivision. The treasurer had on hand $28.55 in cash, $20 in flour and $12.45 in wheat.

Later Settlement in "The Point"

Bunkerville, settled January 6, 1877, was named for Edward Bunker, a member of the Mormon Battalion. Latterly to a degree it has become connected with Arizona through the fact that lands in its vicinity are to be irrigated from a reservoir to be established upon the Virgin within Arizona. January 24, 1877, there were visitors of notable sort, Capt. Daniel W. Jones and company, on their way to a location in the Salt River Valley of Arizona. Bunkerville had elaborate organization under the United Order, and it is agreed that the large amount of irrigation work accomplished hardly could have been done under any other

126

plan. The organization lasted until the summer of 1879, it being found that some of the members, "through their economy and industry were gathering and, laying up in abundance, while others, through carelessness and bad management, were wasting the funds of the company, each year being increasing in debt." This was very unsatisfactory to those whose ambition was to assure at least the necessaries of life.

The Mesquite settlement, across the Virgin from Bunkerville, was established in 1880, but was abandoned a few years later, again to be settled in 1895, from Utah.

There was a returning of the Saints to the Muddy Valley early in 1881, the Patterson ranch, which included the town of Overton, being purchased by Mrs. Elizabeth Whitmore of St. George. Among the names of the settlers was at least one of Arizona association, that of Jesse W. Crosby. In 1892, when visited by Andrew Jenson, in the locality of the main four settlements of the older occupation were only a score of families.

Salt Mountains of the Virgin

Arizona lost one asset of large value in the transfer of the Virgin River section to Nevada. Therein is an enormous salt deposit, locally called the Salt Mountain, though three such deposits are along the Virgin between St. Thomas and the Colorado River. One of them is described as cropping out along the foot of a high bluff of brown clay, exposed for 80 feet in height from the base of the hill, though the depth below its surface is unknown. The salt is obtained by blasting, as it is too hard to dig with picks. It is of excellent quality and of remarkable purity. In early days, from this deposit was obtained the salt needed in southern Nevada, southwestern Utah and much of Arizona, steamers carrying it down the Colorado southward. W. H. Johnson was in early charge of the salt mines. is widow now is resident in Mesa.

127

Writing about Overton, an early historian gives details of the happiness that comes to an individual who relies wholly upon the produce of his land and who lives apart from what is called civilization and its evils. He tells of the sense of comfort, security and satisfaction felt by the brethren who own the land whereon their homes are set and are not afraid of a little expense of bone and muscle to sustain themselves comfortably.

They dress as well or better than those in more favored circumstances, set a plentiful table and enjoy such peace and quiet that seldom falls to the lot of people in these troublous times. No profaning is heard; the smoking, chewing and drinking habits are strangers to the "hope of Israel" here; no racing of horses at breakneck speed through the streets is endured in our peaceful little town; in fact the only complaint is, and not without just cause, that it is rather too quiet.

Along this same line, Dellenbaugh wrote of the southern Utah settlements:

As pioneers the Mormons were superior to any class I have ever come in contact with, their idea being homemaking and not skimming the cream off the country with a six-shooter and a whiskey bottle. One of the first things the Mormon always did in establishing a new settlement was to plant fruit, shade trees and vines and the like, so that in a very few years there was a condition of comfort only attained by a non-Mormon settlement after the lapse of a quarter of a century. Dancing is a regular amusement among the Mormons and is encouraged by the authorities as a harmless and beneficial recreation. The dances were always opened by prayer.

In the journal of Major J. W. Powell, under date of August 30, 1869, there is special mention of the hospitable character of the Mormons of the Virgin River section. They had been advised by Brigham Young to look out for the Powell expedition and Asa (Joseph Asay) and his sons continued to watch the river, though a false report had come that the Powell expedition was lost. They were looking for wreckage that might give some indication of the fate of the explorers when Powell's boats appeared.

128

Powell was very appreciative of Asay's kindness and wrote enthusiastically of the coming, next day from St. Thomas, of James Leithead, with a wagonload of supplies that included melons.

Chapter Twelve

The United Order

Development of a Communal System

At one stage of Church development there was disposition to favor the establishment in each village of the Saints of communal conditions, wherein work should be done according to the ability of the individual. Crops and the results of all industry were to be gathered at a common center for common benefit. Something of the same sort was known among the Shakers and other religious sects in eastern states. Thus in Utah was founded the United Order, which, however, at no time had any direct connection with the central Church organization.

The best development of the idea was at Brigham City, Utah, sixty miles north of Salt Lake City, where the movement was kept along business lines by none other than Lorenzo Snow, later President of the Church of Jesus Christ of Latter-day Saints and the officer credited with having first put that great organization upon a business footing. He established a communal system that proved a potent beneficial force both for the individual and the community. The start was in 1864, with the establishment of a mercantile business, from which there were successive expansions to include about forty industries, such as factories at which were made felt and straw hats, clothing, pottery, brooms and brushes, harnesses and saddles, furniture, vehicles and tinware, while there were three sawmills, a large woolen mill and a cotton goods mill, the last with large attached cotton acreage, in southern Utah. There were 5000 sheep, 1000 head of stock cattle and 500 cows, supplying a model dairy and the community meat market. The settlement was self-clothed and self-fed. Education had especial attention and all sorts of entertainment of meritorious character were fostered. Members of the Order labored in their own industries, were paid good wages in scrip and participated in the growth of general values. In 1875 the value of the products reached $260,000.

By 1879 there had been departure from the complete unity of the United Order plan, though eleven departments still remained intact. There had been adverse circumstances, through which in nine months had been lost about $53,000. The woolen mill, a model, twice had been destroyed by fire. There had been jealousies outside the movement, through which a profitable railroad contract had been ruined, and federal authorities had taxed the scrip issue about $10,000 per annum. The first assessment was paid, but later was turned back. But, with all these reverses piled upon the people, the unity remained intact, and today, upon the foundation laid by the United Order and its revered local leader, Brigham City is one of the most prosperous communities of the intermountain region.

Edward Bellamy, the writer, became so much interested in what he had heard of the United Order in Brigham City, that he made a special trip to Utah in 1886, to study its operation. He spent three days with President Lorenzo Snow, listening to his experiences and explanation of the movement. As a result of this lengthy interview, Mr. Bellamy, the following year, wrote his book, "Looking Backward."

Another example of the operation of the United Order was in Kane County, Utah, about eighteen miles north of the Arizona line. In March, 1871, there was re-settlement of Long Valley, where two towns, Berryville and Winsor, had been deserted because of Indian encroachments. The new settlers mainly came from the breaking up of the

131

Muddy Mission settlements in Nevada, Long Valley having been suggested by President Brigham Young as a possible location. About 200 of the former Muddy residents entered the valley in March, 1871, founding Glendale and Mount Carmel. The residents of the latter, in March, 1874, organized into the United Order. The following year, a number who wished to practice the Order in its fullness, founded a new settlement, midway between Glendale and Mount Carmel, and named it Orderville. This settlement still is in existence, though the communistic plan had to be broken up about 1883, there having arisen a spirit of competition and of individual ambition. The plan of operation was comprehensive of many features, yet simple. The community ate in a common dining hall, with kitchen and bakery attached. Dwelling houses were close together and built in the form of a square. There were work shops, offices, schoolhouse, etc., and manufactories of lumber and woolen products.

Not a General Church Movement

There had been an idea among the adherents to the Order that they were fulfilling a Church commandment. They were disabused by Apostle Erastus Snow, who suggested that each occupation be taken up by small companies, each to run a different department. There was conference with the First Presidency, but the Church declined responsibility sought to be thrown upon it. So there were many defections, though for years thereafter there was incorporation, to hold the mills and machinery, lands and livestock.

The United Order by no means was general. It was limited to certain localities and certain settlements, each of which tried to work out its own problems in its own way, entirely without connection with any other community of the sort. In a few instances the plan proved successful, but usually only where there was some directing leader of integrity and business acumen, such as at Brigham City.

FOUNDERS OF THE COLORADO FERRIES

1—John L. Blythe   2—Harrison Pearce
3—Daniel Bonelli   4—Anson Call

CROSSING THE COLORADO RIVER AT SCANLON'S FERRY

The United Order principle was used, with varying degrees of relative success, in a number of northern Arizona settlements, especially in the early camps on the lower Little Colorado, as noted elsewhere.

The Jones party, that founded Lehi, was organized for traveling and working under the United Order, drawing from a common storehouse, but each family, nevertheless, looked out for its own interest. The United Order lasted until the end of Jones' control of the colony.

An attempt was made in the early part of 1880 at Mesa, to organize, under the laws of Arizona, to carry out the principles of the United Order as far as practicable. A corporation was formed, "The Mesa Union," by President Alex. F. Macdonald, Geo. C. Dana, Timothy Mets, Hyrum Smith Phelps and Chas. H. Mallory. About the only thing done by this organization was to purchase some land, but this land later was taken by members of the Church.

Mormon Cooperative Stores

In the economy and frugality that marked, necessarily, the early days of the Mormon people, there naturally was resort to combination in the purchases of supplies and in the marketing of products. When the United Order declined, there was resort to another economic pioneer enterprise, the cooperative store, established in many of the new communities. Each store, to an extent, was under local Church supervision and, while open to the trade of all, still was established primarily for the benefit of the brethren. Under early-day conditions, the idea undoubtedly was a good one. Mercantile profits were left within the community, divided among many, while the "Co-op" also served as a means through which the community produce could be handled to best advantage.

In the north, June 27, 1881, at Snowflake, with Jesse N. Smith at its head, was organized a company that started a cooperative store at Holbrook, taking over, largely for debt, a store that had been operated by John W. Young

133

at old Holbrook. In January, 1882, this establishment was left high and dry by the moving of Holbrook station a mile and a half west to Berardo's, or Horsehead Crossing. There was difficulty in getting a location at the new site, so this store, in February, 1882, was moved to Woodruff.

In January, 1881, at Snowflake was started a "Co-op" that merged into the Arizona Cooperative Mercantile Institution. The following month, under David K. Udall, a similar institution was opened at St. Johns, where there was attached a flouring mill. Both at St. Johns and Snowflake were cooperative livestock herds.

One of the most extensive enterprises of this sort was started in Mesa in September, 1884, with Chas. I. Robson, George Passey and Oscar M. Stewart at its head. The first stock was valued at $45, yet in 1894, the Zenos Cooperative Mercantile & Manufacturing Institution had a paid-up capital stock of over $25,000 and a two-story building, and had paid dividends ranging from 10 to 50 per cent annually.

Almost every phase of communal effort now appears to have been abandoned in Arizona Mormon business life, probably because found unnecessary in the latter-day development in which the membership of the Church has had so large a share.

The Author feels there should be addition of a statement that the Church is far from acceptance of the European idea of communism, for one of its tenets is, "Thou shalt not be idle, for he that is idle shall not eat of the bread nor wear the garments of the laborer." Nothing of political socialism ever was known in the United Order.

Chapter Thirteen

𝔖𝔭𝔯𝔢𝔞𝔡𝔦𝔫𝔤 𝔍𝔫𝔱𝔬 𝔑𝔬𝔯𝔱𝔥𝔢𝔯𝔫 𝔄𝔯𝔦𝔷𝔬𝔫𝔞

Failure of the First Expeditions

The first attempt from the north of the Mormon Church to colonize within the present limits of Arizona failed. It was by means of an expedition placed in charge of Horton D. Haight. A number of the colonists met March 8, 1873, in the old tabernacle in Salt Lake City, and there were instructed by President Brigham Young. At Winsor Castle they were warned to be friendly to but not too trustful of the Indians and not to sell them ammunition, "for they are warring against our government." The route was by way of Lee's Ferry, the crossing completed May 11. On the 22d was reached the Little Colorado, the Rio de Lino (Flax River) of the Spaniards. From the ferry to the river had been broken a new road, over a tolerably good route. There was no green grass, and water was infrequent, even along the Little Colorado, it being found necessary to dig wells in the dry channel. Twenty-four miles below Black Falls there was encampment, the road blocked by sand drifts.

On June 1 there returned to the expedition in camp an exploring party, under Haight, that had been absent eight days and that had traveled 136 miles up the river. There was report of the trip that the country was barren, with narrow river bottoms, with alkaline soil, water bad and failing, with no spot found suitable in which to settle. There also appeared to be fear of the Apache. So the expedition painfully retraced its steps to Navajo Springs, sending ahead a dispatch to President Young, giving a full

135

report of conditions and making suggestion that the settlement plan had better be abandoned. At Moen Copie on the return was met a party of 29 missionaries, under Henry Day.

An interesting journal of the trip was written by Henry Holmes of the vanguard. He was especially impressed with the aridity of the country. He thought it "barren and forbidding, although doubtless the Lord had a purpose in view when He made it so. Few of the creeks ran half a mile from their heads. The country is rent with deep chasms, made still deeper by vast torrents that pour down them during times of heavy rains." There were found petrified trees. One of them was 210 feet long and another was over five feet across the butt, this in a land where not a tree or bush was found growing. Holmes fervently observed, "However, I do not know whether it makes any difference whether the country is barren or fruitful, if the Lord has a work to do in it," in this especially referring to the Indians, among whom there could be missionary effort. Jacob Miller acted as secretary of the expedition.

On the back track, the company all had ferried to the north bank of the river by July 7, although there had to be improvised navigation of the Colorado, for the ferry-boat had disappeared in the spring flood and all that remained was a little skiff, behind which the wagon bodies were floated over. In all, were ferried 54 wagons, 112 animals, 109 men, 6 women and a child.

This first company had been called from different parts of Utah and was not at all homogeneous, yet traveled in peace and union. The members assembled morning and evening for prayers, at which the blessings of the Lord were asked upon themselves and their teams and upon the elements that surrounded them.

President Young directed the members of the 1873 party to remain in Arizona, but the message was not received till the river had been passed. The following year he ordered another expedition southward. According to a journal of Wm H. Solomon, who was clerk of the party, departure from Kanab was on February 6, 1874. John L. Blythe (who had remained at Moen Copie after the 1873 trip) was in charge. With Blythe was his wife. Ira Hatch took his family. Fifteen other individuals were included. Progress southward was stopped at Moen Copie by reports of a Navajo uprising. Most of the party returned to Utah after a few weeks, leaving behind Hamblin, Hatch and Tenney.

Missionary Scouts in Northeastern Arizona

When the unsuccessful expedition turned back to Utah in the summer of 1873, there remained John L. Blythe of Salt Lake and a number of other missionaries. They located among the Indians on the Moen Copie, where they sowed the ground and planted trees and grapevines, also planting at Moabi, about seven miles to the southwest. Blythe remained at Moen Copie, alone with his family, until 1874, including the time of the Indian trouble more particularly referred to in this volume in connection with the work of Jacob Hamblin.

The failure of the Haight expedition in no wise daunted the Church authorities in their determination to extend southward. In general, reports that came concerning the Little Colorado Valley were favorable. Finally, starting from Salt Lake October 30, 1875, was sent a scouting expedition, headed by Jas. S. Brown, who had a dozen companions when he crossed into Arizona. This party made headquarters at Moen Copie, where a stone house was built for winter quarters. Brown and two others then traveled up the Little Colorado for a considerable distance, not well defined in his narrative, finding a fine, open country, with water plentiful and with grass abundant, with good farming land and timber available. The trio followed the Beale trail westward to a point southwest of the San Francisco Mountains, where there was crossing back to the Little

137

Colorado. Christmas Day, before Moen Copie was reached, the scouts were placed in serious danger by a terrific snowstorm. Brown returned to Salt Lake with his report, January 14, 1876, after traveling 1300 miles, mainly on horseback.

Here might be stated that Brown was none other than a Mormon Battalion member who had participated in the discovery of gold at Sutter's Fort in California. At some time prior to coming to Arizona he had lost a leg, shot off by hunters who had mistaken him for a bear. He should not be confounded with Capt. James Brown of the Battalion.

Foundation of Four Settlements

The first Presidency apparently had anticipated Brown's favorable report, for quick action was had immediately thereafter. Four companies, each of fifty men and their families, were organized, under Lot Smith, Jesse O. Ballenger, George Lake and Wm. C. Allen. The 200 missionaries were "called" from many parts of Utah, but mainly from the north and around Salt Lake. There was no formal gathering of the companies. Each member went southward as he could, to report to his leader on the Little Colorado. The assembling point was Kanab. Thence there was assemblage of groups of about ten families each, without reference to companies. An entertaining detail of this journey lately was given the Historian in Phoenix by David E. Adams, captain of one of the Tens.

The leading teams reached Sunset Crossing on the Little Colorado March 23, 1876, the migration continuing for many weeks thereafter. Allen, Smith and Lake continued up the river twenty miles, to a point about five miles east of the present site of St. Joseph.

From exact data furnished by R. E. Porter of St. Joseph is learned that Allen's company settled at the point where this march ended, establishing Allen's Camp. There was later change to a point one mile east of the present

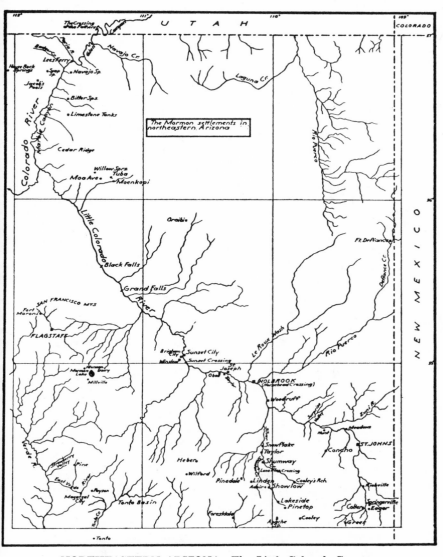

NORTHEASTERN ARIZONA—The Little Colorado Country

location, a site maintained till 1877. The name was changed January 21, 1878, to St. Joseph, after Prophet Joseph Smith.

Lot Smith's company retraced, to establish Sunset, three miles north of Sunset Crossing, on the north side of the river.

Lake's company established itself across the river, three miles south and west of the present site of St. Joseph. The settlement was named Obed.

Ballenger's company located four miles southwest of Sunset Crossing, on the south side of the river, near the site of the present Winslow.

Genesis of St. Joseph

There was quick work in the way of settlement at Allen's Camp, where the first plowing was on March 25, 1876, by John Bushman and Nathan Cheney. Jacob Morris immediately commenced the construction of a house. Two days later an irrigation ditch was surveyed and on the following day John Bushman got out the first logs for a diversion dam. April 3, Bushman sowed the first wheat. A temporary structure was built for protection and for storage. May 26 the name of Allen City was given the settlement, in preference to a second suggestion, Ramah City. Early in August, 23 men, including Allen, started back to Utah, from which a few returned with their families.

On Allen's return southward with a number of families, the old Spanish Trail was used, in its eastern section, via the San Juan region, with some idea that it might be made the main thoroughfare, for thus would be obviated the ferrying of the Colorado River, either above or below the Canyon. But the way into Arizona through northwestern New Mexico was too long, and the experiment was not considered successful.

In the fall, the families moved into a stockade fort, planned to be 152 feet wide and 300 feet long. Only part of this was finished. Probably twenty or more houses were built within it.

CROSSING THE LITTLE COLORADO

THE OLD FORT AT BRIGHAM CITY

WOODRUFF DAM, AFTER ONE OF THE FREQUENT
WASHOUTS

THE FIRST PERMANENT DAM ON THE LITTLE COLORADO
AT ST. JOSEPH

August 23, 1876, a postoffice was established, with John McLaws in charge. A weekly mail service operated between Santa Fe and Prescott.

The first child in the settlement was Hannah Maria Colson, July 17, 1876. The first death was exactly a year later, that of Clara Gray. The first school district was established and the first school was taught during the winter of 1877-78. Of all the lower Little Colorado settlements, this is the only one now existent.

The present St. Joseph lies only a hundred rods from the main line of the Santa Fe railroad system, 25 miles east of Winslow. The first Allen's Camp, in April, 1876, was three miles east of the present site. There was a change to the western location in June, at the suggestion of Daniel H. Wells, who had followed for an inspection of the new settlements. Later there was survey, nearby, of a townsite, the same that now is occupied. Among the few remaining settlers of the Little Colorado settlements, is Joseph Hill Richards, who writes that he was the first justice of the peace for Yavapai County in that region and the first captain there of territorial militia. He also was prominent in the Church organization.

Struggling with a Treacherous River

Every settlement along the Little Colorado River has known repeated troubles in maintaining its water supply. It would be vain recapitulation to tell just how many times each of the poor struggling communities had to rally back on the sands of the river bed to built up anew the structure of gravel and brush that must be depended upon, if bread were to be secured from the land. The Little Colorado is a treacherous stream at best, with a broad channel that wanders at will through the alluvial country that melts like sugar or salt at the touch of water.

There are instances that stand out in this struggle for water. The first joint dam of Allen's Camp and Obed cost the settlers $5000. It is told that 960 day's work was done on the dam and 500 days more work on the Allen ditch. This dam went down at the first flood, for it raised the water about twelve feet. Then, in the spring of 1877, another dam was built, a mile and a half upstream, and this again washed away. In 1879 the St. Joseph settlers sought the third damsite at LeRoux Wash, about two and a half miles west of the present Holbrook. In 1881 they spent much money and effort on a plan to make a high dam at the site of the first construction, but this again was taken downstream by the river. In 1882, a pile dam was built across the river, and it again was spoiled by the floods. This dam generally was in use until 1891, but had to be repaired almost every year. In the year named, work was started upon what was hoped to be a permanent dam, at an estimated cost of $60,000. In 1894, Andrew Jenson wrote that at least $50,000 had been lost by the community upon its dams. Noting the fact that only fifteen families constituted the population, he called St. Joseph "the leading community in pain, determination and unflinching courage in dealing with the elements around them."

St. Joseph, as early as 1894, had completed its eighth dam across the river. Jos. W. Smith wrote of the dedication of the dam, in March of that year. He remarked especially upon the showing of rosy-cheeked, well-clad children, of whom the greater part of the assemblage was composed, "showing that the people were by no means destitute, even if they had been laboring on ditches and dams so much for the last eighteen years."

The main prayer of the exercise was brief, but characteristic: "O Lord, we pray that this dam may stand, if it be Thy will—if not, let Thy will be done." The invocation was effective. The dam stood, as is illustrated within this book.

Decline and Fall of Sunset

Sunset, the lowest of the settlements, was near the present railroad crossing of the river, below the river junction with Clear Creek. There had been a temporary location two miles upstream. The main structure was a stockade, twelve rods square, mainly of drift cottonwood logs. Within were rock-built houses, a community dining hall and a well. Combination was made with Ballenger, across the stream, in the building of a dam, two and a half miles above the settlement.

Apparently the sandy land and the difficulty of irrigating it drove the settlers away, until, finally, in 1885, Lot Smith's family was the only one left upon the ground, and it departed in 1888.

Years later, Andrew Jenson found the rock walls and chimneys still standing. "Everything is desert," he wrote, "the whole landscape looks dreary and forbidding and the lonely graveyard on the hillside only reminds one of the population which once was and that is no more." Only ruin marks the place where once was headquarters of the Little Colorado Stake of Zion. The settlement was badly placed, for floods came within a rod of the fort and covered the wheat fields.

Lot Smith wrote in poetic vein, "This is a strange country, belonging to a people whose lands the rivers have spoiled." Very practically, however, he wrote of good lands and slack water supply, "though the river shows it would be a mighty rushing torrent when the rains commence in summer, with the appearance of being 25 miles broad, and the Indians told us that if we are indeed to live where we are encamped, we had better fix some scaffolding in the trees."

In August, 1878, a correspondent of the Deseret News wrote from Sunset that for a week the rain had been pouring down almost incessantly, that the whole bottom was covered with water, that some of the farms were submerged and grain in shocks was flooded, that the grain of Woodruff was entirely destroyed, the grist mill of Brigham City inundated and the grain stacks there were deep in water, with the inhabitants using boats and rafts to get around their farms.

Village Communal Organization

The settlements all established themselves under the United Order. Early in 1876 one of the settlers wrote from Allen's Camp, "It is all United Order here and no beating around the bush, for it is the intention to go into it to the full meaning of the term." This chronicler, John L. Blythe, April 11, 1876, again wrote, "The companies are going into the United Order to the whole extent, giving in everything they possess, their labor, time and talent." In August there was a report from the same locality that "the people are living in a united system, each laboring for the good of all the community and an excellent feeling prevails."

The communal system was given formal adoption at Allen's Camp April 28, 1877, when articles were agreed upon for a branch of the United Order. June 5, 1877, with Wm. C. Allen presiding, there was an appraisal of property and a separation of duties. Henry M. Tanner (who still is in St. Joseph), was secretary, John Bushman foreman of the farm, James Walker water master and Moses D. Steele superintendent of livestock. Niels Nielsen was in charge of ox teams and Jos. H. Rogers in charge of horse teams, harness and wagons. The Church historian has given in detail the manner in which the system worked:

From the beginning the Saints at Allen's Camp disciplined themselves strictly according to Church rules. Every morning the Saints, at the sound of the triangle, assembled in the schoolhouse for prayer, on which occasion they would not only pray and sing, but sometimes brethren would make brief remarks. The same was resorted to in the evening. They did not all eat at the same table (a common custom followed in the other camps), but nevertheless great union, peace and love prevailed among the people, and none seemed to take advantage of his neighbor. Peace, harmony and brotherly love characterized all the settlers at Allen's Camp from the very beginning.

In August, 1878, Samuel G. Ladd wrote from the new

St. Joseph, that the United Order worked harmoniously and prosperously. In that year manufacturing of brooms was commenced by John Bushman. Up to 1882 each family was drawing from one common storehouse. In 1883 the Order was dissolved at St. Joseph and the stewardship plan adopted. Each family received its part of the divided land and a settlement of what each man originally had put into the Order. Proforma organization of the Order was continued until January, 1887.

Hospitality Was of Generous Sort

From Sunset Crossing Camp, G. C. Wood wrote, in April, 1876, "The brethren built a long shanty, with a long table in it and all ate their meals together, worked together and got along finely." In February, 1878, President Lot Smith wrote the Deseret News in a strain that indicated doubt concerning the efficiency of the United Order system. His letter told:

This mission has had a strange history so far, most who came having got weak in the back or knees and gone home. Some, I believe, have felt somewhat exercised about the way we are getting along, and the mode in which we are conducting our culinary affairs. Now, I have always had a preference for eating with my family and have striven to show that I was willing to enlarge as often as circumstances require, and the same feeling seemed to prevail in these settlements. We have enlarged ourselves to the amount of forty in one day. We have noticed that most people who pass the road are willing to stop and board with us a week or two, notwithstanding our poor provisions and the queer style it was served up.

In July of the same year, Lorenzo Hatch wrote from Woodruff, "At Sunset, Brigham City and Woodruff, the settlements eat at one table, hence we have no poor nor rich among us. The Obed camp also had gone into the United Order in the fullest sense in May, 1876."

Brigham City's Varied Industries

Ballenger, in September, 1878, was renamed Brigham City, in honor of President Brigham Young. Its people were found by Erastus Snow in September, 1878, with a remarkable organization, operating in part under the United Order system. There was a fort 200 feet square, with rocky walls seven feet high. Inside were 36 dwelling houses, each 15x13 feet. On the north side was the dining hall, 80x20 feet, with two rows of tables, to seat more than 150 persons. Adjoining was a kitchen, 25x20 feet, with an annexed bakehouse. Twelve other dwelling houses were mentioned, as well as a cellar and storehouse. Water was secured within the enclosure from two good wells. South of the fort were corrals and stockyards. The main industry was the farming of 274 acres, more than one-half of it in wheat. A pottery was in charge of Brother Behrman, reported to have been confident that he could surpass any of the potteries in Utah for good ware. Milk was secured from 142 cows. One family was assigned to the sawmill in the mountains. J. A. Woods taught the first school. Jesse O. Ballenger, the first leader, was succeeded in 1878 by George Lake, who reported that, "while the people were living together in the United Order they generally ate together at the same table. The Saints, as a rule, were very earnest in their endeavors to carry out the principles of the Order, but some became dissatisfied and moved away." Discouragement became general, and in 1881 all were released from the mission. The settlement practically was broken up, the people scattering, though without dissension.

Some went to Forest Dale, and later to the Gila River, and some left Arizona altogether. There was a surplus from the experiment of about $8000, which went to the Church, after the people had drawn out their original capital, each taking the same number of animals and the same amount of property contributed originally. In 1882 only a couple of families were left and an added surplus of $2200 was used by the Church in settling the Gila country. In 1890 only the family of Sidney Wilson remained on the old site of Brigham City. The Brigham City water-power grist mill built in 1878, a present from the Church, was given to the people of Woodruff, but was not used.

The abandonment of Brigham City should not be blamed to the weakness of a communistic system. There had been frequent failures of crops and there had come a determination to find a locality where nature would smile more often upon the barley, so scouts were sent to the San Juan country in Utah, the Salt River country and to the Gila. George Lake, Andrew Anderson and George W. Skinner constituted the Gila party. Near Smithville they bought land, a transaction elsewhere referred to. Anderson and Skinner, in December, 1880, returned to Brigham City. At that point a business meeting was called at once and the authorities of the United Order approved the purchases made.

January 1, 1878, was announced a census of the settlement of the Little Colorado country. Sunset had 136 inhabitants, Ballenger 277, Allen's Camp 76. Woodruff 50 and Moen Copie 25, a total of 564, with 115 families.

Brief Lives of Obed and Taylor

The settlement of Obed, three miles southwest of St. Joseph, directly south of old Allen's Camp and across the river, bears date from June, 1876, having been moved a short distance from the first camp ground. At that time was built a fort of remarkable strength, twelve rods square. In places, the walls were ten feet high. There were bastions, with portholes for defense, at two of the corners, and portholes were in the walls all around. The camp at the start had 123 souls. Cottonwood logs were sawed for lumber. The community had a schoolhouse in January, 1877, and a denominational school was started the next month, with Phoebe McNeil as teacher. The settlement was not a happy one. The site was malarial, selected against Church instructions, and there were the usual troubles in the washing away of brush and log dams. The population drifted away, until there was abandonment in 1878.

147

Taylor was a small settlement on the Little Colorado, about three miles below the present St. Joseph, and should not be confounded with the present settlement of the same name near Snowflake. This first Taylor was established January 22, 1878, by eight families, mainly from Panguitch and Beaver, Utah. In the United Order they built a dining hall, a quarter-mile back from the river and organized as a ward, with John Kartchner at its head. But there was discouragement, not unnaturally, when the river dam went out for the fifth time. Then, in July, 1878, members of the settlement departed, going to the present site of Snowflake on Silver Creek. They included a number of Arkansas immigrants. There had been little improvement outside of the stockade and dining hall, and for most of the time the people lived in their wagons.

THE COLORADO FERRY AND RANCH AT THE MOUTH OF THE PARIA

By courtesy of Dr. George Wharton James

LEE CABIN AT MOEN AVI

MOEN COPIE WOOLEN MILL
First and Only One in Arizona

Chapter Fourteen

Travel, Missions and Industries

Passing of the Boston Party

Keen interest in the Southwest was excited early in 1876 by a series of lectures delivered at New England points by Judge Samuel W. Cozzens, author of "The Marvellous Country." There was formed the American Colonization Company, with Cozzens as president. Two companies of men, of about fifty individuals each, were dispatched from Boston, each man with equipment weighing about thirty pounds. The destination was a fertile valley in northeastern Arizona, a land that had been described eloquently, probably after only casual observation. The end of the Santa Fe railroad was in northern New Mexico. There the first party purchased four wagons and a number of mules from a grading contractor, Pat Shanley, afterward a cattleman in Gila County.

The best story at hand of the Bostonians is from one of them, Horace E. Mann, who for years has been a prospector and miner and who now is a resident of Phoenix. He tells that the journey westward was without particular incident until was reached, about June 15, the actual destination, the valley of the Little Colorado River, on the route of the projected Atlantic & Pacific Railroad. The travelers were astonished to find the country already taken up by a number of companies of Mormon colonists.

In New England the Mormons were considered a bloodthirsty people, eager to slay any Gentile who might happen along. It is not to be intimated that the Bostonians were mollycoddles. They appear to have been above even the

149

average of the time, manly and stalwart enough, but the truth is, as told by Mr. Mann, the expedition did not care either to mingle with the Mormons or to incur danger of probable slaughter. Therefore, the parties hurried along as fast as possible. The same view is indicated in a recent interview with David E. Adams, of one of the Mormon settlements. He told the Historian that he found the Bostonians suspicious and fearful. At that time the Utah people still were living in their wagons. They were breaking ground and were starting upon the construction of dams in the river. The second Boston party passed June 23.

At Sunset Crossing Mann and three of his companions entered upon an adventure assuredly novel in arid Arizona. They constructed a raft of drift cottonwood and thought to lighten the journey by floating down the river. It was found that the stream soon bent toward the northward, away from the wagon trail. Sometimes there were shoals that the raft had to be pushed over and again there were deep whirlpools, around which the raft went merrily a dozen times before the river channel again could be entered. The channel walls grew higher and higher until, finally, the navigators pulled the raft ashore and resumed their journey on foot, finding their wagon in camp at the Canyon Diablo crossing. There, apparently considering themselves safe from massacre, was an encampment of a week or more.

At the Naming of Flagstaff

Mann, his bunkie, George E. Loring (later express agent at Phoenix), a Rhode Islander named Tillinghast and three others formed an advance party westward. This party made camp at a small spring just south of San Francisco Mountains, where Flagstaff is now. Mann remembers the place as Volunteer Springs in Harrigan Valley. While waiting for the main party to come up, the advance guard hunted and explored. Mann remembers traveling up a little valley to the north and northwest to the big LeRoux Springs, below which he found the remains of a burnt cabin and of a stockade corral, possibly occupied in the past as a station on the transcontinental mail route.

With reference to the naming of Flagstaff, Mr. Mann is very definite. He says that, while waiting for the main party, this being late in June, 1876, and merely for occupation, the limbs were cut from a straight pine tree that was growing by itself near the camp. The bark was cut away, leaving the tree a model flagstaff and for this purpose it was used, the flag being one owned by Tillinghast and the only one carried by the expedition. The tree was not cut down. It was left standing upon its own roots. This tale is rather at variance with one that has been of common acceptance in the history of Flagstaff and the date was not the Fourth of July, as has been believed, for Mann is sure that he arrived in Prescott in June. The main section of the first party came a few days later, and was on the ground for a celebration of the centennial Fourth of July that centered around the flagstaff.

Mann also remembers that Major Maynadier, one of the leaders of the expedition, surveyed a townsite for Flagstaff, each of the members of the expedition being allotted a tract. The second party joined the first at Flagstaff. Word had been received that mechanics were needed at Prescott and in the nearby mines, with the large wages of $6 a day, and hence there was eagerness to get along and have a share in the wealth of the land. It remains to be stated that all the men found no difficulty in locating themselves in and around Prescott and that no regret was felt over the failure of the original plan.

Southern Saints Brought Smallpox

One of the few parties of Southern States Saints known for years in any of the Stakes of Zion joined the poverty-stricken colonists on the Little Colorado in the fall of 1877. Led by Nelson P. Beebe, it numbered about 100 individuals, coming through New Mexico by wagon, with a first stop at Savoia. The immigrants were without means or food and there had to be haste in sending most of them on westward, more wagons being sent from the Little Colorado camps for their conveyance. At Allen's Camp was a burden of sickness, mainly fever sufferers from the unfortunate Obed. To these visitors were added seventy of the "Arkansas Saints," who came October 4. Yet the plucky Allenites not only divided with the strangers their scanty store of bread, but gave a dance in celebration of the addition to the pioneers' strength. The arrivals brought with them a new source of woe. One of their number, Thomas West, had contracted smallpox at Albuquerque and from this case came many prostrations.

Fort Moroni, at LeRoux Spring

One of the most important watering places of northeastern Arizona is LeRoux Spring, seven miles northwest of Flagstaff on the southwestern slope of the San Francisco Mountains. This never-failing spring was a welcome spot to the pioneers who traveled the rocky road along the 35th parallel of latitude. San Francisco Spring (or Old Town Spring) at the present Flagstaff, was much less dependable and at the time of the construction of the Atlantic & Pacific railroad in 1881-2, water often was hauled to Flagstaff from the larger spring, at times sold for $1 a barrel.

The importance of this water supply appears to have been appreciated early by the long-headed directing body of the Mormon Church. Early in 1877, under direction of John W. Young, son and one of the counselors of Brigham Young, from the Little Colorado settlements of St. Joseph and Sunset, was sent an expedition that included Alma Iverson, John L. Blythe and Jos. W. McMurrin, the last at this writing president of the California Mission of the Church, then a boy of 18.

According to Ammon M. Tenney, this LeRoux spring was known to the people of the Little Colorado settlements as San Francisco spring. Mr. McMurrin personally states his remembrance that the expedition proceeded along the

152

Beale trail to the spring, near which was built a small log cabin, designed to give a degree of title to the water and to the locality, probably also to serve as a shelter for any missionary parties that might travel the road. There is no information that it was used later for any purpose.

The men were instructed to build a cabin at Turkey Tanks, on the road to the Peaks, this cabin to be lined with pine needles and to be used as a storage icehouse, Counselor Young expressing the opinion that there would be times in the summer heat of the Little Colorado Valley when ice would be of the greatest value. The tanks were hardly suitable for this purpose, however, and the icehouse was not built.

Location of the LeRoux spring by the Iverson-Blythe party in 1877 appears to have been sufficient to hold the ground till it was needed, in 1881, by John W. Young, in connection with his railroad work. About sixty graders and tie cutters were camped, mainly in tents, on LeRoux Prairie or Flat, below the spring, according to Mrs. W. J. Murphy, now of Phoenix, a resident of the Prairie for five months of 1881, her husband a contractor on the new railroad. She remembers no cattle, though deer and antelope were abundant.

Stockaded Against the Indians

In the early spring came reports of Indian raids to the eastward. So Young hauled in a number of double-length ties, which he set on end, making a stockade, within which he placed his camp, mainly of tents. Later were brush shelters within, but the great log house, illustrated herein, was not built until afterward. Thereafter was attached the name of Fort Moroni, given by Young, who organized the Moroni Cattle Company. At the time of the coming of the grade to Flagstaff, Young also had a camp in the western end of the present Flagstaff townsite.

Fort Moroni was acquired about 1883 by the Arizona Cattle Company. The large building was used as a mess house. The stockade ties were cut down to fence height and eventually disappeared, used by the cowboys for fuel.

An entertaining sidelight on the settlement of what later generally was known as Fort Valley has been thrown by Earl R. Forrest of Washington, Penn., in early days a cowboy for the Arizona Cattle Company. He writes that the building formed one side of a 100-foot square, with the stockade on the other three sides. In his day, the name of the ranch was changed to Fort Rickerson, in honor of Chas. L. Rickerson, treasurer of the company. Capt. F. B. Bullwinkle, the manager, a former Chief of the Chicago Fire Department, and a lover of fast stock, was killed near Flagstaff, thrown from a stumbling horse while racing for the railroad station. Thereafter the property passed into the possession of the Babbitt Brothers of Flagstaff. The old building was torn down late in 1920.

In August, 1908, the first forest experiment station in the United States was established in Fort Valley.

The great spring is used only for watering cattle, and the spring at Flagstaff appears to have been lost in the spread of civilization.

LeRoux spring was named for Antoine LeRoux, principal guide of the famous survey expedition of Lieut. A. W. Whipple, along the 35th parallel, in 1853. Incidentally, this is the same LeRoux who was principal guide of the Mormon Battalion.

Mormon Dairy and the Mount Trumbull Mill

Mormon Mountain, Mormon Lake and Mormon Dairy still are known as such, 28 miles southeast of Flagstaff. The Dairy was established in September, 1878, by Lot Smith, in what then was known as Pleasant Valley, in the pines, sixty miles west of Sunset. In that year 48 men and 41 women from Sunset and Brigham City, were at the Dairy, caring for 115 cows and making butter and cheese. Three good log houses had been built.

Seven miles south of Pleasant Valley (which should not be confounded with the Tonto Basin Pleasant Valley of sanguinary repute), was the site of the first sawmill on the Mogollon Plateau, upon which a half-dozen very large plants now operate to furnish lumber to the entire Southwest. This mill, probably antedated in northern Arizona only at Prescott, first was erected, about 1870, at Mount Trumbull, in the Uinkaret Mountains of northwestern Arizona, to cut lumber for the new temple at St. George, Utah, fifty miles to the northward. This mill, in 1876, was given by the Church authorities to the struggling Little Colorado River settlements. Taken down in August by the head sawyer, Warren R. Tenney, it was hauled into Sunset late in September and soon was re-erected by Tenney, and, November 7, put into operation in the pine woods near Mormon Lake, about sixty miles southwest of Sunset, soon turning out 100,000 feet of boards. Its site was named Millville. The mill, after the decline of the first settlements, passed into the possession of W. J. Flake. In the summer of 1882, it was transferred to Pinedale and in 1890 to Pinetop. It now is at Lakeside, where, it is assumed, at least part of the original machinery still is being operated. Its first work at Pinetop was to saw the timbers for a large assembly hall, or pavilion, to be used for the only conference ever held that included all the Arizona Stakes.

Also in the timber country are to be noted Wilford, named in honor of President Wilford Woodruff, and Heber, named for Heber C. Kimball, small settlements fifty miles southwest of St. Joseph, established in 1883 from St. Joseph and other Little Colorado settlements, for stock raising and dry farming. John Bushman is believed to have been the first Mormon resident of the locality. Log houses were built and at Wilford was a schoolhouse, which later was moved to St. Joseph, there used as a dwelling. When a number of the brethren went into Mexican exile, their holdings were "jumped" by outsiders. Wilford has been entirely vacated, but Heber still has residents.

Where Salt Was Secured

Salt for the early settlements of northern Arizona very generally was secured from the salt lake of the Zuni, just east of the New Mexican line, roughly 33 miles from St. Johns. As early as 1865, Sol Barth brought salt on pack mules from this lake to points as far westward as Prescott. In the records of a number of the Little Colorado settlements are found references to where the brethren visited a salt lake and came back with as much as two tons at a load. This lake is of sacred character to the Zuni, which at certain times of the year send parties of priests and warriors to the lake, 45 miles south of the tribal village. There is elaborate ceremonial before salt is collected. Undoubtedly the lake was known to prehistoric peoples, for salt, probably obtained at this point, has been found in cliff ruins in southern Colorado, 200 miles from the source of supply. The Zuni even had a special goddess, Mawe, genius of the sacred salt lake, or "Salt Mother," to whom offerings were made at the lake. Warren K. Follett, in 1878, told that the lake lies 300 feet lower than the general surface of the country. The salt forms within the water, in layers of from three to four inches thick, and is of remarkable purity.

The Hopi secured salt from a ledge in the Grand Canyon, below the mouth of the Little Colorado, about eighty miles northwest of their villages. At the point of mining, sacrifices were made before shrines of a goddess of salt and a god of war. The place has had description by Dr. Geo. Wharton James, whose knowledge of the gorge is most comprehensive.

On the upper Verde and in Tonto Creek Valley are salt deposits, though very impure. Upper Salt River has a small deposit of very good sodium chloride, which was mined mainly for the mills of Globe, in the seventies. The Verde

GRAND FALLS ON THE LITTLE COLORADO RIVER

ORIGINAL FORT MORONI WITH ITS STOCKADE

FORT MORONI IN LATER YEARS

deposit now is being mined for shipment to paper mills of its sodium sulphate. Reference elsewhere is made to the salt mines of the Virgin River Valley.

The Mission Post of Moen Copie

One of the most interesting early locations of the Mormon Church in Arizona was that of Moen Copie, about 75 miles southeast of Lee's Ferry. The name is a Hopi one, signifying "running water" or "many springs." The soil is alkaline, but it is a place where Indians had raised crops for generations. The presiding spirit of the locality was Tuba, the Oraibi chief, who had been taken by Jacob Hamblin to Utah, there to learn something of the white man's civilization.

Joseph Fish wrote that at an early date Moen Copie was selected as a missionary post by Jacob Hamblin and Andrew S. Gibbons and that in 1871 and 1872, John L. Blythe and family were at that point.

Permanent settlement on Moen Copie Creek was made December 4, 1875, by a party headed by Jas. S. Brown. There was establishment of winter quarters, centering in a stone house 40x20 feet, with walls twenty inches thick. The house was on the edge of a cliff, with two rows of log houses forming three sides of a square.

Indians Who Knew Whose Ox Was Gored

The Author is pleased to present here a tale of Indian craft, delightfully told him by Mrs. Elvira Martineau (Benj. S.) Johnson, who, in 1876, accompanied her husband to Moen Copie, where he had been sent as a missionary. July 4 the women had just prepared a holiday feast when Indians were seen approaching. The men were summoned from the fields below the cliff. Leading the Indians was a Navajo, Peicon, who, addressing Brown as a brother chieftain, thrust forward his young son, dramatically stating that the lad had killed three cows owned at the settlement of Sunset and offering him for any punishment the whites might see fit to inflict, even though it be death. Brown mildly suggested that the Sunset people should be seen, but that he was sure that all they would ask would be the value of the animals. During the protracted argument a party of accompanying Utes came into the discussion, threatening individuals with their bows and arrows. The Navajos were fed and then was developed the truth. It was that the men of Sunset had killed three Indian cattle and the wily chief had been trying to get Brown to fix a drastic penalty upon his own people. Brown went with the Navajos to Sunset, there to learn that the half-starved colonists had killed three range animals, assumed to have been owner- less. The matter then was adjusted with little trouble and to the full satisfaction of the redskins.

In September, 1878, Erastus Snow visited Moen Copie, where the inhabitants comprised nine families, with especial mention of Andrew S. Gibbons, of the party of John W. Young and of Tuba. There had been a prosperous season in a farming way.

This visit is notable from the fact that on the 17th, Snow and others proceeded about two miles west of north and at Musha Springs located a townsite, afterward named Tuba City. Tuba City was visited in 1900 by Andrew Jenson, who found twenty families resident, with one fam- ily at the old Moen Copie mission and three families at Moen Abi, seven miles to the southwest.

A Woolen Factory in the Wilds

Primarily the Tuba settlement was a missionary effort, with the intention of taking the Gospel into the very center of the Navajo and Hopi country. Agriculture flourished a all times, with an abundant supply of water for irrigation· But there was an attempt at industry and one which would appear to have had the very best chance of success. The Navajo and Hopi alike are owners of immense numbers of sheep. The wool in early days almost entirely was utilized by the Indians in the making of blankets, this on rude hand

158

looms, where the product was turned out with a maximum of labor and of time. John W. Young, elsewhere referred to in connection with the establishment of Fort Moroni and with the building of the Atlantic and Pacific railroad, thought he saw an opportunity to benefit the Indians and the Church, and probably himself, so at Tuba City, in the spring of 1879, he commenced erection of a woolen factory, with interior dimensions 90x70 feet. The plant was finished in November, with 192 spindles in use. In the spring of 1880 was a report in the Deseret News that the manufacture of yarns had commenced and that the machinery was running like a charm. Looms for the cloth-making were reported on the way. Just how labor was secured is not known, but it is probable that Indians were utilized to as large an extent as possible. There is no available record concerning the length of time this mill was operated. It is understood, however, that the Indians soon lost interest in it and failed to bring in wool. Possibly the labor supply was not ample and possibly the distance to the Utah settlements was too great and the journey too rough to secure profit. At any event, the factory closed without revolutionizing the Navajo and Hopi woolen industry. In 1900 was written that the factory "has most literally been carried away by Indians, travelers and others." Old Chief Tuba took particular pride in watching over the remains of the factory, but after his death the ruination of the building was made complete. Some of the machinery was taken to St. Johns.

Lot Smith and His End

In general the Saints at Tuba appear to have lived at peace with their Indian neighbors, save in 1892 when Lot Smith was killed. The simple tale of the tragedy is in a Church record that follows:

On Monday, June 20, 1892, some Indians at Tuba City turned their sheep into Lot Smith's pasture. Brother Smith went out to drive the sheep away, and while thus engaged he got into a quarrel

159

with the Indians and commenced shooting their sheep. In retaliation the Indians commenced firing upon Lot Smith's cows and finally directed their fire against Lot Smith himself, shooting him through the body. Though mortally wounded, he rode home, a distance of about two miles, and lived about six hours, when he expired. It is stated on good authority that the Indians were very sorry, as Smith always had been a friend to them.

The Author here might be permitted to make reference to the impression generally held in the Southwest that Lot Smith was a "killer," a man of violence, who died as he had lived. Close study of his record fails to bear out this view. Undoubtedly it started in Utah after his return from Mormon Battalion service, when he became a member of the Mormon militia that harassed Johnston's army in the passes east of the Salt Lake Valley. There is solemn Church assurance that not a life was taken in this foray, though many wagons were burned in an attempt, October 3, 1857, to delay the march of the troops. Smith (who in no wise was related to the family of the Prophet Joseph) became a leader in the Deseret defense forces, but there is belief that in all his life he shed no blood, unless it was in connection with a battle with the Utes near Provo, in February, 1850. In this fight were used brass cannon, probably those that had been bought at Sutter's Fort by returning Mormon Battalion members. According to a friendly biographer, "There never was a man who held the life and liberty of man more sacred than did Lot Smith." Ten years after his death there was re-interment of his remains at Farmington, Utah.

Moen Copie Reverts to the Indians

In 1900 Moen Copie ward embraced 21 families and about 150 souls. There had been an extension of the Navajo reservation westward and the Indians, though friendly, had been advised to crowd the Mormons out, on the ground that the country in reality belonged to the aborigines. There was no title to the land, which had not been surveyed and which was held only by squatter rights. There

160

had been some success in a missionary way, but conditions arose which made it appear best that the land be vacated to the Indians. There was much negotiation and at the end there was payment by the government of $45,000, this divided among the whites according to the value of their improvements and acreage.

In this wise the Mormon settlement of Tuba City was vacated in February, 1903, the inhabitants moving to other parts of Arizona and to Utah and Idaho. A large reservation school has been established on the Wash, many Indians there being instructed in the arts of the white man, while government farmers are utilizing the waters of the stream and of the springs in the cultivation of a considerable acreage. A feature of this school is that fuel is secured, at very slight cost, from coal measures nearby.

Woodruff and Its Water Troubles

Closely following settlement of the ephemeral lower Little Colorado towns came the founding of Woodruff, about 25 miles upstream from St. Joseph and about twelve miles above the present Holbrook. It is still a prosperous town and community, though its history has been one in which disaster has come repeatedly through the washing away of the dam which supplies its main canal with water from the Little Colorado and Silver Creek.

In the locality the Mormons were antedated by Luther Martin and Felix Scott. The section was scouted in December, 1876, by Joseph H. Richards, Lewis P. Cardon, James Thurman and Peter O. Peterson, from Allen's Camp, and they participated in starting a ditch from the river. There appeared to have been no indication of occupancy when, in March, 1877, Ammon M. Tenney passed through the valley and determined it a good place for location. In the following month, however, Cardon and two sons, and Wm. A. Walker came upon the ground, with other families, followed, three weeks later, by Nathan C. Tenney, father of Ammon M., with two sons, John T. and Samuel, Hans

161

Gulbrandsen and Charles Riggs. For about a year the settlement was known simply as Tenney's Camp. L. H. Hatch was appointed to take charge in February, 1878. About that time the name of Woodruff was adopted, in honor of President Wilford Woodruff, this suggestion made by John W. Young. The first settlement was in a rock and adobe fort, forming a half square. There was a common dining room as, for a while, there was adherence to the system of the United Order. It is told that all save two of the settlers participated and there is memorandum of how three sisters were detailed weekly for cooking, with girls as assistants.

In February, 1882, was survey of the present townsite, on which John Reidhead built the first house. This townsite was purchased from the Atlantic and Pacific Railroad Company, in May, 1889, for $8 an acre. At first it had not been appreciated that the town had not been built upon government land.

The history of Woodruff has in it much of disastrous incident through the frequent breaking of the river dams. In May, 1880, the dam had to be cut by the settlers themselves, in order to permit the water to flow down to St. Joseph, where there was priority of appropriation. At several times, the Church organization helped in the repair or building of the many dams, after the settlers had spent everything they had and had reached the point of despair. At suggestion of Jesse N. Smith in 1884, all the brethren in the Stake were called upon to donate one day each of labor on the Woodruff dam. Up to 1890, the dam had been washed out seven times and even now there is trouble in its maintenance.

Of passing interest is the fact that President Wilford Woodruff, after whom the settlement was named, was a visitor to Woodruff on at least two occasions, in 1879, and in 1887, when an exile from Utah. He was at Moen Copie when there came news, which later proved erroneous, that pursuers had crossed at Lee's Ferry. Then, guided by Richard Gibbons, he rode westward, making a stop of a few days at Fort Moroni.

Holbrook Once Was Horsehead Crossing

Holbrook, on the Little Colorado, county seat of Navajo County, shipping point on the Santa Fe railroad system for practically all of Navajo and Apache Counties, had Mormon inception, under its present name, that of an Atlantic and Pacific railroad locating engineer, F. A. Holbrook. The christening is said to have been done in 1881 by John W. Young, then a grading contractor, applied to a location two miles east of the present townsite. Young there had a store at his headquarters. Later the railroad authorities established the town on its present location.

The settlement, since the first coming of English-speaking folk, had been known as Horsehead Crossing. For years before the railroad came, a roadside station was kept at the Crossing by a Mexican, Berardo, whose name was differently spelled by almost every traveler who wrote of him. One of the tales is from E. C. Bunch, who came as a young member of the Arkansas immigration in 1876, and who later became one of the leaders in Arizona education. He tells, in referring appreciatively to Mexican hospitality, that "Berrando's" sign, painted by an American, read, "If you have the money, you can eat." But the owner, feeling the misery coldheartedness might create, wrote below, "No got a money, eat anyway." Berardo loaned the colonists some cows, whose milk was most welcome.

Chapter Fifteen

𝕾𝖊𝖙𝖙𝖑𝖊𝖒𝖊𝖓𝖙 𝕾𝖕𝖗𝖊𝖆𝖉𝖘 𝕾𝖔𝖚𝖙𝖍𝖜𝖆𝖗𝖉

Snowflake and its Naming

Snowflake, one of the most prosperous of towns of Mormon origin, lies 28 miles almost south of Holbrook, with which it was given railroad connection during 1919. The first settler was James Stinson who came in 1873, and who, by 1878, had taken out the waters of Silver Creek for the irrigation of about 300 acres. In July, 1878, Stinson (later a resident of Tempe) sold to Wm. J. Flake for $11,000, paid in livestock.

July 21, the first Mormons moved upon the Stinson place. They were Flake, James Gale, Jesse Brady, Alexander Stewart and Thomas West, with their families, most of them from the old Taylor settlement. Others followed soon thereafter, including six Taylor families, headed by John Kartchner, they taking the upper end of the valley.

Actual foundation of the town came in an incident of the most memorable of the southwestern trips of Erastus Snow. He and his party arrived at the Kartchner ranch September 26, 1878, the location described by L. John Nuttall of the party as "a nice little valley." As bishop was appointed John Hunt of Savoia, who was with the Mormon Battalion, and who remained in the same capacity till 1910. Flake's location was considered best for a townsite and to it was given the name it now bears, honoring the visiting dignitary and the founder. The townsite was surveyed soon thereafter by Samuel G. Ladd of St. Joseph, who also laid out several ditch lines. Even before there was a town, there was a birth, that of William Taylor Gale, son of James Gale.

ERASTUS SNOW
In Charge of Pioneer Arizona Colonization

JOSEPH W. McMURRIN

ANTHONY W. IVINS

January 16, 1879, arrived Jesse N. Smith, president of the newly-created Eastern Arizona Stake, appointed on recommendation of Erastus Snow. After trying to negotiate for land at St. Johns, he returned, and he and his company concluded to locate in Snowflake, where they took up lots not already appropriated. The farming land went in a drawing of two parcels each to the city lot owners, who thus became possessed of twenty acres each. Joseph Fish headed a committee on distribution, which valued each city lot at $30, each first-class farming plot of ten acres at $110 and each second-class plot at $60, giving each shareholder property valued at $200, or ten head of stock, this being at the rate that Flake paid for the whole property. Flake took only one share.

The Mormon towns usually were of the quietest, but occasionally had excitement brought to them. On one such occasion at Snowflake, December 8, 1892, was killed Chas. L. Flake, son of Wm. J. Flake. A message had come from New Mexico asking detention of Will Mason, a desperado said to have had a record of seven murders. Charles and his brother, Jas. M., attempted the arrest. Mason fired twice over his shoulder, the first bullet cutting James' left ear, and then shot Charles through the neck. Almost the same moment a bullet from James' pistol passed through the murderer's head, followed by a second.

Of modern interest, indicative of the trend of public sentiment, is an agreement, entered into late in 1920, by the merchants of Snowflake and the towns to the southward, to sell no tobacco, in any form.

Snowflake was the first county-seat of Apache County, created in 1879, the first court session held in the home of Wm. J. Flake. At the fall election, the courthouse was moved to St. Johns. In 1880, by the vote of Clifton, which then was within Apache County, Springerville was made the county seat. In 1882, St. Johns finally was chosen the seat of Apache County government.

Joseph Fish, Historian

The first consecutive history of Arizona, intended to be complete in its narration, undoubtedly was that written by Joseph Fish, for many years resident in or near Snowflake. Though Mr. Fish is a patriarch of the Mormon Church, his narration of events is entirely uncolored, unless by sympathy for the Indians. His work never had publication, a fact to be deplored. A copy of his manuscript is in the office of the State Historian, and another is possessed by Dr. J. A. Munk, held by him in his library of Arizoniana in the Southwestern Museum at Garvanza, Cal.

The history has about 700 pages of typewritten matter, treating of events down to a comparatively late date. Mr. Fish has a clear and lucid style of narration and his work is both interesting and valuable. Though of no large means, he gathered, at his home on the Little Colorado, about 400 books and magazines, and upon this basis and by personal interviews and correspondence he secured the data upon which he wrote. He is a native of Illinois, of Yankee stock, and is now in his eightieth year. He came to Arizona in 1879 and the next year was in charge of the commissary department for the contract of John W. Young in the building of the Atlantic and Pacific railroad. His first historical work was done as clerk of the Eastern Arizona Stake. In 1902 he began work on another historical volume, "The Pioneers of the Rocky Mountains." He now is resident in Enterprise, Utah.

Another historic character resident in the Stake was Ralph Ramsey, the artist in wood who carved the eagle that overspreads the Eagle gate in Salt Lake City.

Taylor, Second of the Name

Taylor, the second settlement of the name in the Mormon northeastern occupation, lies three miles south of Snowflake (which it antedates). It is on Silver Creek, which is spanned by a remarkable suspension bridge that connects two sections of the town. When the first Mormon

166

residents came, early in 1878 the settlement was known as Bagley. Then there was to be change to Walker, but the Postoffice Department objected, as another Walker existed, near Prescott. The present name, honoring John Taylor, president of the Church, was adopted in 1881, at the suggestion of Stake President Jesse N. Smith.

The first settler was James Pearce, a noted character in southwestern annals, son of the founder of Pearce's Ferry across the Colorado at the mouth of Grand Wash, at the lower end of the Grand Canyon. James Pearce was a pioneer missionary with Jacob Hamblin among the Paiutes of the Nevada Muddy region and the Hopi and Navajo of northeastern Arizona. He came January 23, 1878, in March joined by John H. Standiford. Other early arrivals were Jos. C. Kay, Jesse H. and Wm. A. Walker, Lorenzo Hatch, an early missionary to the northeastern Arizona Indians, Noah Brimhall and Daniel Bagley. A ditch was surveyed by Major Ladd, who did most of such work for all the settlements, but the townsite, established in 1878, on the recommendation, in September, of Erastus Snow, was surveyed in December by a group of interested residents, led by Jos. S. Cardon, their "chain" being a rope. The irrigation troubles of the community appear to have been fewer than those of the Little Colorado towns, though in the great spring flood of 1890 the dams and bridges along Silver Creek were carried away.

Shumway's Historic Founder

Shumway, on Silver Creek, five miles above Taylor, has interest of historical sort in the fact that it was named after an early settler Charles Shumway, one of the most noted of the patriarchs of the Church. He was the first to cross the Mississippi, February 4, 1846, in the exodus from Nauvoo, and was one of the 143 Pioneers who entered Salt Lake with Brigham Young the following summer. In December, 1879, his son, Wilson G. Shumway, accepted a call to Arizona. Most of the winter was spent at Grand

Falls in a "shack" he built of cottonwood logs, roofed with sandstone slabs. In this he entertained Apostle Woodruff, who directed the chiseling of the name "Wilford Woodruff" upon a rock. Charles Shumway and N. P. Beebe bought the mill rights on Silver Creek, acquired through location the previous year by Nathan C. and Jesse Wanslee, brought machinery from the East and, within a year, started a grist mill that still is a local institution. The village of Shumway never has had more than a score of families. Charles Shumway died May 21, 1898. His record of self-sacrifice continued after his arrival in Arizona early in 1880, the first stop being at Concho. There, according to his son, Wilson G., the family for two years could have been rated as among "the poorest of poor pioneers," with a dugout for a home, this later succeeded by a log cabin of comparative luxury. For months the bread was of barley flour, the diet later having variety, changed to corn bread and molasses, with wheat flour bread as a treat on Sundays.

Showlow Won in a Game of "Seven-Up"

Showlow, one of the freak Arizona place names, applied to a creek and district, as well as to a thrifty little settlement, lies about south of Snowflake, twenty miles or more. The name antedates the Mormon settlement. The valley jointly was held by C. E. Cooley and Marion Clark, both devoted to the card game of "seven-up." At a critical period of one of their games, when about all possible property had been wagered, Clark exclaimed, "Show low and you take the ranch!" Cooley "showed low." This same property later was sold by him to W. J. Flake, for $13,000.

The Showlow section embraces the mountain communities of Showlow, Reidhead (Lone Pine), Pinedale, Linden, Juniper, Adair (which once had unhappy designation as "Fools' Hollow"), Ellsworth, Lakeside (also known as Fairview and Woodland), Pinetop and Cluff's Cienega. Cooley, in the Cienega (Sp., marsh) is the site of a large sawmill and is the terminus of a railroad from Holbrook.

168

But the noted scout Cooley, lived elsewhere, at Showlow and at Apache Springs.

The first Mormons to come to Showlow were Alfred Cluff and David E. Adams, who were employed by Cooley in 1876. They were from Allen's Camp, almost driven away by necessity. Others soon came, including Moses and Orson Cluff, Edmund Ellsworth and Edson Whipple, a Salt Lake Pioneer. There was gradual settlement of the communities above listed, generally prior to 1880. While only one member of the faith was killed during the Indian troubles of the eighties, log and stone forts were erected in several of the villages for use in case of need.

Mountain Communities

Out in the woods, twenty miles southwest of Snowflake, is the village of Pinedale, settled in January, 1879, by Niels Mortensen and sons and Niels Peterson. The first location was at what now is called East Pinedale, also known at different times as Mortensen and Percheron. In the following winter, a small sawmill was brought in from Fort Apache and in 1882 came a larger mill, the original Mount Trumbull mill. In that year a townsite had rough survey by James Huff and in 1885 a schoolhouse was built. The brethren had much trouble with desperados, horse and cattle thieves, but peace came after the Pleasant Valley war in Tonto Basin, in which thirty of the range riders were killed.

Reidhead, also known at times as Woolf's Ranch, Lone Pine Crossing, Beaver Branch and Reidhead Crossing, is one of the deserted points of early settlement, historically important mainly in the fact that it was the home of Nathan B. Robinson, killed nearby by Apaches June 1, 1882. Fear of the Indians then drove away the other settlers and, though there was later return, in 1893 was final abandonment. Reidhead lay on Showlow Creek, ten miles above Taylor and ten miles from Cooley's ranch. It was one of the places of first white settlement in northeastern Arizona, a Mexican having had his ranch there even before Cooley came into the country. Then came one Woolf, from whom squatter rights were bought in April, 1878, by John Reidhead, then lately from Utah.

Pinetop, 35 miles south of Snowflake, dates back to March, 1888, when settled by Wm. L. Penrod and sons, including four families, all from Provo, Utah. Progress started with the transfer to Pinetop of the Mount Trumbull mill in 1890. The name is said to have been given by soldiers, the first designation having been Penrod. A notable event in local history was a joint conference in Pinetop, July 4, 1892, with representatives from all Arizona Stakes and attended by President Woodruff's counselors, Geo. Q. Cannon and Jos. F. Smith. For this special occasion was built a pavilion, the largest in Arizona, a notable undertaking for a small community. The structure was destroyed by fire a few years ago.

Forest Dale on the Reservation

In the settlement of what now is southern Navajo County, the Mormon settlers a bit overran the present line of the Apache Indian reservation, where they located early in 1878 upon what now is known as Forest Dale Creek, a tributary of Carrizo Creek. The country is a beautiful one, well watered from abundant rains and well wooded, possibly a bit more favored than the present settlements of Showlow, Pinetop and Lakeside, which lie just north of the reservation line. There is reference in a letter of Llewellyn Harris, in July, 1878, to the settlement of Forest Dale, but the name is found in writings several months before. Harris and several others refer to the Little Colorado country as being in "Aravapai" County. This was in error. The county then was Yavapai, before the separation of Apache County.

The valley was found by Oscar Cluff while hunting in the fall of 1877 and soon thereafter he moved there with his family. In February there followed his brother, Alfred Cluff, who suggested the name. The settlement was started

170

February 18, 1878, by Jos. H. Frisby, Merritt Staley, Oscar Mann, Orson and Alfred Cluff, Ebenezer Thayne, David E. Adams and a few others.

The overruning referred to was not done blindly. Jos. H. Frisby and Alfred Cluff went to San Carlos. There they were assured by Agent Hart that Apache Springs and the creek referred to were not on the reservation, and that the government would protect them if they would settle there. It was understood that the reservation line lay about three miles south of the settlement. This information is contained in a letter signed by Agent Hart and addressed to Colonel Andrews, Eleventh Infantry, commanding Fort Apache. Mr. Hart stated that he would be "glad to have the settlers make permanent homes at Forest Dale, for the reason that the Indians strayed so far from their own lands that it was hard to keep track of them as conditions then were, and that the settlement of the country would have a tendency to hold the Indians on their own lands upon the reservation."

Lieutenant Ray was sent with a detachment of troops and the Indians at Apache Springs were removed and the main body of the settlers, then temporarily located on the Showlow, moved over the ridge into the new valley.

In March, 1878, the settlers included Merritt Staley, Oscar Mann, Ebenezer Thayne, David E. Adams, Jos. H. Frisby, Alfred Cluff, Isaac Follett, Orson Cluff and several unmarried men. In September, Erastus Snow found a very prosperous settlement. A ward organization was established. The first white child, Forest Dale Adams, is now the wife of Frank Webster, of Central, Arizona. Seven springs of good water, known as Apache Springs, formed the headwaters of Carrizo Creek.

In 1879, Missionaries Harris and Thayne appear to have made a mistake similar to that of the Arab who allowed the camel to thrust his nose inside of the tent. They secured permission from the commanding officer of

Fort Apache to allow about a dozen Indian families on the creek. The missionary efforts appear to have failed, and the Indians simply demanded everything in sight. Reports came that the locality really was on the reservation and the white population therefore drifted away, mainly into the Gila Valley. In December, 1879, only three families were left, and the following year the last were gone.

In 1881 rumors drifted down the Little Colorado that Forest Dale, after all, was not on the reservation. So William Crookston and three others resettled the place, some of them from the abandoned Brigham City. Then came the Indian troubles of 1881-82. When Fort Apache was attacked, the families consolidated at Cooley, where they built a fort. Some went north to Snowflake and Taylor. In December, 1881, President Jesse N. Smith of the Eastern Arizona Stake advised the Forest Dale settlers to satisfy the Indians for their claims on the place, and received assurance from General Carr at Fort Apache, that the locality most likely was not on the reservation and that, in case it was not, he would be pleased to have the Mormon settlers there. A new ward was established and William Ellsworth and twenty more families moved in, mainly from Brigham City. In May, 1882, the Indians came again to plant corn and were wrathful to find the whites ahead of them. An officer was sent from Fort Apache and a treaty was made by which the Indians were given thirty acres of planted land.

June 1, 1882, Apaches killed Nathan B. Robinson at the Reidhead place and shot Emer Plumb at Walnut Springs, during a period of general Indian unrest. Soon thereafter, President Smith advised the settlers that they had better look for other locations, as the ground was on the reservation.

In December, Lieutenant Gatewood, under orders from Captain Crawford (names afterward famous in the Geronimo campaign to the southward) came from Fort Apache

JOSEPH FISH
An Arizona Historian

¡JOSEPH H. RICHARDS OF ST. JOSEPH
One of the few original settlers who still lives on the Little
Colorado

A GROUP OF ST. JOSEPH PIONEERS AND
HISTORIAN ANDREW JENSON

SHUMWAY AND THE OLD MILL ON SILVER CREEK

and advised the settlers they would be given until the spring to vacate. The crops were disposed of at Fort Apache and the spring of 1883 found Forest Dale deserted, houses, fences, corrals and every improvement left behind. The drift of the settlers was to the Gila Valley.

This Forest Dale affair was made a national matter, January 24, 1916, when a bill was introduced by Senator Ashurst of Arizona for the relief of Alfred Cluff, Orson Cluff, Henry E. Norton, Wm. B. Ballard, Elijah Hancock, Susan R. Saline, Oscar Mann, Celia Thayne, William Cox, Theodore Farley, Adelaide Laxton, Clara L. Tenney, Geo. M. Adams, Charlotte Jensen and Sophia Huff. Later additions were David E. Adams and Peter H. McBride.

The amounts claimed by each varied from $2000 to $15,000. A similar bill had been introduced by the Senator in a previous Congress. In his statement to the Indian Affairs Committee, the Senator stated that the settlements had been on unreserved and vacant Government lands and that the reservation had been extended to cover the tract some time in 1882.

Appended were affidavits from each of the individuals claiming compensation. All told of moving during the winter, under conditions of great hardship, of cold and exposure and loss of property.

David E. Adams, one of the few survivors of the Forest Dale settlement, lately advised the Author that the change in the reservation line undeniably was at the suggestion of C. E. Cooley, a noted Indian scout, who feared the Mormons would compete with him in supplying corn and forage to Fort Apache.

Tonto Basin's Early Settlement

Soon after location on the Little Colorado there was exploration to the southwest, with a view toward settlement extension. At the outset was encountered the very serious obstruction of the great Mogollon Rim, a precipice that averages more than 1000 feet in height for several

173

hundred miles. Ways through this were found, however, into Tonto Basin, a great expanse, about 100 miles in length by 80 in width, lying south and southwest of the Rim, bounded on the west by the Mazatzal Mountains, and on the south and southeast by spurs of the Superstitions and Pinals. The Basin itself contains a sizable mountain range, the Sierra Ancha.

The first exploration was made in July, 1876, by Wm. C. Allen, John Bushman, Pleasant Bradford and Peter Hansen. Their report was unfavorable, in considering settlement. In the fall of the following year there was exploration by John W. Freeman, John H. Willis, Thomas Clark, Alfred J. Randall, Willis Fuller and others. They returned a more favorable report. In March, 1878, Willis drove stock into the upper Basin and also took the first wagon to the East Verde Valley. He was followed by Freeman and family and Riel Allen. Freeman located a road to the Rim, from Pine Springs to Baker's Butte, about forty miles. Price W. Nielson (or Nelson) settled on Rye Creek, in 1878. In the following year was started the Pine settlement, about twenty miles north of the East Verde settlement, with Riel Allen at its head. There is record that most of the settlers on the East Verde moved away in 1879, mainly to Pine, and others back to the Little Colorado. However, the Author, in September of 1889, found a very prosperous little Mormon settlement on the East Verde, raising alfalfa, fruit and livestock. It was called Mazatzal City and lay within a few miles of the Natural Bridge, which is on the lower reaches of Pine Creek before that stream joins the East Verde.

A settlement was in existence at least as late as 1889 on upper Tonto Creek. The first resident was David Gowan, discoverer of the Natural Bridge, he and two others taking advantage of the presence of a beaver-built log dam, from which an irrigating canal was started. The first of the Mormon settlers at that point, in 1883, were

John and David W. Sanders, with their families, they followed by the Adams, Bagley and Gibson families. This location was a very lonely one, though less than ten miles, by rocky trail, from the town of Payson. It was not well populated, at any time, though soil, climate and water were good.

Erastus Snow in 1878 made formal visit to the Tonto settlements. He found on Rye Creek the Price Nelson and Joseph Gibson families, less than a mile above where the stream entered Tonto Creek. Thereafter were visited the East Verde settlements, from which most of the men had gone to southern Utah after their families and stock, and Pine Creek and Strawberry Valley, where later was considerable settlement.

According to Fish, the first settlement in Tonto Basin was by Al Rose, a Dane, in 1877, in Pleasant Valley, though he lived for only a few months in a stockade home which he erected. Then came G. S. Sixby and J. Church from California. There followed Ed. Rose, J. D. Tewksbury and sons, the Graham family and James Stinson, the last from Snowflake. Sixby is renowned as the hero of a wonderful experience in the spring of 1882, when, his brother and an employe killed, he held the fort of his log home against more than 100 Indians, the same band later fought and captured by Capt. Adna R. Chaffee in the fight of the Big Dry Wash.

There was good reason for the delayed settlement of Tonto Basin, for it was a region traversed continually by a number of Indian tribes. It was a sort of No Man's Land, in which wandered the Mohave-Apache and the Tonto, the Cibicu and White Mountain Apaches, not always at peace among themselves. Several times the Pleasant and Cherry Creek Valleys were highways for Indian raids of large dimensions. The Pleasant Valley war, between the Tewksbury and Graham factions cost thirty lives. No Mormon participated.

Most of the land holdings necessarily were small. The water supply is regular in only a few places. Hence it is natural that most of the Mormons who settled, moved on, to better agricultural conditions found farther southward. Abandonment of all Tonto Basin settlements was authorized at a meeting of President Woodruff with the heads of the Arizona Stakes, held at Albuquerque August 14, 1890.

Chapter Sixteen

𝕷𝖎𝖙𝖙𝖑𝖊 𝕮𝖔𝖑𝖔𝖗𝖆𝖉𝖔 𝕾𝖊𝖙𝖙𝖑𝖊𝖒𝖊𝖓𝖙𝖘

Genesis of St. Johns

One of the most remarkable of Arizona settlements is St. Johns, 58 miles southeast of Holbrook, its railroad station. Though its development has been almost entirely Mormon and though it is headquarters for the St. Johns Stake of the Church, its foundation dates back of the Mormon occupation of the valley of the Little Colorado.

Very early in the seventies, New Mexican cattle and sheep men spread their ranges over the mountains into the Little Colorado Valley and there were occasional camps of the Spanish-speaking people. In 1872 a mail carrier, John Walker, had built a cabin on the river, five miles below the site of St. Johns. As early as 1864 the locality had been visited by Solomon Barth, a Jewish trader, who dealt with the Indians as far eastward as Zuni and who, on burros, packed salt from the Zuni salt lake to the mining camps of the Prescott section. Barth, oddly enough, for a while had been connected with the Mormons, at the age of 13, a new arrival from Posen, East Prussia, joining his uncle in a push-cart caravan to Salt Lake. Later he was in San Bernardino, there remaining after the 1857 exodus, to go to La Paz, Arizona, in 1862. In 1864 he carried mail on the route from Albuquerque to Prescott, as contractor. In November, 1868, he was captured by Apaches, but was liberated, with several Mexican associates, all almost naked, reaching the Zuni villages, on foot, four days later. For food they shared the carcass of a small dog. In 1870 he was post trader at Fort Apache, then known as Camp Ord, in the year of its establishment. In 1873, a game of cards at El Badito (Little Crossing), a settlement on the Little Colorado, on the St. Johns site, determined his future terrestrial place of residence. From his adversaries, New Mexicans, he won several thousand head of sheep and several thousand dollars. Then he left the life of the road and settled down.

A. F. Banta, a pioneer of Arizona pioneers, then known by his army name of Charlie Franklin, tells that he was at Badito (Vadito) in 1876, the place then on a mail route southward to Fort Apache and the military posts on the Gila. In the same connection, James D. Houck, in 1874, contracted to carry mail across the Little Colorado Valley, between Fort Wingate and Prescott. Another mail route was from Wingate to St. Johns and Apache.

Sol Barth and his brothers, Morris and Nathan, settled at St. Johns in the fall of 1873, with a number of New Mexican laborers. At once was commenced construction of a dam across the Little Colorado and of ditches and there was farming of a few hundred acres adjoining the site of the present town. In all, Barth laid claim to 1200 acres of land, though it proved later he had only a squatter title. With him originated the name of St. Johns, at first San Juan, given in compliment to the first female resident, Senora Maria San Juan Baca de Padilla. With this conspicuous exception, all saintly names in Arizona were bestowed by either Catholic missionaries or by Mormons.

Ammon M. Tenney, a scout of Mormondom second only to Jacob Hamblin, in 1877 at Kanab received from President Brigham Young instructions to go into Arizona and select places for colonization. He visited many points in western New Mexico and eastern Arizona, but his recommendation was confined to St. Johns, Concho, sixteen miles west of St. Johns, The Meadows, eight miles northwest, and Woodruff.

With the Tenney report in mind, in January, 1879, St.

Johns was visited by Jesse N. Smith, just arrived in Arizona to be president of the Little Colorado Stake. But Smith was unable to make terms with Barth and his Mexican neighbors and turned back to Snowflake.

Land Purchased by Mormons

Under instructions from the Church, Ammon M. Tenney returned to St. Johns late in 1879 and, November 16, succeeded in effecting the purchase of the Barth interests, including three claims at The Meadows. The purchase price was 770 head of American cows, furnished by the Church, though 100 were loaned by W. J. Flake. The value of the livestock, estimated at $19,000, in later years was donated by the Church toward the erection of the St. Johns academy. Other land purchases later were made by arriving members.

Tenney was the first head of the colony, which was started in December, by the arrival of Jos. H. Watkins and Wm. F. James, missionaries sent from Ogden, who came with their families. In December, Apostle Wilford Woodruff, later President of the Church, held the first religious meeting, this at the home of Donasiano Gurule, a New Mexican. The Church authorities were active in their settlement plans and at a quarterly Stake conference in Snowflake, March 27, 1880, 190 souls were reported from the St. Johns branch.

A few days after the conference, Apostle Woodruff located a townsite one and a half miles below the center of the present site. This location, though surveyed and with a few houses, was abandoned the following September, on recommendation of Apostles Erastus Snow and Francis M. Lyman, for higher ground, west and north of the Mexican village. In the summer of 1880 the settlement, named Salem, was given a postoffice, but the Mormon postmaster appointed, Sixtus E. Johnson, failed to secure his keys from a non-Mormon, E. S. Stover, incumbent at San Juan.

A notable arrival, October 9, 1890, was David K. Udall,

called from Kane County, Utah, to serve as bishop of St. Johns ward. With continuous ecclesiastical service, he now is president of St. Johns Stake, elevated in July, 1887.

Occupation of the new townsite started early in October, 1880, the public square designated by President Jesse N. Smith on the 9th. Twenty square-rod city lots were laid off in blocks 24 rods square, with streets six rods wide. In the spring of 1881 the farming land was surveyed into forty 40-acre blocks, these later subdivided. During the winter of 1881 was built a log schoolhouse, through private donations. The first teacher was Mrs. Anna Romney. The first church was a "bowery" of greasewood.

That the years following hardly were ones of plenty is indicated by the fact that in the spring of 1885 President John Taylor issued a tithing office order for $1000 and $1187 more was collected in Utah stakes, to aid the St. Johns settlers in the purchase of foodstuffs and seed grain.

A. F. Banta started a weekly newspaper, "The Pioneer Press," soon after occupation of the townsite, this journal in January, 1883, bought by Mormons and edited by M. P. Romney.

Wild Celebration of St. John's Day

There was a wild time in St. Johns on the day of the Mexican population's patron saint, San Juan, June 24, 1882, when Nat Greer and a band of Texas cowboys entered the Mexican town. The Greers had been unpopular with the Mexicans since they had marked a Mexican with an ear "underslope," as cattle are marked, this after a charge that their victim had been found in the act of stealing a Greer colt. The fight that followed the Greer entry had nothing at its initiation to do with the Mormon settlers. Assaulted by the Mexican police and populace, eight of the band rode away and four were penned into an uncompleted adobe house. Jim Vaughn of the raiders was killed and Harris Greer was wounded. On the attacking side was wounded Francisco Tafolla, whose son in later years was killed while

180

FIRST MORMON SCHOOL, CHURCH AND BOWERY AT
ST. JOHNS

DAVID K. UDALL AND HIS FIRST RESIDENCE
AT ST. JOHNS

ST. JOHNS IN 1887
Sol Barth's House with the Tower

THE STAKE ACADEMY AT ST. JOHNS

serving in the Arizona Rangers. It was declared that several thousand shots had been fired, but there was a lull, in which the part of peacemaker was taken up by "Father" Nathan C. Tenney, a pioneer of Woodruff and father of Ammon M. Tenney. He walked to the house and induced the Greers to surrender. The Sheriff, E. S. Stover, was summoned and was in the act of taking the men to jail when a shot was fired from a loft of the Barth house, where a number of Mexicans had established themselves. The bullet, possibly intended for a Greer, passed through the patriarch's head and neck, killing him instantly. The Greers were threatened with lynching, but were saved by the sheriff's determination. Their case was taken to Prescott and they escaped with light punishment.

In the fall of 1881 the community knew a summary execution of two men and there were other deeds of disorder, but in no wise did they affect the Mormon people, save that the lawless actions unsettled the usual peaceful conditions.

Disputes Over Land Titles

It is not within the province of this work to deal in matters of controversial sort, especially with those that may have affected the religious features of the Mormon settlement but there may be mention of a few of the difficulties that came to the people of St. Johns in their earlier days.

The general subject of land titles in the Mormon settlements that came within the scope of railroad land grants has been referred to on other pages. In St. Johns there was added need for defense of the squatter titles secured from Barth and the Mexicans, while there was assault on the validity of the occupation of the townsite. On several occasions, especially in March, 1884, there was attempted "jumping" of the choicest lots and there was near approach to bloodshed, prevented only by the pacific determination of Bishop Udall. The opposition upset a house that had been placed upon one lot and riotous conditions prevailed for hours. Reinforcements quickly came from outlying Mormon settlements and firearms were carried generally in self defense. A number of lawsuits had to be defended, at large expense. There was friction with the Mexican element, which lived compactly in the old town, just east of the Mormon settlement, and clashes were known with a non-Mormon American element that had political connection with the Mexicans.

About May 18, 1884, was discovered a plot to waylay and harm Apostle Brigham Young, Jr., and Francis M. Lyman, on the road to Ramah, but a strong escort fended off the danger. In the Stake chronicles is told that the brethren for a time united in regular fasting and prayer, seeking protection from their enemies.

Irrigation Difficulties and Disaster

St. Johns had its irrigation troubles, just as did every other Little Colorado settlement, only on a larger scale. In the beginning of the Mormon settlement, claim was made by the Mexicans upon the larger part of the river flow. Later there was compromise on a basis of three-fifths of the flow to the Mormons and two-fifths to the Mexicans, and in 1886 a degree of stability was secured by formation of the St. Johns Irrigation Company. A large dam, six miles south of St. Johns, created what was called the Slough reservoir. However, this dam was washed out in 1903, after years of drouth. Then were several years of discouragement and of loss of population.

Thereafter came the idea of building a larger dam at a point twelve miles upstream, creating a reservoir to be drained through a deep cut. The plan was approved by the Church, which appropriated $5000 toward construction. There was formation of an irrigation company, to which was attached the name of Apostle F. M. Lyman, who had taken a personal interest in the improvement. A Colorado company provided one-half the necessary capital and the community the balance, and plans were made for the reclamation of 15,000 acres upon higher land than had been irrigated before. After expenditure of $200,000, the dam was completed and the reservoir filled. Construction was faulty and in April, 1915, the dam was washed away, with attendant loss of eight lives and with large damage to flooded farms below. There was reorganization of the Lyman Company and about $200,000 more was spent, with the desired end of water storage still unreached. Then came appeal to the State, which, through the State Loan Board, advanced large sums, taking as security mortgages on the land and dam. State investment in the Lyman project today approximates $800,000. The dam now is about finished and is claimed to be a structure that will stand all flood conditions.

Meager Rations at Concho

Concho was a Mexican village, at least a dozen years established, when the first Mormon settlers arrived. The name probably is from the Spanish word "concha," a shell. The settlement lies sixteen miles west of St. Johns. There were two sections, the older, in which Spanish was spoken and in which stock raising was the main occupation, and the Mormon settlement, a mile up the valley, in which there was effort to exist by agriculture on what was called a "putty" soil, with lack of sufficient water supply. The first of the Mormons to come was Bateman H. Wilhelm, who arrived in March, 1879. Soon thereafter Wm. J. Flake and Jesse J. Brady purchased the main part of the valley, the former paying for his half interest eight cows, one mule, a set of harness and a set of blacksmith tools. Before the end of the year, about thirty Saints were resident in the locality, some of the later arrivals being David Pulsipher, a Mormon Battalion member, Geo. H. Killian and Chas. G. Curtis. A townsite was roughly surveyed by brethren who laid their stakes by the North Star. September 26, 1880, there was organization of a Church ward and there was assumed the name of Erastus, in honor of Erastus

183

Snow, who then was presiding at a Snowflake conference. This name was abandoned for that of Concho at a Church meeting held in St. Johns December 6, 1895. In later years, the Mormon residents, after building a reservoir and expending much effort toward irrigation, generally have turned from agriculture to stock raising.

Hunt is an agricultural settlement seventeen miles down the stream from St. Johns and one mile below a former Mexican settlement, near San Antonio, above which at some time subsequent to 1876 there settled an army officer named Hunt, who left the service at Fort Apache and whose descendants live in the county. The first Mormon settler was Thomas L. Greer in 1879, the old Greer ranch still maintained, a mile east of the present postoffice. Thereafter, the location was known as Greer Valley. In 1901, D. K. Udall became a resident and in that year his wife, appointed postmaster, was instrumental in naming the office and locality after her father, John Hunt, of the Mormon Battalion, who had a farm in the locality a year or so thereafter, though not actually resident.

The Meadows purchase, eight miles northwest of St. Johns, was occupied November 28, 1879. Among the settlers was the famous Indian missionary, Ira Hatch.

Walnut Grove, twenty miles south of St. Johns, was settled early in 1882 by Jas. W. Wilkins and son, who bought Mexican claims. There was trouble over water priorities on the flow of the Little Colorado and the place now has small population, much of it Spanish-speaking.

Springerville and Eagar

Valle Redondo (Round Valley), 32 miles southeast of St. Johns, was the original name of the Springerville section. The first settler was Wm. R. Milligan, a Tennessean, who established a fort in the valley in 1871. The name was given in honor of Harry Springer, an Albuquerque merchant, who had a branch store in the valley. A. F. Banta states that the first town was across the Little Colorado from the present townsite. Banta was the first postmaster, in Becker's store.

The first Mormons on the ground, in February, 1879, were Jens Skousen, Peter J. Christofferson and Jas. L. Robertson, from St. Joseph. Soon thereafter came Wm. J. Flake, with more cows available for trade, giving forty of them to one York, for a planted grain field. Flake did not remain. In March came John T. Eager, who located four miles south of the present Springerville, in Water Canyon, and about the same time arrived Jacob Hamblin, the scout missionary. The latter took up residence in the Milligan fort and was appointed to preside over the Saints of the vicinity, but remained only till winter.

In 1882, President Jesse N. Smith divided Round Valley into two wards, the upper to be known as Amity and the lower as Omer. In 1888 the people of these wards established a townsite, two miles above and south of Springerville, which was a Spanish-speaking community. The new town, at first known as Union, later was named Eagar, after the three Eagar brothers.

A Land of Beaver and Bear

Nutrioso, sixteen miles southeast of Springerville, is very near the dividing ridge of the Gila and Little Colorado watersheds. The name is a combination of nutria (Sp., otter) and oso (Sp., bear). "Nutria" was applied to the beaver, of which there were many. The first English-speaking settler was Jas. G. H. Colter, a lumberman from Wisconsin, who came to Round Valley in July, 1875, driving three wagons from Atchison, Kansas, losing a half year's provision of food to Navajos, as toll for crossing the reservation. He grew barley for Fort Apache, getting $9 per 100 pounds. In 1879, at Nutrioso, he sold his farm, for 300 head of cattle, to Wm. J. Flake. The Colter family for years had its home four miles above Springerville, at Colter, but the founder is in the Pioneers' Home at Prescott. One of the sons, Fred, was a candidate for Governor of Arizona in 1918.

Flake parcelled out the land to John W., Thos. J., Jas. M. and Hyrum B. Clark, John W., J. Y., and David J. Lee, Geo. W. Adair, Albert Minerly, Adam Greenwood, George Peck and W. W. Pace, the last a citizen of later prominence in the Gila Valley. The grain they raised the first season, 1700 bushels, chiefly barley, was sent as a "loan" to the Little Colorado settlers, who were very near starvation.

In 1880 was built a fort, for there was fear of Apaches, who had been wiping out whole villages in New Mexico. There was concentration in Nutrioso of outlying settlers, but the Indians failed to give any direct trouble. A sawmill was started in 1881 and a schoolhouse was built the following year. A postoffice was established in 1883.

In Lee's Valley, sixteen miles southwest of Springerville, is Greer, established by the Saints in 1879. The first to come were Peter J. Jensen, Lehi Smithson, James Hale, Heber Dalton and James Lee. In 1895, was added a sawmill, built by Ellis W. Wiltbank and John M. Black. The name Greer was not applied till 1896. The postoffice dates from 1898.

Altitudinous Agriculture at Alpine

Alpine, in Bush Valley, near the southern edge of Apache County, four miles from the New Mexican line, has altitude approximating 8000 feet and has fame as probably being the highest locality in the United States where farming is successfully prosecuted. Greer is about the same altitude. The principal crop is oats, produced at the rate of 1000 bushels for every adult male in the community. Crop failures are unknown, save when the grasshoppers come, as they have come in devouring clouds in a number of years. The location is a healthful and a beautiful one, in a valley surrounded by pines. Anderson Bush, not a Mormon, was the first settler, in 1876. March 27, 1879, came Fred Hamblin and Abraham Winsor, with their families. For years there were the wildest of frontier con-

186

ditions, between outlaws and Indians. The latter stole horses and cattle, but spared Mormon lives. This was the more notable in that many villages of Spanish-speaking people were raided by the redskins in New Mexico. Naturally, the settlers huddled together, for better defense. In 1880 the log homes were moved into a square, forming a very effective sort of fort, nearly a mile southeast of the present townsite. Until that time the community had kept the name of Frisco, given because of the nearby headwaters of the San Francisco River. In 1881 most of the settlers moved over to Nutrioso for protection, but only for a few weeks. Alpine is the resting place of the bones of Jacob Hamblin, most noted of southwestern missionaries of his faith.

In 1920 the County Agricultural Agent reported that only two farmers in the United States were growing the Moshannock potato, Frederick Hamblin at Alpine and Wallace H. Larson at Lakeside.

In Western New Mexico

Luna, in New Mexico, twelve miles east of Alpine, Arizona, was on the sheep range of the Luna brothers, who did not welcome the advent of the first Mormon families, those of the Swapp brothers and Lorenzo Watson, February 28, 1883. Two prospectors had to be bought out, to clear a squatter's title. In the summer came "Parson" Geo. C. Williams, also a pioneer of Pleasanton. The first name adopted was Grant, in honor of Apostle Heber J. Grant, this later changed to Heber, as there was an older New Mexican settlement named Grant's. But even this conflicted with Heber, Arizona (named after Heber C. Kimball), and so the original name endures, made official in 1895. The first house was a log fort. A notable present resident is Frederick Hamblin, brother of Jacob and of the same frontier type. There is local pride over how he fought, single-handed, with a broken and unloaded rifle, the largest grizzly bear ever known in the surrounding Mogollon

Mountains. This was in November, 1888. The bear fought standing and was taller than Hamblin, a giant of a man, two inches over six feet in height. The rifle barrel was thrust down the bear's throat after the stock had been torn away, and upon the steel still are shown the marks of the brute's teeth. The same teeth were knocked out by the flailing blows of the desperate pioneer, who finally escaped when Bruin tired of the fight. Then Hamblin discovered himself badly hurt, one hand, especially, chewed by the bear. The animal later was killed by a neighbor and was identified by broken teeth and wounds.

New Mexican Locations

As before noted in this work, the Mormon Church sought little in New Mexico in the pioneering days, for little opportunity existed for settlement in the agricultural valleys. In western New Mexico, however, the country was more open and there was opportunity for missionary effort. Missionaries were in the Navajo and Zuni country in very early days and at the time of the great Mormon immigration of 1876 already there had been Indian conversions.

In that year, by direct assignment from President Brigham Young, then at Kanab, Lorenzo Hatch, later joined by John Maughn, settled in the Zuni country, at Fish Springs and San Lorenzo. Thereafter, on arrival of other missionaries, were locations at Savoia and Savoietta. It should be explained that these names, pronounced as they stand, are rough-hewn renditions of the Spanish words cebolla, "onion," and cebolleta, "little onion." Nathan C. Tenney and sons were among the colonists of 1878.

In 1880 were Indian troubles that caused abandonment of the locations, but a new start was made in 1882, when a number of families came from the deserted Brigham City and Sunset. A new village was started, about 25 miles east of the Arizona line, at first known as Navajo, but later as Ramah. The public square was on the ruins of an ancient

FOUNDERS OF NORTHERN ARIZONA TOWNS

1—Henry W. Miller   2—Wm. C. Allen
3—George Lake   4—Wm. J. Flake   5—Charles Shumway
6—Geo. H. Crosby, Sr.   7—J. V. Bushman

A FEW MORE PIONEERS

1—Almeda McClellan
2—Mrs. A. S. Gibbons
3—Mary Richards
4—Joseph Foutz
5—Virginia Curtis

6—Benj. F. Johnson
7—Martha Curtis
8—Josephine Curtis
9—Wm. N. Fife
10—J. D. Fife

Indian pueblo. Ira Hatch came in the fall. A large degree of missionary success appears to have been achieved among the Zuni, with 165 baptisms by Ammon M. Tenney, but at times there was friction with Mexican residents. The land on which the town stood later had to be bought from a cattle company, which had secured title from the Atlantic and Pacific Railroad Company.

Bluewater, near the Santa Fe railroad, about thirty miles northeast of Ramah, is a Church outpost, established in 1894 by Ernst A. Trietjen and Friehoff G. Nielson from Ramah. For a while, from 1905, it was the home of C. R. Hakes, former president of the Maricopa Stake. Bluewater now is a prosperous agricultural settlement, with assured stored water supply and an excellent market available for its products.

Most southerly of the early New Mexican Church settlements was Pleasanton, on the San Francisco River, in Williams Valley, and sixty miles northwest of Silver City. The first settler was Geo. C. Williams, who came in 1879. At no time was there much population. Jacob Hamblin here spent the few last years of his life, dying August 31, 1886. His family was the last to quit the locality, departing in 1889.

Chapter Seventeen

Economic Conditions

Nature and Man Both Were Difficult

To the struggle with the elements, to the difficulties that attended the breaking of a stubborn soil and to the agricultural utilization of a widely-varying water supply, to the burdens of drouth and flood and disease was added the intermittent hostility of stock interests that would have stopped all farming encroachment upon the open range. Concerning this phase of frontier life in Arizona, the following is from the pen of B. H. Roberts:

The settlers in the St. Johns and Snowflake Stakes have met with great difficulties, first on account of the nature of the country itself, its variable periods of drouth, sometimes long-continued, when the parched earth yields little on the ranges for the stock, and makes the supply of water for irrigation purposes uncertain; then came flood periods, that time and again destroyed reservoir dams and washed out miles of irrigating canals. This was also the region of great cattle and sheep companies, occupying the public domain with their herds, sometimes by lease from the government, sometimes by mere usurpation. The cattle and sheep companies and their employees waged fierce war upon each other for possession of the range, and both were opposed to the incoming of the settlers, as trespassers upon their preserves. The stock companies often infringed upon the settlers' rights, disturbed their peace, ran off their stock and resorted to occasional violence to discourage their settling in the country. Being "Mormons," the outlaw element of the community felt that they could trespass upon their rights with impunity, and the civil officers gave them none too warm a welcome into the Territory. The colonists, however, persisted in their efforts to form and maintain settlements in the face of all these discouraging circumstances. The fighting of the great cattle and sheep companies for possession of range privileges is now practically ended; the building of more substantial reservoirs is mastering the flood problems and the drouth periods at the same time, and the Saints, by the uprightness of their lives, their industry, perseverance, and enterprise, have proven their value as citizens in the commonwealth, until the prejudices of the past, which gave them a cold reception on their advent into Arizona, and slight courtesy from the older settlers, have given way to more enlightened policies of friendship; and today peace and confidence and respect are accorded to the Latter-day Saints of Arizona.

A view of early-day range conditions along the Little Colorado lately was given by David E. Adams:

> When we came to Arizona in 1876, the hills and plains were covered with high grass and the country was not cut up with ravines and gullies as it is now. This has been brought about through overstocking the ranges. On the Little Colorado we could cut hay for miles and miles in every direction. The Aztec Cattle Company brought tens of thousands of cattle into the country, claimed every other section, overstocked the range and fed out all the grass. Then the water, not being held back, followed the cattle trails and cut the country up. Later, tens of thousands of cattle died because of drouth and lack of feed and disease. The river banks were covered with dead carcasses.

Breaking the ground in Arizona was found a very serious task, even on the plains or where Nature had provided ample rains. Where industry created an oasis, to it ever swarmed the wild life of the surrounding hills or deserts. Prairie dogs, rabbits and coyotes took toll from the pioneer farmer, sometimes robbing him of the whole of the meager store of foodstuffs so necessary to maintain his family and to secure his residence. From 1884 to 1891 there were occasional visitations, in the Little Colorado Valley, of grasshoppers. For several years the settlement of Alpine was reported "devastated" and for a couple of years at Ramah the crops were so taken by grasshoppers that the men had to go elsewhere for work to secure sustenance for their families. St. Johns, Erastus and Luna all suffered severely at times from insect devastation. Winters were of unusual severity.

Railroad Work Brought Bread

Just as the Saints of Utah benefited by the construction

of the Central and Union Pacific railroads, so there was benefit in northeastern Arizona through the work of building the Atlantic and Pacific railroad in 1880-82. John W. Young and Jesse N. Smith, joined by Ammon M. Tenney, in the spring of 1880 took a contract for grading five miles, simply to secure bread for the people of the Little Colorado Valley. During the previous winter there had been a large immigration from Utah, where, erroneously, it had been reported the Arizonans had raised good crops, so comparatively little food was brought in. The limited crop of 1879 soon was consumed and the spring found the settlers almost starving. Lot Smith had loaned the people a quantity of wheat the previous season and much of the crop was due him.

Young and Smith went as far as Pueblo, where they secured their contract and on their return made arrangements with merchants at Albuquerque for supplies. The first contract was for a section about 24 miles east of Fort Wingate, N. M., and to that point in July went all the men who could possibly leave home. The first company was from Snowflake, Jesse N. Smith taking about forty men. Soon thereafter, flour was sent back to the settlements and there was grateful relief. After a while, Smith drew out of the railroad work. Tenney returned to the railroad the following year to assist Young in filling a contract for the grading of 100 miles and the furnishing of 50,000 ties.

The work on the railroad, while securing food in a critical period, still caused neglect of agriculture at home, where the few men remaining, together with the women and children, had to labor hard.

Burden of a Railroad Land Grant

The settlers on the Little Colorado appear to have had something more than their share of land trouble. Not only were hardships in their journeyings thither, with following privations in the breaking of the wilderness for the use of mankind, but there came an additional and serious blow

192

when even title to their hard-earned lands was disputed, apparently upon adequate legal ground. The best story at hand concerning this feature of early life on the Little Colorado is found in the Fish manuscript, told by one who was on the ground at the time and who participated in the final settlement:

In March, 1872, the General Government gave a railroad land grant of every alternate section of land bordering the proposed Atlantic and Pacific railroad, extending out for forty miles each side of said road, through the public lands of the United States in the Territories of New Mexico and Arizona. The rule was that any lands settled upon, prior to the date of the grant, should be guaranteed to the settler, and the railroad be indemnified with as much land as was thus taken up on an additional grant of ten miles each side, called lieu lands, just outside the forty-mile limits of the main grant. In the fall of 1878 and the winter of 1879, when the settlers arrived on the ground where Snowflake and Taylor now stand, they supposed the railroad grant would doubtless lapse, as there was then no indication that the road would be built. They bought the Stinson ranch, paying an enormous price for it. The Government had not then surveyed the land and the government sections were not then open for entry at the land office. But early in 1880 the railroad company began building its road west from Albuquerque. In May of said year, Jesse N. Smith, on behalf of the settlers of Snowflake, applied to the railroad company for the railroad lands they occupied, and received the assurance that they, the settlers, should have the first right to their land, and the first refusal thereof, and that the price would not be raised on account of their improvements. The railroad company even furnished blank applications, which a number of the settlers made out and filed with the company, which were afterwards ignored. About this time capitalists and moneyed men, many of them foreigners, began turning their attention to cattle raising in our Territory. Among others, a company known as the Aztec Land and Cattle Company was organized, composed mostly of capitalists from the east. This company bought a very large block of the railroad lands, including Snowflake and Taylor, and all in that vicinity. The new owners immediately served notice on the settlers that they must buy or lease the railroad portion, the odd-numbered sections of the land they occupied. The settlers appointed Jesse N. Smith and Joseph Fish a committee to represent their claims, but no definite understanding could be obtained from the local officers of the company, all such business being referred to the central office in New York City. The railroad company not having sold the land

193

at Woodruff, it served a similar notice on the settlers there, and it seemed that they would all be compelled to abandon their improvements and move away. In this emergency, the settlers, who were of the Mormon faith, applied to the Presidency of the Church for relief. An estimate of the value of the improvements of the settlers was made and the amount was found to so far exceed the probable cost of the land that the Presidency of the Church appropriated $500 for the expenses and sent Brigham Young, Jr., and Jesse N. Smith east to negotiate a purchase. They started on their mission in the latter part of February, 1889. They finally, on April 2, 1889, closed a contract in New York City for seven full sections of land at $4.50 per acre, one-fifth of the price being paid down, and Jesse N. Smith giving his note for the remainder, to run four years at 6 per cent interest; one-fourth the amount to be paid at the end of each year, and the interest to be added and paid every half year.

While in New York they also bargained with J. A. Williamson, the railroad land commissioner, for one section of land at Woodruff at $8 per acre, one-half at the expiration of each year, with 6 per cent interest to be added each half year. Payment was made for the last purchase in Albuquerque, the contract being closed May 3, 1889. The Mormon Church furnished much of that money for these purchases, receiving back a small portion, as individuals were able to pay the same, and appropriating the remainder for the benefit of schools and reservoirs in the vicinity of said towns.

Little Trouble With Indians

It is notable that the settlers on the Little Colorado had very little actual trouble with the Indians, with the Navajo of the north or the Apache of the south. The Indians were frequent visitors to the settlements and were treated with usual Mormon hospitality. There were no depredations upon the livestock, and when the peace of the settlements was disturbed it was by the white man and not by the red brother. During the time of the building of the Atlantic and Pacific railroad, there was an Indian scare. This originated in the outbreak of Nockedaklinny, a medicine man of the Coyoteros, who, August 30, 1881, was killed in the Cibicu country, a day's travel from Fort Apache, by troops led by Col. E. A. Carr, Fifth Cavalry. Two days later the Indians attacked Camp Apache itself, after killing eight men on the road, and the post probably was saved

194

from capture by the hurried return of its commander, with his troops. He left behind seven of his men, having been treacherously fired upon by 23 Indian scouts, whom he had taken with him. A number of murders were committed by the Indians in northern Tonto Basin, but the insurrection extended no farther northward than Camp Apache. Still it created great uneasiness within the comparatively unprotected settlements of the river valley. June 1, 1882, was the killing of Nathan B. Robinson, this the only Indian murder of a Mormon in this section.

Church Administrative Features

While this work in no wise seeks to carry through any records of Church authority, it happens that the leader in each of the southwestern migrations and settlements was a man appointed for that purpose by the Church Presidency and the greater number of the settlers came by direct Church "call." In the case of the Little Colorado settlements, this "call" was not released till January, 1900, in a letter of President Lorenzo Snow, borne to St. Johns by Apostle (now President) Heber J. Grant. The several organizations of the northeastern districts are set forth, with official exactness, by Historian Roberts, as follows:

On January 27, 1878, the Latter-day Saints who had settled on the Little Colorado, in Navajo (then Yavapai) County, under the leadership of Major Lot Smith, by that time grouped into four settlements, were organized into a Stake of Zion, with Lot Smith as president and Jacob Hamblin and Lorenzo H. Hatch as counselors. Three of the settlements were organized into wards, a bishop being appointed in each; the fourth was made a" branch" with a presiding elder. This was the first stake organization effected in Arizona. Before the expiration of the year, viz., 27th December, President John Taylor directed that the settlements forming further up the Little Colorado in Apache County, be organized into a Stake. A line running southward from Berardo's (now Holbrook, on the Santa Fe railroad), was to be the dividing line between the two Stakes thus proposed. The western division was to be the Little Colorado Stake, and the eastern division, Eastern Arizona Stake of Zion. The division of the Stakes on these lines was not carried out at that time; the Little Colorado

Stake, constituted of the wards already mentioned at its organization, continued for several years, while the Eastern Arizona Stake had within its jurisdiction, for a number of years, the settlements on Silver Creek, in the southeast corner of Navajo County, and also the settlement of St. Johns near the headwaters of the Little Colorado, and other minor settlements in Apache County. In 1887, however, the directions of President Taylor, with reference to the division of these settlements into two Stakes, were carried into effect. The name of the Eastern Arizona Stake, however, was changed at the time of the reorganization, July 23, 1887, to St. Johns Stake, David K. Udall, bishop of St. Johns, being chosen President, with Elijah Freeman and Wm. H. Gibbons as counselors. Later, viz., December 18, the settlements on the west side of the line running south from Holbrook, on upper Silver Creek, Woodruff Ward, and the fragments of settlements formerly constituting the Little Colorado Stake, by now discontinued, were organized under the name of the Snowflake Stake of Zion, Jesse N. Smith, formerly of the Eastern Arizona Stake, being made President.

Here there may be notation that David K. Udall, still president at St. Johns, is one of the very oldest in seniority in such office within the Church. At Snowflake today the president is Samuel F. Smith, son of Jesse N. Smith, who died in his home town June 5, 1906.

STAKE PRESIDENTS

1—Lot Smith, Little Colorado 2—Jesse N. Smith, E. Ariz. and Snowflake
3—Samuel F. Smith, Snowflake 4—David K. Udall, St. Johns
5—Christopher Layton, St. Joseph 6—Andrew Kimball, St. Joseph

SNOWFLAKE ACADEMY
Destroyed by Fire Thanksgiving Day, 1910

PRESENT SNOWFLAKE ACADEMY
Dedicated Thanksgiving Day, 1913—Cost $35,000

Chapter Eighteen

Extension Toward Mexico

Dan W. Jones' Great Exploring Trip

The honor of leading Mormon pioneering in south-central Arizona lies with Daniel W. Jones, a sturdy character, strong in the faith. He had been in the Mexican war, in 1847, as a Missouri volunteer, and had remained in Mexico till 1850. In the latter year he started for California, from Santa Fe, and, in the Provo country of Utah, embraced Mormonism within a settlement that had treated him kindly after he had accidentally wounded himself. About that time he dedicated himself to life work among the Indians, the Lamanites of the Book of Mormon. He appeared to be successful thereafter in gaining the confidence of the red men and in carrying out the policy so literally expressed by Brigham Young, "It is cheaper to feed the Indians than to fight them." Speaking Spanish, he helped in translation by Meliton G. Trejo, of a part of the Book of Mormon.

The printing done, a missionary party was started southward September 10, 1875, from Nephi, Utah, its members being, besides Jones, J. Z. Stewart, Helaman Pratt, Wiley C. Jones, a son of the leader, R. H. Smith, Ammon M. Tenney and A. W. Ivins. The journey was on horseback, by way of Lee's Ferry and the Hopi Indian villages and thence to the southwest. At Pine Springs, in the Mogollons, were met Dr. J. W. Wharton and W. F. McNulty, who told them something of Phoenix and the Salt River Valley and who advised settlement in the upper valley.

Jones' personal story of his impressions of the future

197

metropolis of the State and of the Salt River Valley possibly should be given in his own language:

We were much surprised on entering Salt River Valley. We had traveled through deserts and mountains (with the exception of the Little Colorado Valley, a place which we did not particularly admire) for a long ways. Now there opened before us a sight truly lovely. A fertile looking soil and miles of level plain. In the distance the green cottonwood trees; and, what made the country look more real, was the thrifty little settlement of Phoenix, with its streets planted with shade trees for miles. Strange as it may seem, at the time we started, in September, 1875, the valley of Salt River was not known even to Brigham Young.

Our animals were beginning to fail, as they had lived on grass since leaving Kanab. We bought corn at 4 cents a pound and commenced feeding them a little. Although Salt River Valley is naturally fertile, owing to the dryness of the climate, there is no grass except a little coarse stuff called "sacaton."

We camped on the north side of the river. On making inquiry, we learned that Tempe, or Hayden's Mill, seven miles further up the river, would be a better place to stop for a few days than Phoenix. C. T. Hayden, being one of the oldest and most enterprising settlers of the country, had built a grist mill, started ranches, opened a store, blacksmith shop, wagon shop, etc.

On arriving at Hayden's place, we found the owner an agreeable, intelligent gentleman, who was much interested in the settlement and development of the country, he being a pioneer in reality, having been for many years in the west, and could sympathize with the Mormon people in settling the deserts. He gave us much true and useful information about the country and natives. Here we traded off some of our pack mules and surplus provisions. We had already traded for a light spring wagon, finding that the country before could be traveled with wagons. We remained here a few days, camping at the ranch of Mr. Winchester Miller. His barley was up several inches high, but he allowed us to turn our animals into his fields and treated us in a kind, hospitable manner. The friendly acquaintance made at this time has always been kept up. Mr. Miller was an energetic man, and manifested a great desire to have the Mormons come there and settle. He had already noticed the place where the Jonesville ditch is now located. He told me about it, saying it was the best ditch site on the river. What he said has proved true. We wrote to President Young, describing the country.

The party tried some proselyting among the Pimas and

198

Papagos. At Tucson they met Governor Safford who offered welcome to Mormon colonists. Sonora was in the throes of revolution, so they passed on to El Paso, on the way talking to a camp of Apaches, given permission by the agent, Thos. T. Jeffords. The San Pedro Valley was looked over for possible settlement.

In January, 1876, the party passed the international line at Paso del Norte. Jones claimed this to have been the first missionary expedition that ever entered Mexico. The party found it a good land and started back in May with a rather favorable impression of the country for future settlement. Return was by way of Bowie, Camp Grant and the Little Colorado. At Allen's Camp were met Daniel H. Wells, Brigham Young, Jr., and Erastus Snow, with whom return to Utah was made. President Young was met late in June, at Kanab, there expressing appreciation of the determination that had brought Jones through every difficulty in the ten months of journeying.

The Pratt-Stewart-Trejo Expedition

Of notable interest is the fact that certain members of the Jones expedition were so deeply interested in what they saw that they made request for immediate return. So, October 18, 1876, there started southward, from Salt Lake, at the direction of the Church Presidency, another expedition, in character missionary, rather than for exploration. It embraced Helaman Pratt, Jas. Z. Stewart, Isaac J. Stewart, Louis Garff and George Terry. Meliton G. Trejo joined at Richfield. Phoenix was reached December 23, there being found several families of the Church who had come the previous year. The day the missionaries arrived happened to be exactly thirty years after the date on which the Mormon Battalion passed the Pima villages on the Gila River, just south of Phoenix. The members of the party worked all over southern Arizona, especially among the Mexicans and Indians.

In February of 1877 headquarters were at Tubac. In

199

April, after a Mexican trip, a letter was received from President Brigham Young asking that Sonora be explored as a country for possible settlement. Later in May the Stewarts started eastward, in continuing danger from hostile Apaches after they had crossed the San Pedro. On the road, while the missionaries were passing, a mail rider was killed. At Camp Bowie the Apaches were found beleaguering the post. East of that point the Stewarts had to replace a wagon tire just as they were passing a point of Apache ambush. Return to Utah was in December, 1877. It was concluded that border settlements better had wait on Indian pacification.

Trejo was a remarkable character. He was of aristocratic Castilian birth and had been an officer in the Spanish army in the Philippines. It would appear that he became interested in the Mormon doctrine, which, in some manner, had reached that far around the earth, and that he resigned his commission and straightway went to Utah. There his knowledge of Spanish, backed by good general schooling, made him valuable as a translator, though his English was learned in the Jones family. His later work was in Arizona and Mexico, as a missionary, his home in 1878 moved to Saint David on the San Pedro, where he died a few years ago. He was a fluent writer and sent many interesting letters to the Deseret News. In January, 1878, he wrote from Hayden's Ferry:

We are now between the Salt and Gila Rivers, on a very extensive rich plain, covered with trees and small brush, watered in some places by means of canals from the two rivers named. The river dams and canals are very easy made, on account of the solid bottoms of the rivers and pure farming clay of the plain. In fact, the people who are now living here find it very easy to get good farms in one or two years without much hard labor. They unite as we do in making canals. The climate is one of the most delightful in the world and until a few years ago, one of the most healthy too, but lately the people have been troubled with fevers, which nobody seems to know the cause. The water is good and the sky is clear, there being no stagnant pools; the ground is dry and the winds blow freely in every direction. I don't believe these fevers are naturally in the country, but are caused by the people not taking proper care of themselves.

An interesting letter has been found, dated at Tubac, March 4, 1877, addressed to President Brigham Young and written by Elder Jas. Z. Stewart. It told that the country is "better than the north part of the Territory, from the fact that the land is as good, if not better, the water is good and regular and the climate more pleasant." He referred to the ruins of whole towns, to the rich mines, to the abundance of game and to the drawback of Apache raids. He described the southern Arizona Mexicans as "all very poor, having no cows, horses, houses nor lands and but very little to live on. Though they live for days on parched corn, they are willing to divide their last meal with a stranger. They are industrious, but ignorant, it being seldom you can find one who can write."

Start of the Lehi Community

The reports from the south gave ample encouragement to expansion ideas within the First Presidency. So, after due deliberation, was organized another Jones expedition for the settlement of the land.

As letters of the time are read and instructions found, it becomes the more evident that President Brigham Young and his counselors had in view a great plan of occupation of the intermountain valleys, reaching down into Mexico, or beyond. It was a time when the Church was growing very rapidly and when new lands were needed for converts who were streaming in from Europe or from the eastern States. Logically, the expansion would be southward, though there was disadvantage of very serious sort in the breaking of continuity of settlement by the Grand Canyon of the Colorado River and by the deserts that had to be passed to reach the fertile valleys of the southland.

When the second Jones party started, according to an official account, "President Young sat with a large map of America before him, while saying that the company of mis-

201

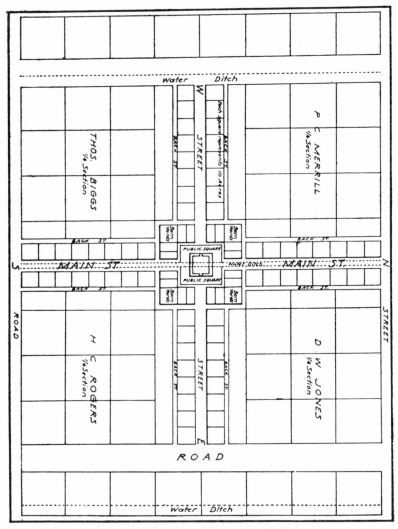

GROUND PLAN OF LEHI

sionaries called were to push ahead as far as possible toward the Yaqui country in Mexico, which would finally be the objective point; but if they could not reach that country they might locate on the San Pedro or Salt River in southern Arizona."

In either case there would be a station on the road, or a stepping stone to those who later would go on to the far south. President Young also said to the brethren on that occasion that if they would do what was right and be guided by the spirit of inspiration, they would know the country as they passed through, and would know where to locate, the same as did the Pioneers when they first reached the valley of the Great Salt Lake.

The pioneering expedition was organized in St. George, in southwestern Utah. In the party were 83 individuals, the family heads being Jones, Philemon C. Merrill, Dudley J. Merrill, Thomas Merrill, Adelbert Merrill, Henry C. Rogers, George Steele, Thomas Biggs, Ross R. Rogers, John D. Brady, Joseph McRae, Isaac Turley and Austin O. Williams.

Start was made January 17, 1877. The way was through Beaver Dams to the mouth of the Virgin. That profiteering was not unknown in those early days is shown by the fact that the expedition, at Stone's Ferry on the Colorado, had to pay ferriage of $10 per wagon. Much of this cost was borne by Joseph McRae, who turned over one wagon, some horses and a little money to the ferryman.

To the southward was found a road, well-traveled in those days, that led from the Fort Mohave ferry to Prescott. But Prescott, then the capital, was left to one side and a direct route was taken from Chino Valley, through Peeples Valley and Wickenburg, to Phoenix. At the latter point there was agreement that the travelers had about reached the limit of their resources and of the strength of their horses. There was remembrance of the valley section of which Winchester Miller had told. So determination to stop was reached in a council of the leaders. There was fear, apparently well grounded, that claim jumpers would cause trouble if the destination of the party became known. On this account, departure from Phoenix was not by way of Hayden's Ferry, but by the McDowell road, as far as Maryville, an abandoned military subpost and station on Salt River, at the Maricopa Wells-McDowell road ford. Here the river was crossed, and the weary immigrants were at their journey's end. The day was March 6, 1877. The camp was at the site of the canal head, the settlement later placed a few miles below.

Henry C. Rogers took charge of the construction of the ditch, started the day after arrival. Ross R. Rogers was the engineer. His only instruments were a straight edge and a spirit level. This still is known as the Utah ditch. Its first cost was $4500. There was the planting of a nursery by George Steele, the trees kept alive by hauling water to them. Jones wrote to Salt Lake that Salt River was at least four times as big as the Provo and had to be tapped through deep cuts, as the channel was "too expensive to dam."

Sunday, May 20, 1877, Jones baptized his first Indians in Salt River, four of the "Lamanites" being immersed. In July, 1877, Fort Utah was located as a place of protection. It was built upon the cross line of four quarter-sections of land, enclosed with an adobe wall, and with a well, on the inside, 25 feet deep. The families lived there while the men went out to work.

President Young soon wrote Jones in a vein indicating that the stop on Salt River was considered merely a camp on the way still farther southward, saying:

We should also like to know what your intentions are with regard to settling the region for which you originally started. We do not deem it prudent for you to break up your present location, but, possibly next fall, you will find it consistent to continue your journey with a portion of those who are now with you, while others will come and occupy the places vacated by you. We do not, however, wish

LEADERS OF UNSUCCESSFUL EXPEDITIONS

1—Horton D. Haight   2—Jacob Miller
3—Daniel H. Wells   4—Lorenzo W. Roundy

ON THE DESOLATE SANDY ROAD TO THE
COLORADO CROSSING

THE FIRST EXPEDITION INTO MEXICO

Wiley C. Jones   A. W. Ivins
Heleman Pratt   D. W. Jones   Jas. Z. Stewart

THE SECOND PARTY SENT TO MEXICO

1—Jas. Z. Stewart   2—Meliton G. Trejo
3—George Terry 4—Isaac J. Stewart   5—Heleman Pratt

you to get the idea from the above remarks that we desire to hurry you away from where you are now, or to enforce a settlement in the district to which you refer, until it is safe to do so and free from the dangers of Indian difficulties; but we regard it as one of the spots where the Saints will, sooner or later, gather to build up Zion, and we feel the sooner the better.

Transformation Wrought at Camp Utah

The newcomers found pioneering conditions very harsh indeed, for it is a full man's task to clear away mesquite and brush and to dig a deep canal. Joseph A. McRae made special reference to the heat, to which the Utah settlers were unaccustomed. He wrote, "as summer advanced, I often saturated my clothing with water before starting to hoe a row of corn forty rods long, and before reaching the end my clothes were entirely dry." But there was raised an abundance of corn, sugar cane, melons and vegetables, and, in spite of the heat, the health of the people was excellent.

Concerning the early Jonesville, a correspondent of the Prescott Miner wrote:

The work done by these people is simply astounding, and the alacrity and vim with which they go at it is decidedly in favor of co-operation or communism. Irrespective of capital invested, all share equally in the returns. The main canal is two and a half miles long, eight feet deep, and eight feet wide. Two miles of small ditch are completed and four more are required. Their diagram of the settlement, as it is to be, represents a mile square enclosed by an adobe wall about seven feet high. In the center is a square, or plaza, around which are buildings fronting outward. The middle of the plaza represents the back yards, in which eleven families, or eighty-five persons are to commingle. They are intelligent, and all Americans.

The settlers, with their missionary turn of mind, were pleased to find the Indians of southern Arizona friendly and even inclined to be helpful. One chief offered to loan the settlers seed corn and wheat. The Indians gathered around to listen to whatever discourse the Saints should offer, the latter, at the same time energetically wielding shovels on a canal that "simply had" to be built in a given time.

205

An appreciated feature was that Salt River abounded in fish, supplementing very acceptably the plain diet on which the pioneers had been subsisting. Possibly it was as well that the Saints had rules against the use of table luxuries. One pioneer of the Lehi settlement told how his family had lived for weeks almost entirely upon wheat, which had been ground in a coffee mill and then cooked into mush, to be eaten with milk. "We thought ourselves mighty fortunate to have the milk," he said.

Soon after the settlement of Camp Utah, Jones' methods of administration excited keen opposition among the brethren. There was special objection to his plan that the settlement should receive Indians on a footing of equality, this being defended as a method that assuredly would tend toward the conversion of the Lamanites speedily and effectively.

Jones was fair in his statement of the matter, and hence special interest attaches to his own story of the earliest days of the settlement:

We commenced on the ditch March 7, 1877. All hands worked with a will. Part of the company moved down on to lands located for settlements. Most of the able-bodied men formed a working camp near the head of the ditch, where a deep cut had to be made.

We hired considerable help when we could procure it, for such pay as we could command, as scrub ponies, "Hayden scrip," etc. Among those employed were a number of Indians, Pimas, Maricopas, Pagagos, Yumas, Yaquis and one or two Apache-Mohaves. The most of them were good workers.

Some of the Indians expressed a desire to come and settle with us. This was the most interesting part of the mission to me, and I naturally supposed that all the company felt the same spirit, but I soon found my mistake, for, on making this desire of the Indians known to the company, many objected, some saying that they did not want their families brought into association with these dirty Indians. So little interest was manifested by the company that I made the mistake of jumping at the conclusion that I would have to go ahead whether I was backed up or not. I learned afterward that if I had been more patient and faithful, I would have had more help, but at the time I acted according to the best light I had and determined to stick to the Indians.

This spirit manifested to the company showing a preference to the natives, naturally created a prejudice against me. Soon dissatisfaction commenced to show. The result was that most of the company left and went on to the San Pedro, in southern Arizona, led by P. C. Merrill. After this move, there being but four families left, and one of these soon leaving, our little colony was quite weak.

Departure of the Merrill Party

It was a sad blow to the settlement when the Merrill company departed, in August, 1877, leaving only the Jones, Biggs, Rogers and Turley families. Nearly all the teams available went with the Merrills, thus delaying completion of the canal, which at that time had reached the settlement. The fort also was left in an incomplete state. The few left behind mainly were employed by Chas. T. Hayden of Tempe, who was described as, "so very kind to the brethren and their families, giving them work and furnishing them with means in advance, on credit, so that they might subsist."

A very interesting item in a letter written by Jones is:

This country is so productive and easy of cultivation, but, notwithstanding, this colony was too poor at seed time to buy a common plow. From present prospects, we hope to be able to save up and have enough for seed and plow the coming season. You speak of the ancient Egyptians using a crooked stick for plowing; if you will call down here soon, we can show you some 300 acres of good wheat patch plowed by our colony with a crooked stick plow, without so much as a ram's horn point.

Probably Jones included a part of the holdings of his Indian wards in this demonstration of primeval agriculture. For years following the advent of the white man, the Pima Indians habitually plowed by means of a crooked mesquite stick, connected by a rope to a pole, tied firmly across the horns of a couple of oxen.

Whatever the dissension between Jones and the other pioneers, he appeared at all times to have been popular with his Indian wards. This is evidenced by the fact that to the north of Lehi is a thriving Pima-Papago Mormon settlement, known as Papago ward. Dan P. Jones followed his

207

father in its administration. A few years ago it had a population of 590 Indians, mainly Pimas, and of four white families, headed by Geo. F. Tiffany, with an Indian counselor, Incarnacion Valenzuela. This counselor has been described by Historian Jenson as "one of the most intelligent Indians I have ever met. He speaks Spanish fluently, as well as the Papago and Pima language; he also understands English, but does not like to speak it." Henry C. Rogers also was a successful Indian missionary. Tiffany's son now is in charge of the Lehi Indians.

Besides the Indians directly belonging to the ward, is a record of 1500 baptized Mormon Indians, mainly Papago, in the desert region to the southward, as far as the Mexican line.

Sunday schools and meetings are held in the Papago ward schoolhouse, built a few years ago. The Indians farm and raise stock; some of them live in good houses and all are learning the habits and ways of their neighbors, who have been their friends from the beginning.

Jones was charged by the people of Phoenix and Tempe with protection of Indians who had trespassed upon crops. He was warned by the Indian agent at Sacaton that he must cease his proselyting, a warning he calmly ignored. He seemed to have had assistance generally from the military authorities at Camp McDowell, about fifteen miles northward, for a time commanded by Capt. Adna R. Chaffee, Sixth Cavalry. Trouble was known with Pima Indians, who lived across the river, where they had been placed a few years before by Tempe settlers, as a possible buffer against Apache raids. This reservation's extension cost Lehi several sections of land.

Altogether, Jones' life in the Salt River Valley was not an easy one. Finally he joined a community in northern Tonto Basin, where his wife and youngest child were killed by accident. After that he moved to Tempe. Thereafter he went to Mexico, where he had mining experience. In the winter of 1884, he helped Erastus Snow and Samuel H. Hill to cross the border at El Paso. His latter days mainly were spent in Utah and California. Early in 1915 he returned to Arizona. His death occurred April 20 of that year, at the Mesa home of a son. His life work is well set out in a book written by himself and published in 1890. The descendants of the sturdy old pioneer are many in southern Arizona and numbers of them have occupied responsible office with credit. A son, Dan. P. Jones of Mesa, is a member of the current Legislature. Other sons and grandsons have been prominent especially in educational work.

Lehi's Later Development

Lehi now is a thriving settlement in bottom lands along Salt River, where growth necessarily is limited. Its schoolhouse is about three miles north of Mesa, which has made by far the greater growth. First known as Camp Utah, or Utahville, for years it was called Jonesville, but finally the postoffice name of Lehi, suggested by Apostle Brigham Young, Jr., has firmly attached.

The first Mormon marriage in the Salt River Valley was at Lehi, that of Daniel P. Jones and Mary E. Merrill, August 26, 1877. The first birth was of their son. The first permanent separate house, of adobe, at Lehi, was built by Thomas Biggs, in the spring of 1878. There was a public school as early as 1878, taught by Miss Zula Pomeroy. In 1880 an adobe schoolhouse was built at a cost of $142, the ground donated by Henry C. Rogers, with David Kimball its main supporter. The following year was built a much better schoolhouse.

The settlement has a townsite of six blocks, each 26 rods square, with streets four rods wide, surveyed in November, 1880, by Henry C. Rogers.

Lehi was badly damaged February 19, 1891, when Salt River reached a height never known before or since. The stream flooded the lower parts of Phoenix and inundated a large part of the farming land at Lehi. A second flood, a few days later, was three feet higher than the first. Five Lehi Indians were drowned and several hundred of them lost their possessions.

Chapter Nineteen

⚔️ℌe 𝔓lanting of 𝔐esa

Transformation of a Desert Plain

Though by no means with exclusive population of the faith, Mesa, sixteen miles east of Phoenix and in the Salt River Valley, today includes the largest organization of the Saints within Arizona and is the center of one of the most prosperous Stakes of the Church. It is beautifully located on a broad tableland, from which its Spanish name is derived, and is the center of one of the richest of farming communities. In general, the soil is of the best, without alkali, and its products cover almost anything that can be grown in the temperate or semi-tropic zones.

At all times since its settlement, Mesa has prospered, but its prosperity has been especially notable since the development, a few years ago, of the Pima long-staple cotton. Nearly every landowner, and Mesa is a settlement of landowners, has prospered through this industry, though it has been affected by the post-war depression. The region is one of comfortable, spacious homes and of well-tilled farms, with less acreage to each holding than known elsewhere in the valley.

Mesa is second only to Phoenix in size and importance within Maricopa County. There are fine business blocks and all evidences of mercantile activity. The farming area is being extended immensely. The community was one of the first to enter the association that secured storage of water at Roosevelt. Thereafter, to the southward came extension of the farming area by means of pumping, this continuing nearly to the Gila River, out upon the Pima

211

reservation. Now there is further extension eastward, and the great plain that stretches as far as Florence is being settled by population very generally tributary to Mesa. It would be idle to speculate upon the future of the city, but its tributary farming country is fully as great as that which surrounds Phoenix.

Mesa was founded by Latter-day Saints from Bear Lake County, Idaho, and Salt Lake County, Utah. The former left Paris, Idaho, September 14, 1877, were joined at Salt Lake City by the others and traveled the entire distance by wagon, using the Lee's Ferry route, and coming over the forested country to Camp Verde.

The immigrants included, with their families, Chas. I. Robson, Charles Crismon (of the San Bernardino colony) of Salt Lake, Geo. W. Sirrine (of the Brooklyn ship party), Francis M. Pomeroy (a '47 pioneer), John H. Pomeroy, Warren L. Sirrine, Elijah Pomeroy, Parley P. Sirrine, all of Paris, Idaho, Wm. M. Newell, Wm. M. Schwartz, Job H. Smith, Jesse D. Hobson and J. H. Blair of Salt Lake. Altogether were 83 individuals.

The valley of the Verde proved a pleasant one, after the cold and hardship known on the plateau, though Christmas was spent in a snowstorm. Both humanity and the horses needed rest. So camp was made at Beaver Head, a few miles from the river, while a scouting party went farther to spy out the land. This party, which went by wagon, included Robson, F. M. Pomeroy, Charles Crismon and G. W. Sirrine.

The scouts, within a few days, had covered about 125 miles that lay between Beaver Head and Camp Utah. Their New Year dinner was taken with Jones, who extended them all welcome. It was proposed that the newcomers settle upon land adjoining that of the first party, but there was a likelihood of crowding in the relatively narrow river valley, and there were attractive possibilities lying along the remains of an ancient canal shown them by Jones.

ORIGINAL LEHI LOCATORS

1—Daniel W. Jones
3—Thomas Biggs

2—Philemon C. Merrill
4—Henry C. Rogers

FOUNDERS OF MESA

Charles Crismon   Francis M. Pomeroy   George W. Sirrine

Legal appropriation of the head of this old water way was made and Crismon was left behind, with a couple of the Camp Utah men as helpers, to start work on the new irrigation project. Incidentally, Crismon made location of land near the heading and thus separated his interests from those of the main party. Later, he started a water-power grist mill on the Grand canal, east of Phoenix. He had rights to a large share in the canal, as well as to lands on the mesa. These he later sold.

Robson, Pomeroy and Sirrine returned to the Verde Valley, to pilot the rested travelers southward. The journey was by way of the rocky Black Canyon road, with difficulty encountered in descending the steep Arastra Creek pass. Fording Salt River at Hayden's Ferry, Camp Utah was reached February 14, 1878. The journey had been a slow one, for cattle had to be driven.

A few days were spent at Camp Utah and then the new arrivals moved upstream five miles, where tents were pitched on a pleasant flat, a couple of miles below the canal heading. There had been conclusion to settle upon the table-land to the southwest. Pomeroy and Sirrine made a rough, though sufficient, survey with straight-edge and spirit level, along what then was named the "Montezuma Canal," eleven miles to a point where a townsite was selected.

Use of a Prehistoric Canal

Nothing short of Providential was considered the finding of the canal, dug by a prehistoric people into the edge of the mesa, which it gradually surmounted. This canal, in all probability, had been cut more than 1000 years before. It could be traced from the river for twenty miles, maintaining an even gradient, possibly as good as could have been laid out with a modern level, and with a number of laterals that spread over a country about as extensively cultivated as at present. A lateral served the Lehi section and other ditches conducted water to the southwest, past the famous ancient city of Los Muertos (later explored by Frank H.

213

Cushing) and then around the southeastern foothills of the Salt River Mountains to points not far distant from the Gila River. The main canal cut through the tableland for two miles, with a top width of even fifty feet and a depth of twelve feet, chopped out in places, with stone axes, through a difficult formation of hardpan, "caliche." The old canal was cleaned out for the necessities of the pioneers, at a cost of about $48,000, including the head, and afterward was enlarged. At the time, there was an estimate that its utilization saved at least $20,000 in cost of excavation. There were 123 miles of these ancient canals.

This canal undertaking was a tremendous one, especially in consideration of the fact that for the first five months the Mesa settlers available for work were only eighteen able-bodied men and boys. The brethren were hardly strong enough in man power to have dug the canal had it not been for the old channel. A small stream was led to the townsite in October, 1878, and in the same month building construction was begun. An early settler wrote:

We were about nine months in getting a small stream of water out at an expense of $43,000 in money and labor, so that we could plant gardens and set out some fruit trees. A man was allowed $1.50 and a man and team $3 per day for labor. Our ditch ran through some formation that would slack up like lime; and as whole sections of it would slide, it kept us busy nearly all the time the following year enlarging and repairing the canal. Our labors only lessened as our numbers increased, and the banks became more solid, so that today (1894) we have a good canal carrying about 7000 inches of water.

It would appear that a tremendous amount of optimism, energy and self-reliance lay in the leaders of the small community, in digging through the bank of a stubborn cliff, in throwing a rude dam across a great flood stream and in planting their homes far out on a plain that bore little evidence of agricultural possibilities, beyond a growth of creosote bush, the Larrea Mexicana. There were easier places where settlements might have been made, at Lehi or Tempe, or upon the smaller streams, but there must have

214

been a vision rather broader than that of the original immigrant, a vision that later has merged into reality far larger and richer than had been the dream.

Within this prosperity are included hundreds of Mormon pioneers and their children. It often is said that the development of a country is by the "breaking" of from three to four sets of immigrants. It is not true of Mesa, for there the original settlers and their stock generally still hold to the land.

Moving Upon the Mesa Townsite

The honor of erection of the first home upon the mesa lies with the Pomeroy family, though it was hardly considered as a house. Logs and timbers were hauled from the abandoned Maryville, an outpost of Fort McDowell, at the river crossing northeast of Fort Utah. It was erected Mexican fashion, the roof supported on stout poles, and then mudded walls were built up on arrowweed latticing. This Pomeroy residence later was used as the first meeting-house, as the first schoolhouse and as the first dance hall, though its floor was of packed earth. It might be added that there were many dances, for the settlers were a light-hearted lot. Most of the settlers re-erected their tents, each family upon the lot that had been assigned.

The first families on the mesa were those of John H. Pomeroy, Theodore Sirrine and Chas. H. Mallory. The Mallory and Sirrine homes quickly were started. Mallory's, the first adobe, was torn down early in 1921.

By the end of November, 1878, all the families had moved from the river camp upon the new townsite.

Early arrivals included a strong party from Montpelier, Bear Lake County, Idaho, the family heads John Hibbert, Hyrum S. Phelps, Charles C. Dana, John T. Lesueur, William Lesueur, John Davis, Geo. C. Dana and Charles Warner. Others, with their families, were Charles Crismon, Jr., Joseph Cain and William Brim from the Salt Lake section. Nearly all of the settlers who came in the earlier

215

days to Mesa were fairly well-to-do, considered in a frontier way, and were people of education. Soon, by intelligence and industry, they made the desert bloom. Canals were extended all over the mesa. In 1879 was gathered the first crop of cereals and vegetables and that spring were planted many fruit trees, which grew wonderfully well in the rich, light soil.

An Irrigation Clash That Did Not Come

The summer of 1879 was one of the dryest ever recorded. Though less than 20,000 acres were cultivated in the entire valley, the crops around Phoenix suffered for lack of water. Salt River was a dry sand expanse for five miles below the Mesa, Utah and Tempe canal headings. The Mormon water appropriation was blamed for this. So in Phoenix was organized an armed expedition of at least twenty farmers, who rode eastward, prepared to fight for their irrigation priority rights. But there was no battle. Instead, they were met in all mildness by Jones and others, who agreed that priority rights should prevail. There was inspection of the two Mormon ditches, in which less than 1000 miners' inches were flowing and then was agreement that the two canal headgates should be closed for three days, to see what effect this action would have on the lower water supply. But the added water merely was wasted. The sand expanse drank it up and the lower ditches were not benefited. There was no more trouble over water rights. Indeed, this is the only recorded approach to a clash known between the Mormon settlers and their neighbors.

Mesa's Civic Administration

In May, 1878, T. C. Sirrine located in his own name the section of land upon which Mesa City now stands, thereafter deeding it to Trustees C. I. Robson, G. W. Sirrine and F. M. Pomeroy, who named it and who platted it into blocks of ten acres each, with eight lots, and with streets 130 feet wide, the survey being made by A. M.

Jones. Each settler for each share worked out in the Mesa canal, received four lots, or five acres. Two plazas were provided.

For many years there was a general feeling that the streets of Mesa were entirely too wide, though it had been laid out in loving remembrance of Salt Lake City, and the question of ever paving (or even of crossing on a hot summer day) was serious. It appears from latter-day development that the old-timers builded wisely, for probably Mesa is alone in all of Arizona in having plenty of room for the parking of automobiles. The main streets have been paved at large expense. In several has been left very attractive center parking, for either grass or standing machines.

Mesa was incorporated July 15, 1883. The first election chose A. F. Macdonald as Mayor, E. Pomeroy, G. W. Sirrine, W. Passey and A. F. Stewart as Councilmen, C. I. Robson as Recorder, J. H. Carter as Treasurer, H. C. Longmore as Assessor, W. Richins as Marshal, and H. S. Phelps as Poundkeeper. All were members of the faith, for others were very few in Mesa at that time.

Growth was slow for a number of years, for in a city census, taken January 4, 1894, there was found population of only 648, with an assessment valuation of $106,000. The 1920 census found 3036.

Mail at first was received at Hayden's Ferry. Soon thereafter was petition for a postoffice. The federal authorities refused the name of "Mesa" on the ground that it might be confused with Mesaville, a small office in Pinal County. So, in honor of their friend at the Ferry, there was acceptance of the name Hayden. Though the Ferry had the postoffice name of Tempe, there ensued much mixture of mail matter. In 1887, there followed a change in the postoffice name to Zenos, after a prophet of the Book of Mormon. In the order of things, Mesaville passed away and then the settlement quickly availed itself of the privilege opened, to restore the commonly accepted designation of Mesa.

217

Foundation of Alma

Alma is a prosperous western extension of Mesa, of which it is a fourth ward. The locality at first, and even unto this day, has borne the local name of Stringtown, for the houses are set along a beautiful country road, cottonwood-bordered for miles. The first settlers of the locality were Henry Standage (a veteran of the Mormon Battalion), Hyrum W. Pugh, Chauncey F. Rogers and Wm. N. Standage, with their families. These settlers constituted a party from Lewiston and Richmond, Cache County, Utah, and arrived at Mesa, January 19, 1880. In that same month they started work on an extension of the Mesa canal, soon thereafter aided by neighbors, who arrived early in 1881. There were good crops. Early in 1882 houses were erected.

Highways Into the Mountains

In 1880, the Mesa authorities took steps to provide a better highway to Globe, this with the active cooperation of their friend, Chas. T. Hayden. Globe was a rich market for agricultural products, yet could be reached only by way of Florence and the Cane Springs and Pioneer road, over the summit of the Pinal Mountains, or by way of the almost impassable Reno Mountain road from McDowell into Tonto Basin, a road that was ridden in pain, but philosophically, by the members of the Erastus Snow party that passed in 1878. The idea of 1880 was to get through the Pinal Mountains, near Silver King. A new part of this route now is being taken by a State road that starts at Superior, cutting a shelf along the canyon side of Queen Creek, to establish the shortest possible road between Mesa and Globe. The first adequate highway ever had from Mesa eastward was the Roosevelt road, later known as the Apache Trail, built in 1905 by the Reclamation Service, to connect the valley with Roosevelt, which lies at the southern point of Tonto Basin.

Tempe, eight miles east of Phoenix on Salt River, was first known as Hayden's Ferry. Its founder was Chas. Trumbull Hayden, a pioneer merchant who early saw the possibilities of development within the Salt River Valley and who built a flour mill that still is known by his name. Arizona's Congressman, Carl Hayden, is a son of the pioneer merchant, miller and ferryman. The name of Tempe (from a valley of ancient Greece) is credited to Darrell Duppa, a cultured Englishman, who is also understood to have named Phoenix. It was applied to Hayden's Ferry and also to a Mexican settlement, something over a half-mile distant, locally known as San Pablo.

Hayden welcomed the advent of the Mormons, led to the country by Daniel W. Jones in 1877, and befriended those who followed, thus materially assisting in the up-building of the Lehi and Mesa settlements.

Tempe, as a Mormon settlement, started July 23, 1882, in the purchase by Benjamin Franklin Johnson, Jos. E. Johnson and relatives, from Hayden, of eighty acres of land that lay between the ferry and the Mexican town. For this tract there was paid $3000. The Johnson party left Spring Lake, Utah, in April and traveled via Lee's Ferry. There was survey of the property into lots and blocks, and the Johnsons at once started upon the building of homes. There was included also a small cooperative store. The foundation was laid for a meeting house, but religious services usually were held in a bowery or in the district schoolhouse that had been built before the Saints came.

In the fall of 1882 there arrived a number of families, most of them Johnsons or relatives. When the Maricopa Stake was organized December 10, 1882, David T. LeBaron was presiding at Tempe. June 15, 1884, Tempe was organized as a ward, successively headed by Samuel Openshaw and Jas. F. Johnson.

219

In August, 1887, most of Tempe's Mormon residents moved to Nephi, west of Mesa, mainly upon land acquired by Benj. F. Johnson, the settlement popularly known as Johnsonville. The departure hinged upon the building of a branch railroad of the Southern Pacific from Maricopa, through Tempe, to Phoenix. An offer was made by a newly-organized corporation for the land that had been taken by the Johnsons, who sold on terms then considered advantageous. Upon this land now is located a large part of the prosperous town of Tempe, within which is a considerable scattering of Mormon families, though without local organization.

Patriarch B. F. Johnson died in Mesa, November 18, 1905, at the age of 87. At that time it was told that his descendants and those married into the family numbered 1500, probably constituting the largest family within the Church membership.

Organization of the Maricopa Stake

The Church history of Mesa started October 14, 1878, when Apostle Erastus Snow, on his memorable trip through the Southwest, at Fort Utah, appointed a late arrival, Jesse N. Perkins, as presiding elder and H. C. Rogers and G. W. Sirrine as counselors. Perkins died of smallpox in northeastern Arizona. In 1880, President John Taylor at St. George, Utah, appointed Alexander F. Macdonald to preside over the new stake. He arrived and took office in February of that year. Macdonald was a sturdy, lengthy Scotchman, a preacher of the rough and ready sort and of tremendous effectiveness, converted in Perth, in June, 1846, and a Salt Lake arrival by ox team in 1854. In 1882, on permanent organization of the Stake, Chas. I. Robson succeeded Sirrine as counselor. Robson December 4, 1887, succeeded to the presidency, with H. C. Rogers and Collins R. Hakes as counselors, Macdonald taking up leadership in the northern Mexican Stakes, pioneering work of difficulty for which he was especially well suited. In

MARICOPA STAKE PRESIDENTS

1—Alexander F. Macdonald   3—Collins R. Hakes
2—Chas. I. Robson
4—Jno. T. Lesueur   5—Jas. W. Lesueur

MARICOPA DELEGATION AT PINETOP CONFERENCE OF THE FOUR ARIZONA STAKES, JULY, 1892

December, 1884, he headed an expedition and surveying party into Chihuahua, Mexico, looking for settlement locations, and secured large landed interests. He became ill at El Paso, on his way back to his home at Colonia Juarez. He died at Colonia Dublan, thirty miles short of his destination, March 21, 1903.

Chas. I. Robson served as President to the day of his death, February 24, 1894. He was of English ancestry, born February 20, 1837, in Northumberland. He was specially distinguished in the early days of Utah through his success in starting the first paper factory known in western America. As a boy, he had worked in a paper factory in England. In 1870, he was warden of the Utah penitentiary.

May 10, 1894, Collins R. Hakes (of the San Bernardino colony) succeeded to the presidency of Maricopa Stake, with Henry C. Rogers and Jas. F. Johnson as counselors. At that time were five organized wards, with 2446 souls, including 1219 Indians in the Papago ward, and to the southward toward Mexico. Mesa then was credited with 648 people of the faith, Lehi 200, Alma 282 and Nephi 104.

In 1905, President Hakes transferred his activities to the development of a new colony of his people at Bluewater, N. M., near Fort Wingate. His death was in Mesa, August 27, 1916.

To the Maricopa Stake Presidency, November 26, 1905, succeeded Jno. T. Lesueur, transferred from St. Johns, where, from Mesa, he settled in 1880. He is still a resident of Mesa. He resigned as president in 1912, the position taken, on March 10 of that year, by his son, Jas. W. Lesueur, who still is in office.

December 20, 1898, first was occupied the Stake tabernacle, 75x45 feet in size, built of brick and costing $11,000. At its dedication were Apostle Brigham Young, Jr., and a number of other Church dignitaries.

A Great Temple to Rise in Mesa

For more than a year plans have been in the making for erection at Mesa of a great temple of the Church, to cost about $500,000. It is to be the ninth of such structures. The others, in the order of their dedication, are (or were): at Kirtland, Ohio, of date 1836; at Nauvoo, Illinois, 1846; at St. George, Logan, Manti and Salt Lake, Utah, and at Laie, Hawaiian Islands. Another is being built at Cardston, Alberta, Canada. The Kirtland edifice was abandoned. That at Nauvoo was wrecked by incendiaries in 1848. The great Temple at Salt Lake, its site located by Brigham Young four days after his arrival, in July, 1847, was forty years in building and its dedication was not till 1893.

Merely in the way of explanation, it may be noted that a Mormon temple is not a house of public worship. It is, as was the Temple of Solomon, more of a sanctuary, a place wherein ecclesiastical ordinances may have administration. It has many lecture rooms, wherein to be seated the classes under instruction, and there is provision of places for the performance of the ordinances of baptism, marriage, confirmation, etc.

Especially important are considered the baptism and blessings (endowments) bestowed vicariously on the living for the benefit of the dead. There also is added solemnity in a temple marriage, for it is for eternity and not merely for time. Due to this is the unusual activity of the Church members in genealogical research. It is believed that the Mormon Church is the only denomination that marries for eternity, this marriage also binding in the eternal family relation the children of the contracting individuals.

The temple administration is separate from that of the Stake in which it may be situated and its doors, after dedication, are closed save to its officers and to those who come to receive its benefits. In the past years these ordinances have been received outside of Arizona, at large

222

expense for travel from this State. Naturally, there has been a wish for location of a temple more readily to be reached by the devout.

The temple idea in Arizona appears to date back to an assurance given about 1870 in St. George by Brigham Young. A prediction was made by Jesse N. Smith about 1882, to the effect that a temple, at some future day, would be reared on the site of Pima in Graham County. The first donation toward such an end was recorded January 24, 1887, in the name of Mrs. Helena Roseberry, a poor widow of Pima, who gave $5 toward the building of a temple in Arizona, handing the money to Apostle Moses Thatcher. This widow's mite ever since has been held by the Church in Salt Lake. Possibly it has drawn good interest, for through the Church Presidency has come a donation of $200,000 to assure the end the widow had wished for.

Another "nest egg," the first contribution received directly for the Mesa edifice, came from another widow, Mrs. Amanda Hastings of Mesa, who, on behalf of herself and children, three years ago, gave the Stake presidency $15.

The new temple, of which there is reproduction herewith of an artist's sketch, is to rise in the eastern part of Mesa upon a tract of forty acres, which is to be a veritable park, its edges occupied by homes. The architects are Don C. Young and Ramm Hansen of Salt Lake. The temple will rise 66 feet, showing as a vast monument upon a foundation base that will be 180x195 feet. This base will contain the offices and preparation rooms. While the structure will be sightly from all sides, on its north will be a great entrance. Between the dividing staircase will be a corridor entry to the baptismal room. The staircase, joined at the second story, will stretch 100 feet in a great flight, its landings successively taking the initiates to the higher planes of instruction. In this respect, the plan is said by Church authorities to be the best of any temple of the faith. The rooms will be ample in size for the instruction of classes of over 100.

The building of the Mesa temple was the primary subject at all meetings of congregations of the faith on September 12, 1920, and from voluntary donations on that day there was added to the temple fund $112,000.

Chapter Twenty

First Families of Arizona

Pueblo Dwellers of Ancient Times

In considering the development features of the settlement of central Arizona, the Author feels it might be interesting to note that the immigrants saw in the Salt River Valley many evidences of the truth of the Book of Mormon, covering the passage northward of the Nephites of old. There was found a broad valley that had lain untouched for a thousand years, unoccupied by Indian or Spaniard till Jack Swilling and his miners dug the first canal on the north side of the river a few years before the coming of the Saints to Jonesville. The valley had lain between the red-skinned agriculturists of the Gila and the Apache Ishmaelites of the hills. There had been no intrusion of Spanish or Mexican grants. The ground had been preserved for utilization of the highest sort by American intelligence.

Yet this same intelligence found much to admire in the works of the people who had passed on. From the river had been taken out great canals of good gradient, and it was clear that they had been dug by a people of homely thrift and of skill in the tilling of the soil. There still were to be seen piles of earth that marked where at least seven great communal houses had formed nuclei for a numerous people. These were served by 123 miles of canals.

These people were not Aztec. According to accepted tradition, the Aztecs passed southward along the western coast, reaching Culiacan, in northwestern Mexico, about 700 A. D., and there named themselves the Mextli. The ancient people of the Salt River Valley probably had

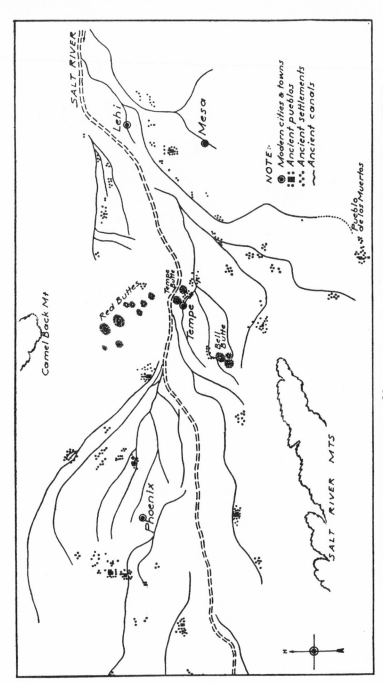

ANCIENT CANALS COVERING 123 MILES, AND PUEBLOS OF SALT RIVER VALLEY

Surveyed by Herbert R. Patrick

moved, or were moving, about that same time. They appear to have been of Toltecan stock and undoubtedly came from the southward, from a land where was known the building of houses and wherein had been established religious cults of notable completeness and assuredly of tenacious hold. Just why they left the Salt River Valley is as incomprehensible as why they entered it, and how long they stayed is purely a matter of conjecture. Probably occupation of the valley was not simultaneous. Probably the leaving was by families or clans, extending over a period of many years. Probably they left on the ending of a cycle of peace, on the coming to the Southwest of the first of the Apache, or of similar marauders, who preyed upon the peaceful dwellers of the plains. That they were people of peace cannot be doubted, people who in the end had to defend their towns, yet sought no aggression.

Evidences of Well-Developed Culture

Possibly a great epidemic, of the sort known to have swept Mexico before the coming of the Spaniard, gravely cut down the numbers of the ancient valley settlers. Near every communal castle is to be found a cemetery, filled with burial urns, their tops usually less than a foot below the surface. These urns (ollas) are filled with calcined human bones. By them are to be found the broken pottery, of which the spirits were to accompany the late lamented on their journey to the happy hunting grounds. These dishes once contained food, intended for the spirit travelers' nourishment. When there was a child, oftimes now is found the clay image of a dog, for a dog always knows the way home. The dog is believed to have been the only domestic animal of the time.

In some cases, in the greater houses, walled into crypts that might have served as family lounging places, have been found the skeletons of those who were of esoteric standing, considered able, by the force of will, to separate spirit from body. In other cases the cleansing and disintegrating

227

effects of fire secured the necessary separation of the spirit from the body.

With these mortuary evidences also are found domestic implements, stone clubs, arrow points and, particularly valuable, prayer sticks and religious implements that clearly show the archaeologist a connection with the pueblo-dwelling peoples who still live, under similar communal conditions, to the northward.

Northward Trend of the Ancient People

That these ancient peoples went north there can be no doubt. North of the valley, nearly fifty miles, on the Verde, is a great stone ruin and beyond it are cavate dwellings of remarkable sort. In Tonto Creek Valley, a dozen miles north of the Roosevelt dam, is an immense ruin built of gypsum blocks. To the eastward, Casa Grande, most famed of all Arizona prehistoric remains, still stands, iron-roofed by a careful government, probably of a later time of abandonment, but still a ruin when first seen by Father Eusebio Kino in 1694. All the way up the Gila, and with a notable southern stem through the Mimbres Valley, are found these same evidences of ancient occupation. Chichilticalli, "the Red House," mentioned by Marco de Niza and by Coronado's historians in 1539-40, lay somewhere near where another group of Mormons again reclaimed the desert soil by irrigation in the upper Gila Valley. Ruins extended from Pueblo Viejo ("Old Town"), above Solomonville, down to San Carlos.

Into the valleys of the Salt and of the Gila, from the north come many waterways. In none of these tributary valleys can there be failure to find evidences of the northward march of the Indians who lived in houses. In this intermediate region, the houses usually, for protection, were placed in the cliffs. Particularly notable are the cave dwellings of the upper Verde and in Tonto Basin, near Roosevelt, and in the Sierra Anchas and near Flagstaff.

Again there was debouchment upon a river valley, that

THE ARIZONA TEMPLE AT MESA

JONATHAN HEATON OF MOCCASIN AND HIS
FIFTEEN SONS—page 98

1—Ira Hatch, Indian Missionary—page 107
2—Thales Haskell, Indian Missionary—page 107
3—Wm. C. Prows, Battalion Member—page 37
4—Nathan B. Robinson, killed by Indians—page 172

of the Little Colorado. Possibly some of the tribes worked eastward into the valley of the Rio Grande. Another section, and for this there is no less evidence than that of Frank Hamilton Cushing, formed at least a part of the forefathers of the Zuni. Swinging to the northwest, the Water House and other clans formed the southern branch of the three from which the Moqui, or Hopi, people are descended. This last is history. The early Mormons remarked upon the pueblo ruins that lay near their first Little Colorado towns, above St. Joseph. These ruins are known to the Hopi as "Homolobi," and much is the information concerning them to be had from the historians of the present hilltop tribes.

Reports of similarity have been so many, there can be no surprise that the earlier settlers from Utah wrote home joyously, telling that proofs had been found of the northern migration so definitely outlined in their ecclesiastical writings, according to the Book of Mormon.

The Great Reavis Land Grant Fraud

For about ten years from 1885 all the lands of the Salt and Gila valleys of Arizona lay under a serious cloud of title. There had been elimination of the Texas-Pacific landgrant, which unsuccessfully had been claimed by the Southern Pacific. Then came the Reavis grant, one of the most monumental of attempted swindles ever known. James Addison Reavis, a newspaper solicitor, claimed a tract 78 miles wide from a point at the junction of the Gila and Salt Rivers, eastward to beyond Silver City, N. M., on the basis of an alleged grant, of date December 20, 1748, by Fernando VI, King of Spain, to Senor Don Miguel de Peralta y Cordoba, who then was made Baron of the Colorados and granted 300 square leagues in the northern portion of the viceroyalty of New Spain. The grant was said to have been appropriated in 1757. Reavis had first claimed by virtue of a deed from one Willing, of date 1867, but there was switching later, Reavis thereafter claiming as agent for his wife, said to have been the last of the Peralta line, but in reality a half-breed Indian woman, found on an Indian reservation in northern California, and one who had no Mexican history whatever. Reavis renamed himself "Peralta-Reavis," and for a while had headquarters for his "barony" at Arizola, a short distance east of Casa Grande, where he maintained his family in state, with his children in royal purple velvet, with monogrammed coronets upon their Russian caps. He arrogated to himself ownership of all the water and the mines and sold quitclaim deeds to the land's owners. It is said that the Southern Pacific bought its right of way from him and that the Silver King and other mines similarly contributed to his exchequer. He claimed Phoenix, Mesa, Florence, Globe, Silver King, Safford and Silver City.

He planned a storage basin on Salt River and another above Florence on the Gila, and advertised that he intended to reclaim 6,000,000 acres on the Casa Grande and Maricopa plains, "thereafter returning to the Gila any surplus water." Just how accurate his figures were may be judged by the fact that government engineers have found that the waters of the Gila, above Florence, are sufficient for the irrigation of not more than 90,000 acres. He viewed things on a big scale, however. At Tonto Basin he was to build a dam 450 feet high and the water was to be taken from the river channel by means of a 44,000-foot tunnel.

Whenever one of his prospective customers failed to contribute, he often deeded the land to a third party. Some of these deeds are to be seen on the records of Maricopa County. His case had been so well prepared that many were deceived, even the lawyers who served him as counsel, including Robert G. Ingersoll. Naturally something approximating a panic for a while was known by the farmers of the valleys affected.

Meanwhile, very largely from moneys obtained as above

noted, Reavis was spending royally at many points. At Madrid, Spain, he had a gorgeous establishment, whereat he even entertained the American Legation. At many points in Mexico, he scattered coin lavishly and accumulated cords of alleged original records and he even found paintings of his wife's alleged ancestors. The grant was taken into politics and was an issue in the congressional campaign of 1887.

About 1898 there was establishment of the United States Court of Private Land Claims, especially for adjudication of many such claims in the Southwest. Reavis' elaborately prepared case tumbled almost from the day it was brought into court. Government agents found bribery, corruption and fraud all along his trail. He had interpolated pages in old record books and had even changed and rewritten royal documents, including one on which the grant was based. Some of his "ancient" documents were found to have been executed on very modern milled paper. On one of them appeared the water mark of a Wisconsin paper mill. Others had type that had been invented only a few years before. The claim was unanimously rejected by the land court and on the same day Reavis was arrested on five indictments for conspiracy. He was convicted in January, 1895, and sentenced to six years in the penitentiary. After serving his sentence, he made a brief confession, telling that he had been "playing a game which to win meant greater wealth than that of Gould or Vanderbilt." The district covered by his claim today has property valued at at least one billion dollars.

When Mesa first was settled, every alternate section was called "railroad land," claimed by the Southern Pacific, under virtue of the old Tom Scott-Texas & Pacific land grant. Early in the eighties, this claim vanished, it being decided that the Southern Pacific had no right to the grant.

Chapter Twenty-one

Near the Mexican Border

Location on the San Pedro River

Much historical value attaches to the settlement of the Saints upon the San Pedro River, even though prosperity there has not yet come in as large a degree as has been known elsewhere within the State. It is not improbable that within the next few years an advance in material riches will be known in large degree, through water storage, saving both water and the cutting away of lands through flood, and that permanent diversion works will save the heart-breaking tasks of frequent rebuilding of the temporary dams heretofore washed out in almost every freshet.

Elsewhere has been told the story of the Daniel W. Jones party that settled at Lehi and of the dissension that followed objections on the part of the majority to the rulings of the stout old elder, whose mind especially dwelt upon the welfare of red-skinned brethren.

There had been general authorization to the Jones-Merrill expedition to go as far southward as it wished. Under this, though not till there had been consultation with the Church Presidency, the greater number of the Lehi settlers left Salt River early in August, 1877. There was expectation that they were to settle on the headwaters of the Gila or on the San Pedro. There must have been a deal of faith within the company, for the departure from camp was with provisions only enough to last two days and there was appreciation that much wild country would need to be passed. But there was loan of the wages of A. O. Williams, a member of the party who had been employed by C. T. Hayden at Tempe, and with this money added provisions were secured.

Necessarily, the journey was indirect. At Tucson employment was offered for men and teams by Thomas Gardner, who owned a sawmill in the Santa Rita Mountains. Much of the money thus earned was saved, for the party lived under the rules of the United Order, and very economically. So, in the fall, with the large joint capital of $400 in cash, added to teams and wagons and to industry and health, there was fresh start, from the Santa Ritas, for the San Pedro, 45 miles distant. The river was reached November 29, 1877.

These first settlers comprised Philemon C., Dudley T., Thomas, Seth and Orrin D. Merrill, George E. Steele, Joseph McRae and A. O. Williams. All but Williams and O. D. Merrill had families.

Ground was broken at a point on the west side of the river, on land that had been visited and located October 14, by P. C. Merrill on an exploring trip. The first camp was about a half mile south of the present St. David and soon was given permanency by the erection of a small stone fort of eight rooms. That winter, for the common interest, was planting of 75 acres of wheat and barley, irrigated from springs and realizing very well.

Malaria Overcomes a Community

As was usual in early settlement of Arizona valleys, malarial fever appeared very soon. At one time, in the fall of 1878, nearly all the settlers were prostrated with the malady, probably carried by mosquitoes from stagnant water. That year also it was soberly told that fever and ague even spread to the domestic animals. At times, the sick had to wait on the sick and there was none to greet Apostle Erastus Snow when he made visitation October 6, 1878. His first address was to an assembly of 38 individuals, of whom many had been carried to the meeting on their beds. It is chronicled by Elder McRae that, "not-

233

withstanding these conditions, the Apostle blessed the place, prophesying that the day would come when the San Pedro Valley would be settled from one end to the other with Saints and that we had experienced the worst of our sickness. When he left, all felt better in body and in spirit." It was a decidedly hot season. "Vegetation grew so rank that a horseman mounted on a tall horse could hardly be seen at a distance of a quarter of a mile. Hay could be cut a stone's throw from our door."

The first death was on October 2, 1878, of the same A. O. Williams whose money had brought the people to the new land.

Possibly the settlement needed the mental and spiritual encouragement of Apostle Snow, for more than a year had passed of hardships and of labor, and, including the Lehi experience, there had been no recompense, unless it might have been in the way of mental and moral discipline.

The early malaria of the Arizona valleys nearly all has disappeared, with the draining of swampy places, the eradication of beaver dams and mosquitoes and the knowledge of better living conditions. Elsewhere has been told of the abandonment of Obed and other early Little Colorado settlements, because of chills and fever. Something of the same sort was known on the upper Gila, from 1882 to 1890, around Pima, Curtis and Bryce. In this same upper Gila Valley, Fort Goodwin had to be abandoned on account of malarial conditions. The same is true of old Fort Grant, across the divide, on the lower San Pedro. The upper Verde, the Santa Cruz and nearly all similar valleys knew malaria at the time of settlement.

According to Merrill, on March 26, 1879, the sick and sorry settlers went into the Huachuca Mountains to summer, but, "the wind blew so much that we moved back to the river, near where Hereford now is, rented some land and put in some crops." This location is just about where the members of the Mormon Battalion, in 1846, had their memorable fight with the wild bulls.   A Merrill report, rendered March 16, 1881, was far from hopeful and asked that the writer be relieved of his responsibilities.

On the Route of the Mormon Battalion

This office has been unable to find any reference connecting Merrill's later experiences in the San Pedro Valley with the time when he was an officer of the Mormon Battalion, though it can be imagined that his later associates had the benefit of many reminiscences of that period of the march just prior to the taking of Tucson.

The San Pedro Valley is a historic locality. Down it passed Friar Marco de Niza, in 1539, and the Coronado expedition of the following year. The waters of the stream were a joyous sight to the Mormon Battalion, when it passed that way during the Mexican War. The country then had been occupied to some extent by Spaniards or Mexicans, who had established large ranches, with many cattle, from which they had been driven by the Apaches, years before the Battalion came. The country once had been the ranging ground of the friendly Sobaipuri Indians, but they too had been driven away by the hillmen and had established a village on the Santa Cruz, near their kinsmen, the Papago, almost on the site where Tucson was founded as a Spanish presidio in 1776.

The river, when the Merrill party came, was found usually in a deep gully, in places twenty feet below the surface of the silty ground.   Naturally, difficulty has attended the attempts to dam the stream.

Chronicles of a Quiet Neighborhood

St. David was named by Alexander F. Macdonald in honor of David W. Patten, a martyr of the Church, who died at the hands of the same mob that killed Joseph Smith. Its first mail was received at Tres Alamos, sixteen miles down the river. A postoffice was established in 1882, Joseph McRae in charge. When the Southern Pacific came through, Benson was established, nine miles to the northward. Tombstone lies sixteen miles to the southeast.

In May, 1880, the present St. David townsite was laid out. John Smith Merrill built the first house. The following year an adobe schoolhouse was built, this used for public gatherings until shaken down by an earthquake, May 3, 1887, happily while the children were at recess. Much damage was done in the town.

The settlement had little or no trouble with Indians, though for nine years Apache bands scouted and murdered in the nearby mountains and committed depredations within the San Pedro Valley, both to the northward and southward.

Early in 1879 John Campbell, a new member, from Texas, built a sawmill, in the Huachuca Mountains, that furnished a diversity of industry, from it much lumber being shipped to Tombstone.

Macdonald was a southern extension of the St. David community on the San Pedro, established in 1882 by Henry J. Horne, Jonathan Hoopes and others, and named in honor of Alexander F. Macdonald, then president of the Maricopa Stake. It was of slow growth, owing to claims upon the lands as constituting a part of the San Juan de las Boquillas y Nogales grant, later rejected. In 1913, nine miles west of St. David, was established the community of Miramonte.

Looking Toward Homes in Mexico

While the Saints were establishing themselves upon the San Pedro and Gila, the Church authorities by no means had lost sight of the primary object of the southern migration. January 4, 1883, Apostle Moses Thatcher, with Elders D. P. Kimball, Teeples, Fuller, Curtis, Trejo and Martineau, left St. David for an exploring trip into Mexico.

September 13, 1884, another party left St. David to explore the country lying south of the line, along the Babispe River, returning October 7, by way of the San

Bernardino ranch, though without finding any locations considered favorable.

In November, 1884, Apostles Brigham Young, Jr., and Heber J. Grant, with a company from St. Joseph Stake, with thirty wagons, went into Sonora, where they were given a hearty welcome by the Yaqui Indians, who expressed hope of a settlement among them.

St. David was the scene of one of the most notable councils of the Church, held in January, 1885, and presided over by none other than President John Taylor, who left Salt Lake City, January 3, and whose party at St. David included also Apostles Joseph F. Smith, Erastus Snow, Brigham Young, Jr., Moses Thatcher and Francis M. Lyman, with other dignitaries of the Church. At St. David were met Jesse N. Smith, Christopher Layton, Alex. F. Macdonald and Lot Smith, presidents of the four Stakes of Arizona. The discussion at this conference appeared to have been mainly upon the Church prosecution, then in full sway, a matter not included within the purview of this work. There was determination to extend the Church settlements farther to the southward. According to Orson F. Whitney:

In order to provide a place of refuge for such as were being hunted and hounded, President Taylor sent parties into Mexico to arrange for the purchase of land in that country, upon which the fugitive Saints might settle. One of the first sites selected for this purpose was just across the line in the State of Sonora. Elder Christopher Layton made choice of this locality. Other lands were secured in the State of Chihuahua. President Taylor and his party called upon Governor Torres at Hermosillo, the capital of Sonora, and were received by that official with marked courtesy.

Historian Whitney states that the Taylor party then went westward by way of the Salt River Valley settlements to the Pacific Coast. And this office has a record to the effect that, in January, President Taylor visited also the settlements of the Little Colorado section and counseled concerning the disposition of several of the early towns of that locality.

Of Arizona interest is the fact that for two and a half years thereafter, the President of the Mormon Church was in exile, till the date of his death, July 25, 1887, in Kaysville, Utah. Much of the intervening time was spent in Arizona and a part of it in Mexico, in the settlements that had been established as places of refuge. His declining months, however, were spent in Utah, even entire communities guarding well the secret of the presence of their spiritual head.

Arizona's First Artesian Well

Possibly the first artesian well known in Arizona was developed in the St. David settlement. In 1885 a bounty of $1500 was offered for the development of artesian water. The reward was claimed by the McRae brothers, who developed a flow of about thirty gallons a minute, but who failed to receive any reward. Five years ago, J. S. Merrill of St. David reported that within the San Pedro Valley were about 200 flowing wells, furnishing from five to 150 gallons a minute. The deepest valley well was about 600 feet. At that time about 2000 acres were irrigated by the St. David canal and by the wells, sustaining a population of about 600 souls.

Development of a Market at Tombstone

It happened on the San Pedro, just as in many other places, that the Mormons were just a little ahead of some great development. September 3, 1877, at Tucson, Ed. Schieffelin recorded the first of his mining claims in Tombstone District, which then lay in Pima County.

Schieffelin's first discovery was several miles from the later site of Tombstone and about four miles from the San Pedro. Later, with Dick Gird and Al Schiffelin, the original discoverer located the lower group of mines in the camp of Tombstone, then established. A number of other settlements sprang up, including the nearby Richmond, Watervale and the mill towns of Charleston and

Contention City, both on the San Pedro ,where water could be secured.

Several miles west of Tombstone, just where Ed. Schieffelin camped at the time of the discovery of his Tombstone claim, is a large monument of cemented rock, under which lie his remains, brought back from the Northwest for interment in the land he loved. His death was on May 12, 1897.

The Tombstone Gold & Silver Milling & Mining Company, of which former Gov. A. P. K. Safford was president, in 1880 owned the original group of Schieffelin claims, of which the Tough Nut was the main property. A stamp mill was built on the San Pedro and a contract entered into with the Mormons to build a dam and ditch, from which it was hoped to secure motive power. Concerning this job, estimated to cost $6000, Merrill later wrote that the contractors found themselves fined $300 for six days' overtime on completion of the job. Joseph McRae's record tells that, in 1879, some of the brethren went up the river, twenty miles above St. David, and put in a rip-rap dam and a mile and a half of ditch at Charleston for the Boston Mining Company. This may have been the Boston & Arizona Smelting & Reduction Company, a Massachusetts corporation which had a twenty-stamp mill and a roasting furnace on the San Pedro, between Charleston and Contention, ten miles from Tombstone. This job returned $6000 in cash.

The mines brought a relative degree of prosperity to the San Pedro settlement, furnishing a ready and profitable market for agricultural products, but especially calling upon all transportation facilities that could be afforded. Teams were busy hauling from the terminus of the railroad at Tucson and at Benson, until, in October, 1882, there was completion of the New Mexico and Arizona railroad, then a Santa Fe corporation, from Benson to Nogales, much of the way through the San Pedro Valley, past St. David and the milling towns. The mines paid $30 a cord for fuel wood and even $40 a ton for hay.

Lean days descended upon the community, however, in the early summer of 1886, when the great pumps of the Grand Central mine were stopped by fire. The following year Tombstone practically was abandoned and the market it had afforded was lost. Not till 1901 did the camp revive. It closed again in June, 1903, by the drowning of the pumps. Latterly the old mines, consolidated, have been worked to some extent by the Phelps-Dodge Corporation, but again have been closed, early in April, 1921.

⚙n tl̩e 𝔘pper ⅁ila

Ancient Dwellers and Military Travelers

Possibly as representative a region as is known in the settlement area of the Mormon people lies for about 25 miles along the Gila River in eastern Arizona, in Graham County, and within St. Joseph Stake. Over a dozen communities are contained within this section and all are distinctly Mormon in settlement and local operation, save Solomonville, at the upper end, and Safford, the county seat and principal town. Most of the land is owned by the Saints, who control, as well, a dozen small canals. Within the Stake have been included Mormon settlements of the San Pedro Valley and those upon the upper Gila, in Greenlee County, extending over into New Mexico and El Paso.

The settlement of the Graham County section of the Gila Valley did not start with the Mormons. Far from it. In the upper end of the cultivated region is one of the most notable groups of ruins in the Southwest. This group, since the coming of the Spaniard, appears to have borne the name of Pueblo Viejo (Sp., "Old Town"). Somewhere farther down the stream is assumed to have been "Chichilticalli," the "red house" mentioned in the chronicles of Marco de Niza and the Coronado expedition.

The valley was traversed, from east to west, by Gen. S. W. Kearny, on his way, with a dragoon escort, in 1846, to take California from the Mexicans, this command, from the Pima villages westward, forming the advance guard for the Mormon Battalion. Much interesting data of the Gila Valley trip was written by Lieutenant Emory, who later

241

was chief of the Boundary Survey. It is notable that in 1846 Mount Graham already was known by that name.

Early Days Around Safford

A few Mexicans were in the valley as early as 1871, farming in the vicinity of Pueblo Viejo, immediately below which later arose the town of Solomonville. In 1872 was the first Anglo-Saxon settlement, a group of farmers coming from Gila Bend, upon the Gila River, where they had attempted farming and had failed because the wandering river had washed away their dams and headgates. These farmers, financed in Tucson for the building of the Montezuma canal, settled in the vicinity of Safford, where about that time, was established a townsite, named in honor of Gov. A. P. K. Safford who, from Tucson, then was making a tour of that part of Arizona Territory.

One of the very earliest valley residents was D. W. Wickersham, who wrote the Author lately, covering his early experiences. To later serve as the first teacher, he arrived in Safford the summer of 1876, there finding Joshua E. Bailey and Hiram Kennedy, who had come from Gila Bend. Bailey he considers the founder of Safford and believes it was he who named the settlement. Both Bailey and Kennedy came with California troops during the Civil War. The former died in Michigan and Kennedy was murdered in Safford in 1877. Others of the early settlers were Wm. A. Gillespie, John Glasby, John Conley, A. F. Perigo, Edw. E. Tuttle and E. T. Ijams.

In 1876 appeared Isador E. Solomon, who for many years occupied a leading position. He came primarily to burn charcoal for the rude adobe furnaces that had been erected by the Lesynzskys to smelt the free ores of the famous Longfellow mine in Chase Creek Canyon, a few miles above Clifton. For charcoal Solomon found abundant material in an almost unbroken mesquite forest that stretched for many miles along the river. Solomon purchased a road house and small store that had been estab-

242

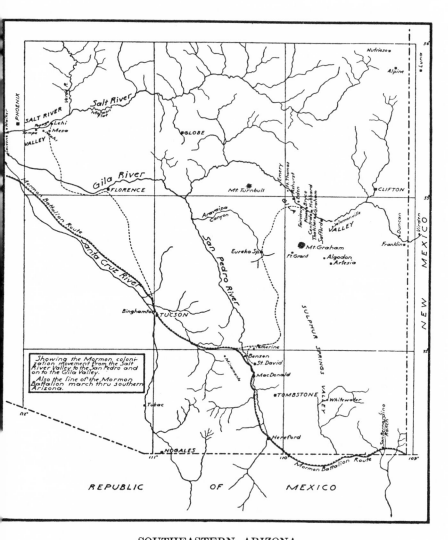

SOUTHEASTERN ARIZONA

The Salt, San Pedro and Gila Valleys and Routes of travel

lished near Pueblo Viejo by one Munson, and the place soon became a trading post for a large extent of country, its importance increasing with the development of the great mining region around Globe. I. E. Solomon still is living, an honored resident of Tucson, his children prominent in the business affairs of the State. Solomonville was so named, in 1878, by none other than Bill Kirkland, who raised the American flag in Tucson in 1856 and who, for a while, carried mail from Fort Thomas to Clifton.

Apostle Erastus Snow appears to have been the first of the Mormon faith to cross this Gila Valley region. His party arrived on the San Pedro River, October 6, 1878. The most easterly point reached in the Gila Valley was at old Camp Goodwin, not far from the present railroad station of Fort Thomas and at the extreme western or lower end of the present farmed area. It would require a separate volume to follow Apostle Erastus Snow on his journeyings through the Southwest, where he appears to have served as a veritable inspector-general for his Church.

On the 1878 trip, L. John Nuttall of Snow's company, writes of passing into the Gila Valley through a rocky canyon, "a terrible place, almost impassable, the dread of all who travel this way." The same road is very little better to this day.

At one point was passed a ridge known as Postoffice Hill, where was found the grave of a white man, killed several years before by Apaches. Every time an Apache passed, he put a rock on the grave mound, at that time about twenty feet square at the base and four feet high. The travelers added another rock, on the principle of, "When in Rome, do as the Romans do."

Mormon Location at Smithville

The Mormon settlement of the Gila Valley was one of the few made without particular and direct instruction from the general Church authorities. It was caused, primarily, by trouble over the land tenure at Forest Dale, in the

244

THE TEEPLES HOME, FIRST HOUSE IN PIMA

THE FIRST SCHOOL HOUSE AT SAFFORD

GILA NORMAL COLLEGE AT THATCHER

mountains to the northward, where settlers, at first permitted, even encouraged by the reservation authorities, finally were advised that they were on Indian land and would have to move. The first question before the colonists immediately became where they should find a new abiding place. All of them had come from the northward, seeking a better location than afforded along the Little Colorado River or in the mountain settlements. So there was determination to see what could be found in the way of farming land on the Gila, to the southward.

In February, 1879, an expedition started over the hills to view the valley of the Gila. It included W. R. Teeples, John Wm. Tanner, Ben Pierce and Hyrum Weech. The last-named told that the party looked over the country and finally selected a location for a town. He wrote, "We traveled from one end of the valley to the other on both sides of the river, looking for the best place to take out a ditch, because we had very little means and could not go to large expense. This (near the location of Smithville, later known as Pima) seemed to be about the easiest place on the river to take out water, so we decided on making the location here."

The Smithville ditch was on the basis of prior location by Gillespie and was extended to cover the Mormon land in 1880. Somewhat higher was the Central ditch, which had been built several years before as far down as the later site of Thatcher and which was extended above Pima in 1882.

Somewhat of a Samaritan was found on the ground in one Markham, from Oregon, from whom were hired a team and wagon and who refused to take any pay. With a pocket compass, Smithville was laid out. The settlement could not be scattered, because Indians and outlaws threatened. Foundations were laid on sixteen corners, each under the name of one of the families expected to come from the north.

The pioneer party then made close investigation of the

valley, traveling up the Gila into New Mexico, and viewed the country around Clifton and along the Blue and Black Rivers. The whole trip took about a month.

The report was, "that the country looked good for stock raising and farming." On March 16, at Moses Cluff's camp, the proposed migration was approved by Stake President Jesse N. Smith, who appointed Jos. K. Rogers to lead it. In the first company were Rogers, Teeples, Weech, Henry D. Dall, William Thompson and the families of all except Weech and Dall. To these were added John and Thomas Sessions and Earlton Haws, making 28 in all. Arrival was on April 8, 1879. The Cluffs (three families) came very soon after the first party. In a later migration came Samuel Curtis, Heber Reed, Edgar Sessions and William Asay.

E. G. Curtis, one of the earliest of the settlers, told that in passing Fort Thomas in March, "the country is found entirely covered with poppies, one of the most beautiful sights I ever expect to see. The grass was high and when the wind would blow it down in great waves, you could see great bunches of antelope."

A Second Party Locates at Graham

In the Church history of Graham Ward is found additional data concerning the early Gila Valley settlement. It is told that, "the settlers of Brigham City on the Little Colorado, getting discouraged because of frequent failures of crops and poor prospects, sent explorers out to look for new locations. Two went to the San Juan country in Utah, two to the Salt River Valley and three, George Lake, Andrew Anderson and George Skinner, to the Gila River." The journey was via Fort Apache, the arrival at Smithville being in the latter part of November, 1880. At the Graham settlement there was purchase of a water ditch and a quit-claim deed to four quarter-sections of land that had been farmed by non-Mormons. The record recites, "it was merely a rustlers' ranch, possessed by horsethieves and speculators who had a small house on it, for which the brethren paid about $1800, in cows valued at $35 per head."

Lake remained in the valley. Anderson and Skinner returned in December to Brigham City, where the authorities of the United Order accepted the purchase. Anderson and Skinner started again for the Gila, accompanied by their families, by Moses M. Curtis and William Hawkins and their families and a number of unmarried men, taking with them seed grain, farming implements, cows, sheep and other animals. Transportation was by ox teams. Christmas Day was spent at St. Joseph on the Little Colorado and New Year at Showlow, arrival on the Gila being in January. Lake, in the meantime, had been joined by Jorgen Jorgensen and Jerome J. Adams, the two who had been sent to the Salt River Valley.

The new arrivals at once set at work, clearing their lands and putting in grain, raising good crops. The manual labor, of the hardest sort, was performed under the conditions of the United Order and on a diet principally of bread and beans. The sheep band was turned over to the Church, as profits of the Order, and the wheat and other products were divided according to the number of families and the number of persons. A stockade fort was built, but the homes for months consisted of sheds or tents and even of the wagons. In 1884, on the newly-surveyed townsite of Graham, was built a meeting house, called the "factory house," with mesquite posts and dirt roof and with walls only of heavy unbleached muslin, which appears to have been called "factory."

One of the early settlements of the Gila Valley is Matthews (successively Matthewsville, Fairview and Glenbar), founded in December, 1880, by Joseph Matthews and family, from Round Valley, and Wm. R. Waddill. In 1881 they built a stockade and though no local Indian depredations were known, in that year the Matthews settlers moved to Pima for better protection. A townsite was selected by the Stake President September 17, 1886, but was not occupied. A resident of note was the first district school teacher, John F. Nash, who came with his father to Arizona in 1874, first settling in Williamson Valley near Prescott. He arrived in the valley in 1881, the progress of the family toward Texas stopped on the Gila by the stealing of a band of Nash horses by "rustlers."

Vicissitudes of Pioneering

Eden, first known as Curtis, lies on the northern side of the Gila, nine miles northwest of Pima. It dates from early in 1881, when there was arrival from Brigham City, Arizona, of a party of United Order settlers, headed by Moses M. Curtis. Though other immigrants occupied holdings nearby, M. M. Curtis and Wm. R. Hawkins were the only residents of the present Eden townsite in 1881. The men first turned their attention toward the construction of a ditch from the river, this completed the following year. For a while the young community was on very short rations. At times there could be only one meal a day, that a meager one of beans, served at noon to the workers, who scarcely could summon strength for more than a half day's labor.

Some of the early settlers built boweries of brush under which they rolled their covered wagons, to secure better protection from the pitiless Arizona summer sun, and with no other home for weeks. There were Indian "scares," as elsewhere told, and life was far from comfortable, with occasional crossing of the Gila at flood to secure protection at the more populous Pima. In January, 1882, was a moving back to five log houses that had been built on the Curtis townsite, but even after that was flight to Pima when word came of an Indian raid. In the fall of 1882 eight families were living in a little stockade fort that enclosed a half acre of ground, near the river. The present townsite was located May 10, 1883.

Thatcher, present Stake headquarters, derives its name from Apostle Moses Thatcher, who was a Christmas visitor in 1882, in company with Apostle Erastus Snow. The first settler was John M. Moody, who came with his family from Utah, arriving when Nature had warm welcome indeed, on July 4, 1881. In 1882 he was joined by the Cluff and Zufelt families and by James Pace of the Mormon Battalion, who built a stockade, and a little later by Hyrum Brinkerhoff and wife Margaret, "Aunt Maggie," who bought and occupied the Moody place. They were prominent among the Southern Utah and Muddy pioneers.

The Thatcher townsite was selected by President Layton May 13, 1883, a school district being established the following month. Among the arrivals of the following year was Samuel Claridge, one of the pioneers of the Muddy section. October 19, 1885, the presidency located a new townsite about one-half mile to the southward and on higher land. Much of the old Moody ranch since the Brinkerhoff purchase has disappeared, from the encroachments of the Gila River.

Bryce, across the river from Pima, dates from January, 1883, when Ebenezer Bryce, Sr., and sons commenced construction of a ditch, completed the next year. The first house was that of Ebenezer P. Bryce, occupied in December, 1884.

Central, between Thatcher and Pima, took its name from the Central canal, which irrigates part of the settlement. Its first settlers were Orson and Joseph Cluff of Forest Dale, from which they came southward in the spring of 1882.

The Hubbard settlement is an outgrowth of the Graham and Bryce wards and is of comparatively late occupation. It is named after Elisha F. Hubbard, Sr., the first ward bishop.

The Layton settlement, named for the first stake president, is one of the most prosperous, and is the third in order of population of the St. Joseph Stake wards. The first settler was Hyrum H. Tippets, who came January 13, 1883, direct from Brigham City, Utah.

The Franklin settlement, above Duncan on the Gila, is about seven miles in length, most of it in Arizona, though lapping over into New Mexico. Its first Mormon settler was Thomas J. Nations, in 1895. He joined, with others of the brethren, in taking out a canal. Thomas A. McGrath is understood to have been the first settler of the locality. The name was given in 1898, at the time of the visit of Apostles John Henry Smith and John W. Taylor, and is in honor of Franklin D. Richards, an apostle of the Church, who in no wise had been associated with Arizona affairs. In the same vicinity, wholly in New Mexico, is the settlement of Virden, mainly populated by refugees from Mexico. In these upper Gila communities the Mormons have created a veritable garden, where careless cultivation had been known.

Graham County was created by the Arizona Legislature in the spring of 1881, the settlement south of the Gila theretofore having been in Pima County. The first county seat was Safford, but county government was transferred to Solomonville by an act of the Legislature in 1883. In 1915, after the setting off of Greenlee County, the courthouse went back to Safford.

Considering the Lamanites

In the entertaining flood of reminiscence that comes from almost any of the devout pioneers, there often is found expression of abiding belief of personal protection extended by Omnipotence. Possibly, save in the development of character by trials and by tribulation, the average pioneer of the faith, from a present viewpoint, would appear to have been little favored, yet thankful devotion ever was present.

One story that indicated celestial intervention in time

of danger, has been told by Orson Cluff. He and several brothers and their families were on the road south from Forest Dale to the Gila, and had camped at a point twenty miles south of Fort Apache. In the morning there was the usual prayer, from which the company arose, refreshed in spirit, for another hard day's journey. A short time later, an Indian told how he was a member of a band of redskins that lay in ambush about the Mormon camp that very morning. The work of massacre was about to begin when the intended victims were seen to drop upon their knees and to lift their hands aloft in supplication. The startled Indians were overcome by some mysterious power and stole away. Possibly they feared that potent "medicine" was being made against them, but the Cluffs are sure that the Holy Spirit had descended to save them for further earthly experience.

The Gila Valley saw much of Indian rapine in its earlier days. The section considered in this chapter lies just east of the San Carlos Apache reservation and is flanked on the northward by the White Mountain reservation. When the California Column, under General Carleton, was established in Arizona in 1863, after beating the Confederates back beyond the Rio Grande, it was found necessary to establish military stations in that locality. Camp Goodwin, named after the first Governor of the Territory, was at the lower end of the valley. A number of years after its abandonment, there was established, five miles to the eastward, Camp Thomas, maintained until after the final subjugation of the hostile Indians. Thomas was a veritable guard post for the Mormon settlers. To the southwest was Camp Grant, in the northern extension of the Sulphur Springs Valley, this post a successor to old Camp Grant, which was at the mouth of Aravaipa Creek, at the junction of that stream with the San Pedro River. To the northward was Fort Apache and to the southward Fort Bowie.

The native Pinaleno Indians of the San Carlos region, while inclined toward spasmodic outbreaks, were not as hostile as their western neighbors, the Mohave and Yuma Apaches. A very dangerous element was added when, in 1876, under direction of the army, Agent John P. Clum moved to San Carlos 325 Indians of the Chiricahua-Apache strain from a reservation in southeastern Arizona. Within a few years, 4500 Indians were concentrated at San Carlos. The Chiricahuas, unsettled and forever yearning to get back to the scene of their marauding along the emigrant road to the southward and in Mexico, constantly were slipping away from the reservation by individuals and by bands, and their highway usually was up the river. In the early eighties the settlers along the Gila lived forever in terror of the savage foe. The military was efficient. Hard-riding troopers would dash forth from one or all of the guardian posts whenever danger threatened, and to these same troops undoubtedly is due the fact that general massacres were not known in and around the Gila Valley towns.

Often the Author finds in the manuscripts of personal experiences that have been accumulated by the score in his office, a note indicating the conditions under which the land was settled. There have been attempts in other parts of this work to make clear the fact that the Mormons always tried to be friendly with the Indians and suffered without protest treatment from the aborigines that would have led to the shedding of blood by others. One interesting little item of this sort is in a record contributed by Mrs. W. R. Teeples. She found the Indians on the Gila River in 1879 were friendly, possibly too much so. She wrote, "When I was cooking pancakes over the fire in our camp, the Indians would sit around watching, and they would grab the cakes out of the pan before they were done, so I had to cover the pancakes up to keep them for ourselves."

Mrs. J. N. Stratton wrote of the same period:

Besides the fear of getting out of food was the greater fear of the Indians. They were on the San Carlos reservation and were supposed to be peaceful, but bands often went out on the warpath and spread terror throughout the country, so the people never knew what to expect from them. The mesquite and sage brush were so thick where Safford's streets and houses are now, that one could only see a little distance, and it was no uncommon occurrence for an Indian to slip out from behind the brush and come walking in at the cabin door, or put his face up against the window and peer in, if the door happened to be closed. One settler who had two doors had her husband nail one up so that when the Indians did come to call on them, she could stand in the other door and keep them from coming in. The mothers never let their children get out of their sight, for fear they would be stolen.

I. E. Solomon and his family had many experiences with the Indians, and in several cases narrowly escaped death. A number of Solomon's employes were killed in the open country toward Clifton.

An interesting chronicle is from Mrs. Elizabeth Hanks Curtis, who came with her family in April, 1881. Incidentally, she is a descendant of the Hanks family, tracing relationship to Abraham Lincoln. A mile above Eden they built a log fort. In September this had to be abandoned, word brought by a friendly Indian of the coming of a large band of Indians and of imminent danger. Will Ransom from Pima provided a raft to cross the river upon and the settlers concentrated at Pima. The settlers were driven into Pima again in April of the following year, after huddling for days in Moses Curtis' cabin. Protection came from Fort Thomas.

Murders by Indian Raiders

July 19, 1882, Jacob S. Ferrin of Pima was killed under circumstances of treachery. A freighting camp, of which he was a member, was entered by a number of Apaches, led by "Dutchy," escaped from custody at San Carlos. Pretending amity, they seized the teamsters' guns and fired

253

upon their hosts. Ferrin was shot down, one man was wounded and the others escaped.

On the morning of December 1, 1885, Lorenzo and Seth Wright were killed by Indians who had been combing the valley for horses. The Wrights had started, with members of a posse, from Layton, and were joined at Solomonville by Sheriff Stevens and two other men, after there had been recovered a number of the stolen horses, for the pursuers rode harder and faster than the fleeing thieves. There had been assumption that the thieves were Mexicans and so there was an element of recklessness in the pursuit that would have been missing had the truth been known, that they were Apaches. The four leading men of the posse were ambushed by the redskins, who had halted by the roadside. Seth Wright was shot from his horse. His brother immediately dismounted and opened fire upon the Indians. Lorenzo's right arm was broken by a bullet, and then, while he was running, he was shot in the back.

This same band had killed a man and a boy at Black Rock and a herdsman at Bear Springs Flat.

May 23, 1886, Frank Thurston of Pima, while starting a lime kiln, six miles from the town, was surprised by eight Apaches and killed. This band passed by the Curtis settlement, driving off a number of horses.

Concerning the Indian situation, James H. Martineau, on June 1, 1886, wrote that the Apaches then were riding in many small bands, but were kept on the move constantly by the vigorous measures of General Miles, and he assumes that the Apache question would have been settled had his predecessor, General Crook, been less dilatory. The writer expressed his conclusion that in military skill, strategy and ability the Indians far excelled their opponents, and details that fifty or sixty Apaches the year before had killed more than 75 white settlers, all the while pursued by seventeen companies of United States troops, without losing a single Indian.

The Mormons of the Gila Valley maintained most amicable relations with their neighbors, but occasionally had to participate in some of the ordinary frontier episodes. James R. Welker, an arrival in Safford in 1883, tells that, "The cowboys had things about their own way for a few years. They would ride right into a town, go straight to the saloon and commence shooting the place up. They were expert with the pistol too. I have seen some very wonderful shots among those cowboys. They did not do much killing around here, but they were pretty wild and did about as they pleased." W. T. Barney wrote, "The rustlers gave us quite a bit of trouble, perhaps even more than the Indians."

The peaceful Saints in the Gila Valley undoubtedly found much that was foreign to their habits of life. A tale of the frolicsome cowboy is told by Isaac P. Robinson of Thatcher, who was in Safford in 1884:

> There were but very few houses in Safford then. About the only business house was the Glasby building, which had a saloon and also a store. The cowboys had things about their own way. They would come into the store and take possession. Mr. Glasby would go out and leave it to them. They would shoot up the store, help themselves to what they wanted, pay for everything they had taken, shoot up the town and go on. But I don't want to see any more of it. You haven't the remotest idea what a lot of trouble they made. This was the main route from the north into Mexico and the principal rendezvous for a lot of those rough characters.

In the way of outlawry, the valley had unwelcome notoriety, when from its rougher element was constituted a band which, May 11, 1889, ambushed Paymaster J. W. Wham of the United States army, on the road between Fort Grant and Fort Thomas, and stole about $28,000 in gold and silver, intended for the pay of the troops at the latter post. An escort of eleven colored infantrymen, led by a sergeant, apparently deserted by the Major, fought well, but was driven away after five of the soldiers had been wounded. Thirteen bandits were understood to have been implicated. Eight individuals were arrested. There was trial at Tucson, where Wham and the soldiers were notably poor witnesses and where the defendants were acquitted.

A Gray Highway of Danger

Just as the Mormon settlements on the Little Colorado providentially were given assistance by the building of the Atlantic and Pacific railroad, just so the struggling pioneers on the Gila found benefit in the opening of the silver and copper mines at Globe. Freight teams were in demand for hauling coke and supplies from the railroad at Willcox and Bowie and for hauling back from the mines the copper bullion. Much of this freighting was done with great teams of mules and horses, veritable caravans, owned by firms such as Tully & Ochoa or M. G. Samaniego of Tucson, but enough was left for the two and four-horse teams of the Mormons, who thus were enabled from the hauling of a few tons of coke to provide provisions for their families and implements for the tilling of their fields.

The road from the railroad to Globe ofttimes was a gray highway of danger. After leaving the Gila towns, it led through the length of the Apache Indian reservation. Usually the teams went in sort of military order. The larger "outfits" had strict rules for defense, each driver with his pistol and rifle and each "swamper" similarly armed. Every night the wagons were drawn into a circle, within which the horses were corralled or tied to the wagon poles, where they were fed. Pickets were kept out and care was incessant day and night.

But, sometimes, a freighter, eager to earn extra pay for a quick trip, or wishing to drive ahead of the cloud of dust that enveloped each large convoy, would push along by himself. Possibly the next day, the train would come to the embers of what had been wagons and their contents. Nearby would be the bodies of the tortured and murdered teamsters. So the careful ones united, remaining at the railroad until at least a score of wagons had accumulated, and then made their way northward, relatively safe through united vigilance.

In 1899 the Gila Valley, Globe & Northern railroad was completed from Bowie, through the Gila Valley towns, to Globe, a distance of 124 miles, though the loss to the freighters was more than balanced by the general good to the community of bettered transportation facilities. Right-of-way through the reservation was accorded by the Indians after a diplomatic distribution to them by a railroad agent of $8000, all in silver coin.

Chapter Twenty-three

Civic and Church Features

Troublesome River Conditions

In the memory of Americans still living, the Gila River through the Safford region, was a relatively narrow stream, over which in places a stone could be tossed. There were occasional lagoons, some of them created by beaver dams—picturesque, but breeding places for mosquitoes and sources of malaria. Camp Goodwin was abandoned because of malarial conditions in 1869-70, troops being transferred to the new post of Camp Ord (Apache).

The river situation of later years has been very different indeed from that known to the pioneers. The lagoons drained and the underbrush, grass and trees cut away, the river floods have had full sweep and, as a result, there has been tremendous loss in the washing away of the lower lying land. The farms have been pushed back toward the mesas. Now under consideration is a comprehensive irrigation system that will cost several millions of dollars, with a great concrete diversion dam above Solomonville and with two head canals that economically will serve both sides of the river.

But in the early days the colonists did what they could, not what economically was advisable. They did not have such trouble as was known along the Little Colorado and their water supply was much larger and somewhat more regular. They took out little canals at different points, with headworks that were easily replaced when washed away.

For a few years around 1910, there appeared a prospect

that the Gila Valley farms would have to be abandoned unless something could be done to stop the flow of tailings from the concentrating mills of the Clifton-Morenci country, on the San Francisco River, a tributary of the Gila. The finely pulverized rock was brought down in the irrigation water and spread out upon the fields in a thick layer, almost impervious to the growth of vegetation. Mit Simms, then a farmer near Safford, tells that the dried tailings upon his farm spread out in a smooth sheet, that could be broken like glass, with a blow from a hammer. The mining companies refused to heed demand to impound their tailings flow, and so the matter was taken into the courts. Decisions uniformly were with the settlers, the matter finally being disposed of in their favor in the United States Supreme Court. Then the companies, using the tailings material for the making of dams, created great tailings reservoirs in the hills near their plants, and filled up valley after valley with the rejected material. Incidentally, they spent in this work enormous sums, believed to have been sufficient to have bought all the farms of the Gila Valley, at the price put upon them ten years ago. This expended money, however, may yet be returned, for plans have been set afoot for leaching copper treasure out of the tailings banks.

Artesian water was struck in the Gila Valley in 1887, according to John A. Lee, understood to have been the first well borer in the artesian district, within which are the present towns of Algodon (otherwise Lebanon) and Artesia. The first water was struck at a depth of 330 feet and better flows were secured with deeper borings down to 1000 feet.

The first few years of the Gila Valley settlement, every alternate section was assumed to be the property of the Texas Pacific Railroad Company, a land grant claimed by the Southern Pacific. This claim was decided against by the United States authorities early in 1885, and the lands thus were thrown open to entry by the settlers. Pima was

259

on railroad land and filing of its townsite formally was accomplished by Mayor W. W. Crockett.

Basic Law in a Mormon Community

Interest attaches to the Church commission, dated February 20, 1883, received by Christopher Layton on his appointment as head of the San Pedro and Gila Valley settlers. It was signed by John Taylor and Jos. F. Smith of the First Presidency and contains instructions and admonitions that might well have served as a basic law of any God-fearing community.

President Layton was instructed to see that the settlers did not scatter themselves promiscuously throughout the land, that surveys be made for townsites, that the people settle in these localities, with facilities for public schools and meeting houses, and that due provision be made to protect the settlers against depredations of the lawless and unprincipled combinations of brigands and other hostile marauders.

A notably interesting paragraph recites, "You will understand that our object in the organization of the Stake of St. Joseph is to introduce the Gospel into the Mexican nation, or that part of it which lies contiguous to your present settlement, and also, when prudence shall dictate and proper arrangements are entered into, that a settlement may commence to be made in that country."

It was recommended, in forming cities either in Arizona or Mexico, "care should be had to place them in proper localities, convenient to land and water, with careful examination of the sanitary conditions. It is the general opinion that it is more healthy and salubrious on the plateaus or mesas than on the low land, the latter of which in your district of country are more or less subject to malarial diseases, which ought, always, when practicable, to be avoided."

The streets should be wide and commodious,with public squares for church, county, school and ornamental purposes.

GILA VALLEY PIONEERS

1—Wm. R. Teeples   2—John M. Moody
3—Jos. K. Rogers   4—Ebenezer Pryce   5—Hyrum Brinkerhoff
6—Samuel H. Claridge   7—Frank N. Tyler

PIONEER WOMEN OF THE GILA VALLEY

1—Elizabeth Hanks Curtis
2—Mrs W. R. Teeples
3—Elizabeth Moody 4—Margaret Brinkerhoff 5—Elizabeth Layton
6—Josephine Wall Rogers
7—Rebecca Claridge

School and church affairs should be kept separate. There was warning against favoritism in the allotment of town lands and a recommendation that the principles of the United Order be approached, without the placing of the communities under rigid rules.

Another interesting paragraph recites, "The order of Zion when carried out, will be that all men should act in the interest of and for the welfare of Zion, and individualism, private speculation and covetousness will be avoided, and that all act in the interest of all and for the welfare of the whole community. We may not, at present, be able to carry out these ideas in full, but without any special formality or rule, we may be approaching these principles as fast as circumstances will admit of it. We profess to be acting and operating for God, and for His Kingdom, and we are desirous that our acts should be in consonance with our professions."

In the selection of elders, care was enjoined that all such persons should be honorable, free from any pernicious or degrading habits, "for if men cannot control themselves, they are not fit to be rulers or leaders in the Kingdom of God."

There was special injunction that the Lamanites, the Indians, be treated with all consideration and shown that the Mormons do not teach one thing and practice another. The Indians should be taught to be "friendly with the government of the United States or Mexico and to live at peace with one another, to be chaste, sober and honest and subject to the law of God."

Tithing of one-tenth was stipulated as in the interest of the people. The new leader was advised that, "God has placed you as a watchman on the walls of Zion and He will hold you accountable for your acts," and he was directed to see that the laws of God were carried out in his community, irrespective of persons or families.

Layton Soldier and Pioneer

Christopher Layton was a rough diamond, almost illiterate, yet possessed of much energy and a keen, practical judgment that served him and his people well through the course of a long life. He was an Englishman, born in Bedfordshire, March 8, 1821. His first practical experience was at 7 years of age, when he kept crows from the wheatfields for the large salary of 56 cents a week, boarding himself. In 1843 he crossed the ocean. Elsewhere is noted his experience with the Mormon Battalion. Following discharge, for a few years he lived in California, finally taking ship from San Francisco back to Liverpool, where he arrived in March, 1850. On the same ship's return, James Pennell led 250 converts to America, landing at New Orleans proceeding by river to St. Louis. and then Utah.

In September, 1852, Layton first saw Salt Lake, arriving at the head of an expedition of 52 wagons, including the first threshing outfit in Utah. In 1856 he was in the Carson Valley of Nevada, where he proceeded toward the very notable undertaking of building a wagon road across the Sierra Nevadas to Hangtown, early Placerville. With the rest of the Utah Saints, he was recalled to Salt Lake in the fall of 1857.

Layton arrived at St. David February 24, 1883. In May he organized wards on the Gila, at Pima, Thatcher, Graham and Curtis, under Jos. K. Rogers, John M. Moody, Jorgen Jorgensen and Moses Curtis. In March of the next year, he organized Layton branch near Safford.

President Layton's own story of his advent in the Gila Valley includes:

The Saints were wanting to settle close together, so I bought a 600-acre tract of land of a syndicate living in Tucson. Then I bought out the squatters' rights and improvements by taking quit-claim deeds of them. Thus I was in a position to help the Saints to get homes. In July I bought 320 acres of Peter Anderson (adjoining the other tract) and laid it out in a townsite which we named Thatcher. I built a three-roomed adobe house in Thatcher ward (it being the

262

second house built on the townsite) and we moved into it. I gave a lot for a schoolhouse and the few Saints who were settling here then built an adobe building on it. The mesquite was so thick that when we tried to go any place we were very fortunate if we did not get lost. I gave the Seventies a lot, but they never made any use of it; also gave the bishop a lot for tithing purposes. The Academy was afterward built on it.

Layton, aided by his many sons, was active in business, as well as in the faith, operating stores, a flour mill, an ice factory and a number of stage lines, one of which stretched all the way from Bowie Station through the Gila Valley, to Globe, and, through the Tonto Basin, to Pine and Fort Verde, the longest stage mail line in the Southwest at the time.

The transfer of headquarters of St. Joseph Stake appears to have been determined upon very soon after the arrival of Layton at St. David. One of his counselors, David P. Kimball, visited Smithville March 10, 1883, and in May Layton himself was on the ground, visiting Smithville (Pima) and Safford. There was approval of the new settlement of Curtis on May 10 and on the 13th was location of the townsite of Thatcher.

At this time there appears to have been determination to move headquarters of the Stake from St. David to Smithville, where the first formal quarterly conference of the Stake was held June 3. No record can be found of this transfer nor of the subsequent change to Thatcher.

A New Leader on the Gila

In 1897 President Layton's health declined and on January 27, 1898, he was released from his spiritual office, to which was appointed Andrew Kimball, this with a letter from President Wilford Woodruff, expressing the highest appreciation of Layton's labors. Christopher Layton left Arizona June 13, 1898, for his old home in Kaysville, Utah, where he died August 7. At a reunion, about six years ago, of the Layton descendants and their families, were present 594 individuals.

Andrew Kimball, successor to the presidency of St. Joseph Stake, had formal installation January 30, 1898, at the hands of Apostles John Henry Smith and John W. Taylor, at the same time there being general reorganization of the Church subdivision. President Kimball, who still most actively is in office, is a son of the noted Apostle Heber C. Kimball, First Counselor to President Brigham Young. President Kimball from the very first showed keen enthusiasm in the work of upbuilding his community. In October of the year of his installation he returned to Utah, like the spies returned from the land of Canaan, bringing equally large stories of the fertility of the new land. Instead of bearing a huge bunch of grapes, he had to take with him photographs, in order to secure reception of his stories of corn that was sixteen feet tall, Johnson grass eight feet high, a sweet potato that weighed 36 pounds, of peaches too big to go into the mouth of a preserving jar, sunflower stalks that were used for fence poles, weeds that had to be cut with an ax and sugar cane that grew four years from one planting. On the strength of his enthusiasm, very material additions were made to the population of the Gila Valley, and the President even yet keeps busy in missionary work, not only of his Church, but work calculated to assist in the upbuilding of the Southwest along irrigated agricultural lines.

Church Academies of Learning

Every Mormon community gives especial attention to its schools, for education in the regard of the people follows closely after their consideration of spiritual affairs. The normal schools of the State always have had a very large percentage of the youth of the faith, training to be teachers.

Three of the four Arizona Stakes maintain academies, wherein the curriculum also carries religious instruction. The largest of the three Church schools, at Thatcher, lately was renamed the Gila Normal College. It was established in January, 1891, under instruction that had

been received over two years before from the genera
Church Board of Education. Its first sessions were in
the meetinghouse at Central, with Joy Dunion as principal.
The second year's work was at Thatcher, where the old
adobe meetinghouse was occupied. Thereafter a tithing
house was used and was expanded for the growing necessities of the school, which has been in continuous operation
ever since, with the exception of two years following 1896,
when the finances of the Stake were at low ebb. The academy was revived on assumption of Andrew Kimball to the
Stake Presidency, under Principal Emil Maeser, he a son
of one of Utah's most noted educators. Andrew C. Peterson has been in charge of the school most of the time since
1906. In 1909 was occupied a new building, erected and
furnished at a cost of about $35,000. Leland H. Creer now
is principal.

At St. Johns the St. Johns Stake Academy was founded
January 14, 1889, with John W. Brown as its first principal.
The present building was dedicated December 16, 1900.
Howard Blazzard now is in active charge, while Stake
President David K. Udall, first president of the Academy's
Board, still occupies the same position, after 27 years of
service.

The Snowflake Stake Academy was founded, with E.
M. Webb in charge, only a week later than that of St.
Johns. The two institutions for many years were the only
means provided for local education, beyond the grammar
grades. At Snowflake industrial and agricultural courses
are given prominence in the curriculum. Thanksgiving
Day, 1910, fire destroyed the large school building, which
was replaced by a more modern structure, that cost
$35,000 and that was dedicated Thanksgiving Day, 1913.
For years the school was directed by Joseph Peterson.

At Mesa, Chandler and Gilbert are maintained semi-
naries, mainly for advanced instruction in Church doctrine.

Chapter Twenty-four

𝔐𝔬𝔟𝔢𝔪𝔢𝔫𝔱 𝔍𝔫𝔱𝔬 𝔐𝔢𝔵𝔦𝔠𝔬

Looking Over the Land

The Mormon settlement of Mexico, as elsewhere told, was a cherished plan of Brigham Young, who saw to the southward a land wherein his Church, its doctrines and influence could find room for expansion. He died while the southern migration started by him still was far short of a Mexican destination, though that country had been explored to an extent by several missionary parties.

The first Mormons to enter Mexico were the soldiers of the Mormon Battalion who, in 1846, passed south of the Gila in Mexican territory, and then entered the present Mexico by a swing of the column southward from the San Bernardino ranch around to the valley of the San Pedro. The D. W. Jones party was the first missionary expedition into Mexico, crossing the Rio Grande at Paso del Norte, the present Juarez, January 7, 1876. The Pratt-Stewart party, including Meliton G. Trejo, was in northern Mexico early in '77, and small missionary parties followed thereafter from time to time.

November 15, 1879, Apostle Moses Thatcher was in Mexico City with J. Z. Stewart and Trejo, there founding the first organization of the Church within the Republic.

Decided impetus was given the southward movement when it became evident that the national prosecution against plural marriage was to be pushed to the extreme. January 4, 1883, with the idea of finding an asylum for the Saints in Mexico, Apostle Thatcher traveled from St. David on the San Pedro, to the southeast as far as Corralitos, where some arrangement was made for lands. In the following September, another party from St. David explored the country along the Babispe River. Still more important, November 2, 1884, Apostles Brigham Young, Jr., and Heber J. Grant investigated the Yaqui River section of Sonora, this with three companies of prospective settlers from the Salt River, Gila and San Pedro Valleys, together with some additions from Salt Lake.

In January, 1885, migration was under personal charge of President John Taylor, who, after a notable conference at St. David, as noted in the history of that section, led a party southward into Sonora and held a satisfactory conference with Governor Torres, yet made no settlement. In the same month, however, notation has been found that Alexander F. Macdonald was at Corralitos, Chihuahua, from Mesa. A few parties were in that locality in February, 1885, one expedition of seventy having come from Arizona, under Captain Noble. Something of a setback was known when, on April 9, 1885, the Governor of Chihuahua ordered departure of all Mormon settlers within his State. Apostles Young and Thatcher, May 18, visited the City of Mexico and secured from the federal government permission for the immigrants to remain.

Colonization in Chihuahua

It was in 1886 that the main Mormon exodus traveled across the border. The way had been prepared by the organization of a Colorado corporation, the Mexican Colonization & Agricultural Company, this under the management of Anthony W. Ivins, a northern Arizona pioneer. This company had been granted the usual colonists' privileges, including the introduction, without duty, of livestock, agricultural implements and household effects, but had no special concessions. It was given the usual exemption from taxation for ten years. Through this company, land was acquired at Colonia Juarez and Colonia Diaz, by purchase from Ignacio Gomez del Campo and others. Payment was made with money that had been donated in Utah and from Church funds.

Colonies were established, in which were consolidated the Mormons already south of the line and the newcomers. Diaz was on the Janos River, near the Mexican town of Ascension, and Colonia Juarez was 75 miles upstream on a branch of the Janos river, the Piedras Verdes. At the former place about 100,000 acres were acquired and at the latter 25,000. A prior settlement at Corralitos had been established in the fall of 1884. Juarez had the first meeting-house, built January 31, 1886, but the town had to be moved two miles, in January, 1887, on discovery that the site was outside of the lands that had been purchased.

Largely from data secured from Mr. Ivins is found much of detail concerning northern Mexican settlement. One important step was the acquirement in 1886, of 100,000 acres of Mexican government timber land in the Sierra Madre Mountains, near Colonia Juarez, and on this tract was established Colonia Pacheco, wherein the main industry was lumbering. Then two other mountain tracts were acquired, of 6000 acres each, upon which were established Colonia Garcia and Colonia Chuichupa, sixteen miles to the southwest of Colonia Juarez. In 1889 was established Colonia Dublan, upon a 60,000-acre tract that was most valuable of all, considered agriculturally. Naturally this became the strongest of all the settlements of the colonist company.

There had been exploration, however, to the westward, in the State of Sonora, and in 1896, a tract of 110,000 acres was acquired on the Babispe River. There was established Colonia Oaxaca. The land was mainly valuable for grazing, but some good farming land was along the river. Twenty-five miles below Oaxaca, three years later was acquired a tract of 25,000 acres, whereon Colonia Morelos was established, to be the center of an agricultural section, with attached grazing land.

As colonization generally was directed from a central agency, each of the colonies had somewhat the same method of establishment and of operation, this founded upon the experience of the people in Utah and Arizona. There would be laid out a townsite, near which would be small tracts of garden land, and farther away larger tracts of agricultural and grazing land, sold to the colonists at cost with ample time for payment, title remaining in the company until all the purchase price had been paid. In each colony one of the very first public works was erection of a schoolhouse, used as a house of worship and for public hall, as well. Graduates from the colony grammar schools could be sent to an academy at Colonia Juarez, where four years' high school work was given. Skilled teachers were secured wherever possible. Instruction was free, both to the children of the colonists and to the Mexicans. Wherever sufficient school maintenance could not be provided, the deficiency was made up by the Church.

In each colony the rough homes of adobe or rock later were replaced by houses of lumber or brick, until, it is told, these Mexican towns were among the best built known in the Southwest.

Agriculture was notably successful. There were fine orchards, vegetables were abundant and good crops of grain and potatoes were known. The best breeds of cattle and horses were imported and improved agricultural machinery was brought in. Hundreds of miles of roads were constructed by the colonists, turned over to the government without cost, and taxation was cheerfully paid on the same basis as known by neighboring Mexican settlements.

Wherever water could be developed were well-surveyed ditches, heading on the Casas Grandes, Janos and Babispe Rivers and their tributaries, though, without reservoirs, there often was shortage of water. Water power was used

269

for the operation of grist and lumber mills and even for electric lighting. By 1912 there were five lumber and shingle mills, three grist mills, three tanneries, a shoe factory and other manufacturing industries and there was added a telephone system, reaching all Chihuahua colonies.

In general, relations with the Mexican government and with the neighboring Mexicans appear to have been cordial. Possibly the best instance of this lies in an anecdote concerning the visit to the Chihuahua State Fair of President Porfirio Diaz. There he saw a remarkable exhibit of industry and frugality presented by the Mormon colonies, including saddles and harness, fruit, fresh and preserved, and examples of the work of the schools. Then it was the General fervently exclaimed, "What could I not do with my beloved Mexico if I only had more citizens and settlers like the Mormons."

The colonists took no part in the politics of the country. Only a few became Mexican citizens. Junius S. Romney stated that in each settlement pride was taken in maintaining the best ideals of American government. Occasionally there was irritation, mainly founded upon the difference between the American and Mexican judicial systems. According to Ammon M. Tenney, in all the years of Mormon occupation, not a single colonist was convicted of a crime of any sort whatever. In 1912 the colonists numbered 4225.

Abandonment of the Mountain Colonies

At the break-up of the Diaz government, May 25, 1911, fear and disorder succeeded peaceful conditions that had been known in the mountain settlements. Sections of Chihuahua were dominated by Villa, Salazar, Lopez, Gomez and other revolutionary leaders. A volume might be written upon the experiences of the colonists on the eastern side of the mountains. There would appear to have been little prejudice against them and little actual antagonism, but they had amassed a wealth that was needed

270

by the revolutionary forces, and there were recurring demands upon them for horses, wagons, supplies, ammunition and finally for all weapons. Patience and diplomacy were needed in the largest degree in the conferences with the Mexican military leaders. Soon it was evident, however, that nothing remained but flight to the United States. July 29, 1912, most of the settlers were hurried aboard a train, almost without time in which to change their clothing. The stores and public buildings were closed. The colonists were huddled, with small personal property, into boxcars or cattle cars and hauled from Colonia Dublan to El Paso. There, there was immediate assistance by the City of El Paso and the United States government, soon reinforced by friends and relatives in Arizona and Utah. At one time 1500 Mormon refugees were encamped in El Paso.

A. W. Ivins tells:

As soon as the colonists were gone, a campaign of looting and destruction was commenced by the Mexican revolutionists and local Mexicans near the colonies. The stores were broken into and looted of hundreds of thousands of dollars worth of merchandise. Private homes were treated in the same manner. Livestock was appropriated, until almost every available thing was carried away or destroyed. There was little wanton destruction of property except at Colonia Diaz, where the better part of the residences and public buildings was burned. The homes and farm buildings were not destroyed.

Some of the colonists returned as soon as a degree of safety was assured, to check up the property remaining and to plan for the eventual return of their people. But again there had to be an exodus, this late in December, 1915. At that time it is told that Villa was only a few miles away, preparing to march upon the Mormon settlements, with all orders given to that end. But in the morning the plans were changed, apparently by celestial intervention, and he marched his men in another direction, into the Galiana Valley.

On one of the flights, after all but the most vigorous of the men had departed, there came peremptory demand for surrender of all arms and ammunition. Some guns were surrendered, but the best had been deposited at a mountain rendezvous. To that point the men hurried and, well-armed and well-mounted, made their way by mountain trails to the border, avoiding conflict with Mexican bands that sought to bar the way.

Sad Days for the Sonora Colonists

In 1905 was known a disastrous flood, which at Oaxaca swept away forty brick houses, though without loss of life. At Morelos a number of houses were swept away and about 1000 acres of choice farming land was rendered worthless. Then Morelos and Oaxaca colonists in the Batepito Valley, nine miles north of Morelos, founded Colonia San Jose, with new canals, in addition to those of the Babispe. In 1912, Colonia Morelos had in granary over 50,000 bushels of wheat, while the orchards, gardens and alfalfa fields had produced an abundance. These Sonora colonists had 4000 acres of cultivated and fenced lands.

A flour mill was operated, succeeding one that had been destroyed by fire of incendiary origin. The Morelos canal had cost $12,000. Many local industries had been established, a good schoolhouse was in each settlement and no saloons were tolerated. In general, there was good treatment from the national Mexican government, though "local authorities had demands called very oppressive and overbearing."

War came to the western colonies in November, 1911, on the arrival of a band of seventy men under Isidro Escobosa, repulsed at El Tigre and fleeing to Morelos, followed by federal cavalry, who are reported to have been at least as destructive as the bandits. Thereafter was continuous grief for the colonists. In June, 1500 federals were quartered on the streets and in the school buildings at Morelos, with open depredations upon the settlers' personal property, and scandalous conditions from which no appeal was effective. There then was demand for wagons and teamsters to accompany the federals. The settlers sent their horses into secret places in the mountains and thus saved most of them. Much the same conditions were known at Oaxaca.

When it became evident that Mexican conditions were unendurable, the sick and the older people were sent into the United States. August 30, 1912, following news that the rebel Salazar, was marching into Sonora, a large number of women and children were sent northward. Sixty wagons constituted the expedition, carrying 450 people. The journey was through a rough country, in which there was one fatal accident, and in the rainy season, with attendant hardship. At Douglas was cordial reception, with assistance by the United States and by citizens. September 3, still more of the women and children went northward, leaving about 25 men in the colonies, as guards.

Occasional parties kept up connection between the border and the colonies for some time thereafter. A few of the expeditions were captured by the Mexicans and robbed.

The colonies had been entirely abandoned for some time when a Mormon party from Douglas returned on a scouting trip. According to a chronicler of the period:

On arriving at the colonies they found that every house had been looted and everything of value taken, sewing machines and furniture ruthlessly smashed up and lying around as debris, while house organs, which were to be found in nearly every Mormon home, were heaps of kindling wood. The carcasses of dead animals lay about the streets, doors and windows were smashed in, stores gutted and the contents strewn everywhere about, while here and there a cash register or some other modern appliance gave evidence of the hand of prejudice-destroying ignorance.

In October, Consul Dye of Douglas made a formal inspection.

Some of the colonists returned when conditions apparently had bettered, and there is at hand a record of what may be considered to have been the final abandonment. In the first days of May, 1914, at Douglas, 92 Americans from the three Sonora colonies, arrived in 21 wagons, being the last of the colonists. They practically had been ordered out, after having been notified by the American Secretary of State that the protection of their country would not be extended to them. Most of their property was left behind, at the mercy of the Mexican authorities.

Congressional Inquiry

In September, 1912, at El Paso, was an investigation under the terms of a Senate resolution, which sought to find whether the Mexican troubles had been incited by American citizens or corporations. Senator Smith of Michigan was chairman of the committee. At the hearings there was repeated inquiry apparently seeking to demonstrate that the Standard Oil Company, to a degree, was responsible for the Madera revolution. There also was considerable inquiry, apparently hostile, seeking to define ulterior reasons why the Mormons should have chosen Mexico as an abiding place. The investigation covered all parts of Mexico where American interests had suffered, and only incidentally touched the Mormon settlements. There was ample evidence to the effect that the Mormons retained their American citizenship and American customs, that they had lived in amity with the former stable Mexican government, that any troubles they may have had were not due to any actions of their own, but to the desire fo loot on the part of the roaming national and revolutionary soldiery and that their departure was forced and necessary. No especial definition seems to have been given to the exact amount of the loss suffered, but there was agreement that the damage done to these American citizens was very large. At the outbreak of the revolution, according to evidence presented, guarantees had been received by the Mormons from both of the major Mexican factions, but, when these guarantees were referred to, General Salazar sententiously observed, "They are but words."

274

Repopulation of the Mexican Colonies

A few valiant souls returned to the colonies and remained as best they could, forming nuclei for others who have drifted back from time to time, though neither their going nor coming was under direct Church instruction.

Early in 1920, President J. C. Bentley of the Juarez Stake told of the revival of the Mexican missions, and in the latter part of the same year, A. W. Ivins, returning from the Chihuahua colonies, told that 779 colonists were found, approximately one-fifth of the total number of refugees. To a degree their property had been maintained and their orchards kept alive by the few who had remained over the troublous period. The academy at Colonia Juarez had been running some time, with 100 students. He told of the great work of reconstruction that would have to be done, in restoration of fences and homes, and expressed confidence that all now would be well under the more stable government that has been provided in the southern republic.

There was restoration of order in Mexico in 1920 and assumption of an apparently stable political government under President Alvaro Obregon, a Sonora citizen, with whom is associated P. Elias Calles, who had somewhat to do with the Morelos-Oaxaca troubles. Assurances have been given that protection will be extended to all immigrants, the Mormon land titles have been accepted and a fresh movement southward has been started across the border. But there are many, possibly a half of those who fled, who will not return. They have established themselves, mainly in Arizona, under conditions they do not care to leave. So, it is probable, further extension southward of the Church plans of agricultural settlement will be a task that will lie upon the shoulders of a younger generation.

Chapter Twenty-five

𝕸𝖔𝖉𝖊𝖗𝖓 𝕯𝖊𝖛𝖊𝖑𝖔𝖕𝖒𝖊𝖓𝖙

Oases Have Grown in the Desert

The Mormons of Arizona today are not to be considered in the same manner as have been their forebears. The older generation came in pilgrimages, wholly within the faith, sent to break the wilderness for generations to come. These pioneers must be considered in connection with their faith, for through that faith and its supporting Church were they sent on their southward journeyings. Thus it happens that "Mormon settlement" was something apart and distinctive in the general development of Arizona and of the other southwestern sections into which Mormon influences were taken. It has not been sought in this work even to infer that Mormons in anywise had loftier aspirations than were possessed by any other pioneer people of religious and law-abiding sort. However, there must be statement that the Mormons were alone in their idea of extension in concrete agricultural communities. Such communities were founded on well-developed ideals, that had nothing in common with the usual frontier spirit. They contained no drinking places or disorderly resorts and in them rarely were breaches of the peace. Without argument, this could have been accomplished by any other religious organization. Something of the sort has been done by other churches elsewhere in America. But in the Southwest such work of development on a basis of religion was done only by the Mormons.

There was need for the sustaining power of Celestial Grace upon the average desert homestead, where the fervent sun lighted an expanse of dry and unpromising land. The task of reclamation in the earlier days would have been beyond the ability and resources of any colonists not welded into some sort of mutual organization. This welding had been accomplished among the Mormons even before the wagon trains started southward. Thereafter all that was needed was industry, as directed by American intelligence.

Prosperity Has Succeeded Privation

Today the Mormon population of Arizona does not exceed 25,000, within a total population of over 300,000. The relative percentage of strength, however, is larger than the figures indicate, this due, somewhat, to the fact that the trend of Mormon progress still is by way of cultivation of the soil. Of a verity, a family head upon a farm, productive and independent, is of larger value to the community and of more importance therein than is the average city dweller.

The immigrant from Utah who came between 1876 and 1886 no longer has the old ox-bowed wagon. His travel nowadays is by automobile. His log or adobe hut has been replaced by a handsome modern home. His children have had education and have been reared in comfort that never knew lack of food. Most of the Mormon settlements no longer are exclusively Mormon. There has come a time when immigration, by rail, has surrounded and enveloped the foundations established by the pioneers.

To the newer generation this work is addressed especially, though its dedication, of right, is to the men and women who broke the trails and whose vision of the future has been proven true. Many of the pioneers remain and share with their children in the benefits of the civilization that here they helped to plant. The desert wilderness has been broken and in its stead oases are expanding, oases filled with a population proud of its Americanism, prosperous through varied industry and blessed with consideration for the rights of the neighbor.

BIBLIOGRAPHY

Bancroft, Hubert Howe,	History of Arizona and New Mexico, History of Nevada, History of California: San Francisco, 1889.
Bartlett, John R.,	Personal Narrative: Appleton, 1854.
Beadle, S. H.,	Western Wilds: Jones Bros., Cincinnati, 1878.
Church Chronology,	Deseret News, Salt Lake.
Church Historian's Office,	Mss. data of Arizona Stakes and Wards.
Cooke, Col. P. St. George,	Conquest of New Mexico and California: Putnam's Sons, New York, 1878.
Dellenbaugh, F. S.,	Breaking the Wilderness: Putnam's Sons, 1908. The Romance of the Colorado River: 1909. A Canyon Voyage, New York, 1908.
Donaldson, Thomas,	Moqui Pueblo Indians: Census Bureau, 1893.
Englehardt, Rev. Zephyrin,	Missions of California: 4 vols., Barry Co., San Francisco, 1905-15.
Farish, Thos. E.,	History of Arizona: 8 vols., Filmer Co., San Francisco, 1915-18.
Fish, Joseph,	Mss. History of Arizona.
Gregory, Herbert,	The Navajo Country: Interior Dept., 1916.
Hamblin, Jacob,	Personal Narrative, by Little: Deseret News, 1909.
Hinton, R. J.,	Handbook to Arizona: Payot-Upham, San Francisco, 1878.
Hodge, F. W.,	Handbook of the American Indians: Bureau of American Ethnology.
James, Dr. Geo. Wharton,	In and Around the Grand Canyon: Little-Brown Co., Boston, 1900.
Jenson, Andrew,	Biographical Encyclopedia: 3 vols. Deseret News, 1900, 1910, 1920.
Jones, D. W.,	Forty Years Among the Indians: Salt Lake, 1890.
Layton, Christopher,	Autobiography (Mrs. Selina L. Phillips, John Q. Cannon): Deseret News, 1911.
McClintock, Jas. H.,	History of Arizona: 2 vols., Clarke Co., Chicago, 1916.

279

Munk, Dr. J. A.,	Arizona Sketches: Grafton Press, N. Y., 1905.
Powell, J. W.,	Canyons of the Colorado: Flood-Vincent, Meadville, Penn., 1895.
Roberts, B. H.,	History of the Mormon Church: Salt Lake.
Standage, Henry,	Mss. Story of Mormon Battalion.
Twitchell, Ralph W.,	Leading Facts of New Mexican History: Torch Press, Cedar Rapids, Ia., 1911.
Tyler, Daniel,	Mormon Battalion: Salt Lake, 1881.
Whitney, Orson F.,	History of Utah: 3 vols., Geo. Q. Cannon Co., Salt Lake, 1892.

MORMON SETTLEMENT PLACE NAMES

(Capital letters indicate present settlement names)
See map of Arizona, page x.

ADAIR, Fools Hollow—2½ m. w. of Showlow
ALGODON, Lebanon—7 m. se. of Thatcher
ALMA, Stringtown—about 1 m. w. of Mesa
Allen City, Allen Camp, Cumorah, ST. JOSEPH—Little Colorado settlement
ALPINE, Frisco, Bush Valley—60 m. se. of St. Johns
Apache Springs—at Forest Dale
Apache Springs—sw. of Pinetop, Cooley's last ranch
Amity and Omer, Union, EAGAR—upper Round Valley
Arivaipa Canyon—western route Gila Valley to San Pedro
ARTESIA—in Gila Valley, about 18 m. se. of Thatcher
ASHURST, Redlands, Cork—about 15 m. nw. of Thatcher

Badger Creek—on Mormon wagon road 10 m. w. of Lee's Ferry
Bagley, Walker, TAYLOR—3 m. s. of Snowflake
Ballenger, Brigham City—was Little Colorado town
Beaver Dams, LITTLEFIELD, Millersburg—nw. corner of State
Beaver Ranch, Woolf Ranch, Lone Pine Crossing, Reidhead—12 m. s. of Snowflake
Berardo, Horsehead Crossing, HOLBROOK—on Little Colorado
Binghampton—6 m. n. of Tucson, near Ft. Lowell
Bisbee—in se. Arizona, near Mexican border
Bitter Springs—on Mormon road, 18 m. s. of Lee's Ferry
Black Falls—on Little Colorado, 56 m. s. of Moen Copie
BLUEWATER—in New Mexico on rr. 107 m. w. of Albuquerque
Bonelli's, STONE'S FERRY—near mouth of Virgin r.
Brigham City, Ballenger—was Little Colorado r. settlement
Buckskin Mountains—between Kanab and Colorado r.
BUNKERVILLE—Muddy settlement, 45 m. sw. of St. George
Burke Tanks—On road Pleasant Valley to Grand Falls
BRYCE—in Gila Valley, 2 m. n. of Pima
Bush Valley, Frisco, ALPINE—60 m. se. of St. Johns

CALLVILLE, Call's Landing—16 m. w. of mouth of Virgin r.
CEDAR RIDGE—on Mormon road, 33 m. s. of Lee's Ferry
Cedar Ridge—10 m. ne. of Pleasant Valley
Cedar Springs—Barney & Norton Double "N" ranch, 30 m. sw. of Thatcher

CENTRAL—3 m. w. of Thatcher, in Gila Valley
CHANDLER—8 m. s. of Mesa
Clark's Ranch—Just off Ft. Apache road, near Showlow
Clay Springs—Snowflake Stake
Cluff's Cienega—6 m. e. of Pinetop, embraces new town of Cooley
COLTER—17 m. se. of Springerville
Columbine—near top of Mt. Graham, Graham Co.
COOLEY—at lumber camp near Pinetop, rr. terminus
Cooley's ranch—At Showlow—C. E. Cooley's first ranch
Cooley's ranch—where C. E. Cooley died, sw. of Pinetop
Cumorah, Allen's Camp, ST. JOSEPH—Little Colorado settlement
CONCHO, Erastus—about half way between Snowflake and St. Johns
Cork, Redlands, ASHURST—15 m. nw. of Thatcher
Crossing of the Fathers, Vado de los Padres, El Vado, Ute Crossing,
    Ute Ford—Colorado river crossing just n. of Utah line
Curtis, EDEN—about 15 m. nw. of Thatcher, in Gila Valley

DOUGLAS—near Mexican border, se. Arizona

EAGAR, Round Valley—2 m. s. of Springerville
Eagle Valley—upper end of Muddy Valley
Eastern Arizona Stake—1878.   Included wards e. of Holbrook in
    ne. Arizona
East Pinedale, PINEDALE—15 m. sw. of Snowflake
East Verde—Mazatzal City—was near Payson, in n. Tonto Basin
EDEN, Curtis—about 15 m. nw. of Thatcher in Gila Valley
Ellsworth—was 1¾ m. s. of Showlow
Emery—w. of Fort Thomas in Gila Valley
Enterprise—was near San Jose, 15 m. e. of Thatcher
Erastus, CONCHO—about half way between Snowflake and St. Johns
Eureka Springs—in Arivaipa Valley about 25 m. sw. of Thatcher

Fairview, LAKESIDE, Woodland—about 30 m. s. of Snowflake
Fairview, Matthews, GLENBAR—10 m. nw. of Thatcher in Gila
    Valley
Fools Hollow, ADAIR—in ravine 2½ m. w. of Showlow
Forest Dale—8 m. sw. of Showlow
FORT DEFIANCE—near N. M. line 30 m. n. of Santa Fe rr.
Fort Milligan—was 1 m. w. of present Eagar
Fort Moroni, Fort Rickerson—7 m. nw. of Flagstaff in LeRoux Flat
Fort Thomas—in Gila Valley, 22 m. nw. of Thatcher
Fort Utah, Utahville, Jonesville, LEHI—3 m. ne. of Mesa
FRANKLIN—near N. M. line 50 m. e. of Thatcher
FREDONIA, Hardscrabble—3 m. s. of Utah line, 8 m. s. of Kanab
Frisco, ALPINE, Bush Valley—near N. M. line 60 m. se. of St. Johns

Gila Valley—in Graham Co., in se. Arizona
GILBERT—6 m. se. of Mesa
GLENBAR, Fairview, Matthews—10 m. w. of Thatcher in Gila Valley
GLOBE—80 m. nw. of Thatcher
GRAHAM—across the Gila river n. of Thatcher
Grand Falls—on Little Colorado, 5 m. below ford and 47 m. below
    Winslow
Grand Wash—leads s. of St. George into Colorado r.
Grant, Heber, LUNA—across N. M. line, 40 m. se. of Springerville
GREER—15 m. sw. of Eagar

HARDYVILLE—landing on Colorado, about 90 m. s. of Callville
Hayden, Zenos, Mesaville, MESA—Headquarters of Maricopa Stake, 16 m. e. of Phoenix
HAYDEN—35 m. s. of Globe
Hayden's Ferry, San Pablo, TEMPE—9 m. e. of Phoenix
Heber, Grant, LUNA—across N. M. line, 40 m. se. of Springerville
HEBER—near Wilford, 50 m. sw. of Holbrook
HEREFORD—on San Pedro, 33 m. s. of St. David
HOLBROOK, Horsehead Crossing, Berardo—on Little Colorado
Horsehead Crossing, Berardo, HOLBROOK—on Little Colorado
House Rock Springs—on Mormon road, 38 m. sw. of Lee's Ferry
HUBBARD—6 m. nw. of Thatcher
HUNT—on Little Colorado, 17 m. nw. of St. Johns

Jacob's Pools—on Mormon road, 27 m. sw. of Lee's Ferry
JOHNSON'S—on Mormon road, 14 m. ne. of Kanab, n. of Utah line
Johnsonville, Nephi—was successor of Tempe ward, 3 m. w. of Mesa
Jonesville, Utahville, Ft. Utah, LEHI—3 m. ne. of Mesa
Joppa—in Snowflake Stake
Junction (City), RIOVILLE—at junction of Muddy r. with Virgin r.
Juniper, LINDEN—8 m. w. of Showlow

KANAB—just n. of Utah line, about 65 m. e. of St. George

LAKESIDE, Fairview, Woodland—ward 30 m. s. of Snowflake
LAVEEN—on Salt River, 12 m. sw. of Phoenix
LAYTON—3 m. e. of Thatcher
Lebanon, ALGODON—in cotton district, 7 m. se. of Thatcher
Lee Valley—15 m. sw. of Eagar
LEE'S FERRY, Lonely Dell—on Colorado r., 18 m. s. of Utah line
LEHI, Jonesville, Utahville, Ft. Utah—ward 3 m. ne. of Mesa
LeRoux Springs and Flat—about 7 m. nw. of Flagstaff, location of Ft. Moroni
Limestone Tanks—on Mormon road, 27 m. s. of Lee's Ferry
LINDEN, Juniper—8 m. w. of Showlow
Little Colorado Stake—first Arizona Stake, embraced Little Colorado settlements
LITTLEFIELD, Beaver Dams, Millersburg—on Virgin r., 3 m. e. of Nevada line
LOGAN, West Point—s. of Muddy r., 15 m. w. of St. Joseph
Lonely Dell, LEE'S FERRY—crossing on Colorado r., 18 m. s. of Utah line
Lone Pine, Beaver ranch, Woolf ranch, Reidhead—12 m. s. of Snowflake
LUNA (Valley), Grant, Heber—across N. M. line, 40 m. se. of Springerville

Macdonald—on San Pedro, 5 m. s. of St. David
MARICOPA STAKE—Headquarters at Mesa
Matthews, Fairview, GLENBAR—10 m. nw. of Thatcher in Gila Valley
Mazatzal City—in Tonto Basin, on East Verde r.
McClellan Tanks—on Mormon road, about 35 m. s. of Lee's Ferry
Meadows—on Little Colorado r., 8 m. nw. of St. Johns
MESA, Hayden, Zenos, Mesaville—Maricopa Stake Headquarters, 16 m. e. of Phoenix

MESQUITE—on n. side of Virgin r., 1 m. w. of Nevada line
MIAMI—6 m. w. of Globe, 86 m. nw. of Thatcher
Milligan Fort—was 1 m. w. of present Eagar
Millersburg, Beaver Dams, LITTLEFIELD—on Virgin r., nw. corner
  of Arizona
Millville—was on Mogollon plateau, 35 m. s. of Flagstaff
Mill Point—6 m. nw. of St. Thomas on Muddy r.
Miramonte—9 m. w. of Benson
Moaby, Moa Ave, Moen Abi, Moanabby—7 m. sw. of Tuba, 60 m.
  s. of Lee's Ferry
MOCCASIN SPRINGS—3 m. n. of Pipe Springs
MOEN COPIE—was mission headquarters, 2 m. s. of Tuba
Mohave Spring—in Moen Copie wash, s. of Tuba
Mormon Dairy—near Mormon Lake, belonged to Sunset and Brigham
  City
Mormon Lake—about 28 m. se. of Flagstaff, 50 m. w. of Sunset
Mormon Road—west extension of Spanish Trail, St. George to Los
  Angeles
Mormon Road—wagon road from Lee's Ferry to Little Colorado r.
Mormon Range—at head of Muddy Valley, now se. Nevada
Mormon Flat—on Apache Trail, Phoenix to Globe, 20 m. ne. of Mesa
Mormon Fort—n. of Las Vegas, in Nevada
Mortensen, Percheron, East Pinedale—Just e. of Pinedale settlement
Mt. Carmel, Winsor—United Order ward in Long Valley n. of Kanab,
  Utah
Mt. Trumbull—in Uinkarat Mnts., 30 m. w. of mouth of Kanab Wash
Mt. Turnbull—37 m. nw. of Thatcher
Muddy, river and valley, in present Nevada, near nw. corner of Arizona
Musha Springs—just s. of Tuba, townsite of Tuba City, n. of Moen
  Copie

Navajo, Savoia, RAMAH—in N. M., 22 m. n. of Zuni, 80 m. ne. of
  St. Johns
Navajo Spring—on Mormon road, 8 m. s. of Lee's Ferry
Navajo Wells—16 m. e. of Kanab, in Utah, foot of Buckskin mts.
Nephi, Johnsonville—was successor of Tempe ward, 3 m. w. of Mesa
NUTRIOSO—17 m. se. of Springerville

Obed—was on Little Colorado r., 3 m. sw., across river, from St. Joseph
Omer and Amity, Union, EAGAR—in lower Round Valley, Apache Co.
OVERTON, Patterson's Ranch—8 m. nw. of St. Thomas, Nevada
ORAIBI—Indian village, about 40 m. se. of Moen Copie
Orderville—was United Order ward in Long Valley, n. of Kanab, in
  Utah

PAPAGO—Indian ward on both sides of Salt r., just nw. of Mesa.
Paria River—enters Colorado r. from n., just above Lee's Ferry
Patterson's Ranch, OVERTON—8 m. nw. of St. Thomas, Nevada
PAYSON—in upper Tonto Basin, 75 m. w. of Showlow
Peach Springs—10 m. ne. of station of same name on Santa Fe, 58
  m. w. of Ash Fork
Pearce's Ferry—Colorado r. crossing at mouth of Grand Wash
Penrod, PINETOP—12 m. se. of Showlow
Percheron, Mortensen, PINEDALE—15½ m. w. of Showlow
PHOENIX—Capital of Arizona, in Salt River Valley

PIMA, Smithville—in Gila Valley, 6 m. nw. of Thatcher
PINE—on Pine Creek, Tonto Basin, 70 m. w. of n. of Roosevelt dam
PINEDALE, Percheron, Mortensen—15½ m. w. of Showlow
Pine Springs—near Pine Creek in Tonto Basin
PINETOP, Penrod—12 m. se. of Showlow
PIPE SPRINGS, Winsor Castle—on Mormon road, 20 m. sw. of
   Kanab
PLEASANTON—in Williams Valley, N. M., 36 m. s. of Luna Valley
PLEASANT VALLEY—location of sawmill and dairy, 25 m. se. of
   Flagstaff
POMERENE—4 m. n. and e. of Benson

RAMAH, Navajo, Savoia—in N. M., 80 m. ne. of St. Johns
RAY—25 m. sw. of Globe
Redlands, ASHURST, Cork—about 15 m. nw. of Thatcher
REIDHEAD, Beaver Ranch, Woolf Crossing, Lone Pine Crossing—
   10 m. s. of Taylor
RICHVILLE, Walnut Grove, 18 m. s. of St. Johns
RIOVILLE, Junction (City)—junction of Muddy r. with Virgin r.
Round Valley, EAGAR—35 m. s. of St. Johns

ST. JOHNS, Salem—St. Johns Stake hdqrs., 60 m. se. of Holbrook
ST. JOHNS STAKE—Embraces eastern Arizona, n. of Graham Co.
ST. DAVID—on San Pedro r., 7 m. se. of Benson in se. Arizona
ST. JOSEPH—5 m. n. of Overton, n. side of Muddy r., now in Nevada
ST. JOSEPH, Allen Camp, Cumorah—on Little Colorado r., 10 m.
   w. of Holbrook
ST. JOSEPH STAKE—embraces se. Arizona, hdqrs. at Thatcher
ST. THOMAS—w. side of Muddy, 1¾ m. above junction with Virgin r.
SAFFORD—3 m. e. of Thatcher
Salem, ST. JOHNS—St. Johns Stake hdqrs., 60 m. se. of Holbrook
Salt Lake—33 m. e. of St. Johns; is in New Mexico
Salt Mountains—Salt deposits on Virgin r., below St. Thomas
San Francisco Mountains—n. of Flagstaff
SAN BERNARDINO, Cal.—about 50 m. e. of Los Angeles
San Bernardino Ranch—in extreme se. corner of Arizona
San Pablo, Hayden's Ferry, TEMPE—9 m. e. of Phoenix
San Pedro—river and valley in se. Arizona
Savoia, Navajo, RAMAH—Savoia was 6 m. e. of present Ramah
SHOWLOW—22 m. s. of Snowflake
SHUMWAY—ward on Silver creek, 7 m. s. of Snowflake
Simonsville—was mill location, 6 m. nw. of St. Thomas
Smithville, PIMA—6 m. nw. of Thatcher, once St. Joseph Stake hdqrs.
SNOWFLAKE—Snowflake Stake hdqrs., 30 m. s. of Holbrook
SNOWFLAKE STAKE—embraces practically Navajo County
Soap Creek (Springs)—on Mormon road, 16 m. sw. of Lee's Ferry
SOLOMONVILLE—e. end of Gila Valley
SPRINGERVILLE—35 m. se. of St. Johns
Stinson Valley—former name of valley in which Snowflake is located
STONE'S FERRY, Bonelli's—Colorado r. crossing, w. of mouth of
   Virgin r.
Strawberry Valley—in n. Tonto Basin
Sulphur Springs Valley—in se. Arizona
Sunset, Sunset Crossing—Little Colorado r. settlement, 25 m. w. of
   St. Joseph

Sunset Sawmill—was 7 m. s. of Mormon Dairy
Surprise Valley—10 m. nw. of Hunt, along Surprise Creek, 27 m. nw. of St. Johns
Surprise Valley—near mouth of Kanab Canyon

Taylor—was settlement across Colorado r., 3 m. w. of St. Joseph
TAYLOR, Bagley, Walker—on Silver Creek, 3 m. s. of Snowflake
TEMPE, San Pablo, Hayden's Ferry—9 m. e. of Phoenix
Tenney's Camp, WOODRUFF—on Little Colorado r., 12 m. ne. of Holbrook
THATCHER—St. Joseph Stake hdqrs., in Gila Valley
Tonto Basin—in central Arizona
TUBA (CITY)—on Mormon road, 60 m. se. of Lee's Ferry
TUBAC—on Santa Cruz r., 42 m. s. of Tucson
Turkey Tanks—about 10 m. ne. of Flagstaff

Union, Omer, Amity, EAGAR—ward embraced Round Valley settlements
Utahville, Fort Utah, LEHI, Jonesville—3 m. ne. of Mesa
Ute Ford, Vado de los Padres, CROSSING OF THE FATHERS—on Colorado r., just n. of Arizona line

Vermilion Cliffs—w. of Colorado r., extending into both Arizona and Utah
VERNON—ward includes Concho and Hunt branches
VIRDEN—just over New Mexico line on Gila r., 8 m. ne. of Franklin

Walker, Bagley, TAYLOR—on Silver Creek, 3 m. s. of Snowflake
Walnut Grove, RICHVILLE—18 m. s. of St. Johns on Little Colorado r.
West Point, LOGAN—s. of Muddy r., 15 m. w. of St. Joseph, Nevada
Whitewater—22 m. e. of Tombstone.
Wilford—6 m. sw. of Heber, 56 m. sw. of Holbrook
Williams Valley—in New Mexico, 36 m. s. of Luna Valley
Willow Springs—on Mormon road, 7 m. nw. of Tuba
Winsor, Mt. Carmel—was United Order ward in Long Valley n. of Kanab
Winsor Castle, PIPE SPRINGS—on Mormon road, 20 m. sw. of Kanab
WOODRUFF, Tenney's Camp—ward on Little Colorado r., 12 m. se. of Holbrook
Woolf Crossing, ranch, Beaver ranch, Lone Pine, Reidhead—10 m. s. of Taylor
Woodland, Fairview, LAKESIDE—3 m. nw. of Pinetop

Zenos, Hayden, Mesaville, MESA—16 m. e. of Phoenix

CHRONOLOGY OF LEADING EVENTS

1846—Feb. 4, Chas. Shumway first to cross Mississippi in exodus from Nauvoo; Feb. 4, "Brooklyn" sailed from New York, with 235 L. D. S.; July 29, arr. San Francisco; July 20, Mormon Battalion left Council Bluffs; Aug. 1, arr. Ft. Leavenworth; 12, left Leavenworth; 23, Col. Allen died; Oct. 9, 1st detachment at Santa Fe; 13, Cooke in command; Sept. 16, families sent to Pueblo; Oct. 19, left Sant Fe; Nov. 21, turned to west; 28, at summit Rockies; Dec. 18, at Tucson; 22, arr. Pima villages.

1847—Jan. 8, Battalion at mouth of Gila; 10, crossed Colorado r.; 29, arr. near San Diego; July 16, discharged; 24, Pres. Young and Utah pioneers reached Salt Lake Valley.

1848—Jan. 24, gold discovered at Sutter's Fort, Cal.

1851—June, Lyman and Rich and about 500 from Utah located San Bernardino, Cal.; fall, Mormons located at Tubac.

1853—First missionaries in Las Vegas district.

1855—May 10, 30 missionaries left Salt Lake for Las Vegas.

1857—Ira Hatch and Dudley Leavitt among Paiutes; Hamblin sees Ives steamer "Explorer;" Sept. 11, Mountain Meadows massacre.

1858—Jan., Ira Hatch sent to Muddy; Feb., Col. Kane treaty with Paiutes; San Bernardino vacated; spring, Hamblin to Colorado r.; first trip across Colorado r.

1859—Oct., Hamblin to Hopi.

1860—Oct., Hamblin to Hopi; Nov. 2, Geo. A. Smith, Jr., killed by Indians near Tuba.

1862—Nov., Hamblin to Hopi.

1863—Feb. 24, Arizona Territory organized from New Mexico; Mar. 18, Hamblin to Hopi; Pipe Springs located by Dr. J. M. Whitmore.

1864—Mar., Hamblin party parleys with Navajos; Moccasin Springs settled; United Order established in Brigham City, Utah, by Lorenzo Snow; Oct., Anson Call directed to establish Colorado r. port, Beaver Dams settled by Henry W. Miller; Dec. 2, Call party at site of Call's landing; 18, work begun at Call's Landing.

1865—Jan. 8, first settlers at St. Thomas on Muddy r., settlement of St. Joseph on Muddy r.; settlement on Paria Creek; Dec., Muddy section organized as Pah-ute County, Arizona.

287

1866—Jan. 8, Whitmore and McIntire killed by Indians near Pipe Springs; June 4, conference with Indians on Muddy r.; Moccasin vacated through Indian troubles; Nov., steamer "Esmeralda" on upper Colorado r.

1867—Jan. 18, Pah-ute county claimed by Nevada; spring, floods caused abandonment of Beaver Dams; Oct. 1, county seat of Pah-ute moved from Callville to St. Thomas.

1868—Feb. 10, trouble with Paiutes on Muddy r.; August 18, destructive fire at St. Joseph; Nov. 1, Andrew S. Gibbons and O. D. Gass started from Callville to Ft. Yuma by boat.

1869—Feb. 8, Junction City (Rioville) established; Feb. 15, Utah organized Rio Virgen County, including Muddy settlements; May 29, Powell started first trip down Canyon; June 12, Davidson family died of thirst on desert near Muddy r.; June 16, Callville abandoned; August, 3 of Powell's men killed by Indians; 29, Powell ended trip below Canyon; Oct., Hamblin at Hopi.

1870—Mar., Brigham Young party visited Muddy settlements; June 14, settlement on Kanab Creek; Sept., Hamblin to Mt. Trumbull with J. W. Powell; Nov. 5, Hamblin peace talk with Navajos at Ft. Defiance; took Chief Tuba to Utah; Dec., determination to abandon Muddy settlements

1871—Spring, abandonment Muddy district; Pah-ute County abolished by Arizona Territory; Aug., Hamblin, with Powell, on second Colorado r. trip; Moccasin Springs re-settled; Moen Copie made mission post;

1872—John D. Lee located at mouth of Paria; June 28, J. H. Beadle at Lee's Ferry.

1873—Mar. 8, Brigham Young instructed Arizona colonists in Salt Lake; spring, L. W. Roundy and Hamblin at Moen Copie; May 1, H. D. Haight party left Utah for Little Colorado Valley; May 22, Haight party on Little Colorado r.; June 30, Haight party turned back.

1874—Jan., Hamblin to Hopi to prevent war; Aug., Hamblin to Ft. Defiance on peace mission.

1875—Feb. 20, Orderville established; Sept. 16, D. W. Jones exploration party left Salt Lake; Oct. 27, Jones party crossed Colorado r.; 30, Jas. S. Brown exploring party left Salt Lake; Dec. 4, Brown party at Moen Copie; 14, Jones party at Tucson.

1876—Jan., Jones party in Mexico; Feb. 3, Little Colorado settlers left Salt Lake; Mar. 23, advance company at Sunset; 24-31, locations of Allen City, Obed, Sunset, Ballenger; 28, work commenced on St. Joseph dam; Apr., location of Tenney's (Woodruff) Camp, on Little Colorado r.; 17, United Order established on Little Colorado r.; Daniel H. Wells and party on Little Colorado r.; May, Boston party passed Little Colorado settlements; June 24, L. W. Roundy drowned in Colorado r.; 27, Obed moved to new location; June, D. W. Jones party returns to Utah; first L. D. S. settlers on Showlow Creek; July 17, exploration of Tonto Basin; 17, first child born in Allen City; 19, Allen City dam washed away; Aug., Lorenzo H. Hatch located at Savoia; Oct. 18, Pratt-Stewart party left Utah for Arizona; Nov. 7, Mt. Trumbull sawmill re-established near Mormon Lake; Dec. 23, Pratt party reached Phoenix; Dec., Harrison Pearce established ferry at mouth of Grand Wash; Hamblin located new route to Sunset, via Grand Wash.

1877—Jan. 6, Jones settlement party organized at St. George by Brigham Young, Bunkerville located, first L. D. S. school in Arizona, at Obed; 17, Jones party left St. George; Mar. 6, arr. Salt River, founded Lehi; Mar. 23, J. D. Lee executed; May 20, first Indian baptism on Salt r.; Aug., Merrill company left Lehi; 29, death of Brigham Young,| Hamblin at Hopi; Sept. 14, start of Idaho-Salt Lake party that founded Mesa; 14, Merrill company on San Pedro r.; Nov. 12, Arkansas L. D. S. arr. on Little Colorado r.; 29, Merrill party location on San Pedro r.

1878—Jan., C. I. Robson and others selected Mesa location; 20, Colorado r. frozen over at Lee's Ferry; 22, location of Taylor on Little Colorado r.; 23, James Pearce first L. D. S. settler on Silver Creek; 27, Little Colorado Stake organized, name of Ballenger changed to Brigham City, name of Allen changed to St. Joseph; Feb. 5, Robson party at Fort Utah; 9, naming of Woodruff; 18, settlers at Forest Dale; May 15, first L. D. S. locations in Tonto Basin; July 21, Flake and Kartchner moved the site of Snowflake; Sept.-Dec., Erastus Snow and party travel in Arizona; Sept. 27, Erastus Snow party located and named Snowflake, selected Jesse N. Smith as President Eastern Arizona Stake; Oct. 26, first settlers on Mesa townsite; Dec., re-settlement of Beaver Dams.

1879—Jan. 16, arr. at Snowflake of Jesse N. Smith; Feb., L. D. S. explorers at Smithville on Gila r.; Mar., L. D. S. settlement in Concho; Apr. 8, Showlow company located at Smithville; Completion of J. W. Young woolen factory at Moen Copie; settlement at Shumway; first session of court in Apache County; Nov. 16, purchase of Barth claims at St. Johns.

1880—Mar. 29, St. Johns townsite selected by Wilford Woodruff; Sept. 19, re-location of St. Johns townsite; Sept. 26, naming of Alpine; fall, re-settlement of Overton; Oct. 6, arr. at St. Johns of D. K. Udall; Nov., land at Graham on Gila r. bought by Brigham City settlers; Dec., settlement of Matthews on Gila r.

1881—Jan., location at Graham; Mar., settlement at Curtis (Eden), trouble with Indians; location of Holbrook; name of Smithville changed to Pima.

1882—Jan. 28, re-location of Holbrook townsite; June 1, N. B. Robinson killed by Indians, Indian troubles in mountain settlements; June 24, N. C. Tenney killed at St. Johns; July, establishment of first paper in Apache County; July 19, L. D. S. settlement at Tempe; Dec. 10, Maricopa Stake organized; Dec. 25, naming of Thatcher.

1883—Jan. 4, location party in Mexico from St. David; 13, settlement of Layton; Feb. 25, establishment of St. Joseph Stake at St.

David; spring, Forest Dale abandoned; Aug. 25, Wilford and Heber organized; Nov., naming of Lehi.

1884—Mar., land jumping in St. Johns; Nov., Young and Grant party visit Yaqui Indian country.

1885—Feb. 9, departure of first L. D. S. Mexican colony; Nov.-Dec., Indian depredations in Gila Valley; Dec. 1, killing of Lorenzo and Seth Wright on Gila r.; Wilford abandoned.

1886—Feb. 9, Andrew S. Gibbons died at St. Johns; Aug. 31, death of Jacob Hamblin at Pleasanton; Sept. 8, Isaac C. Haight died at Thatcher.

1887—Jan. 24, first donation to Arizona temple; May 3, earthquake at St. David; Fredonia settled; July 24, St. Johns Stake organized; Dec. 4, C. I. Robson president of Maricopa Stake; Dec. 18, Snowflake Stake organized.

1889—Jan. 14, St. Johns Stake Academy established; 21, Snowflake Academy established; Apr. 2, Brigham Young Jr., and Jesse N. Smith purchased Little Colorado Valley lands in New York; May 11, Wham robbery, near Ft. Grant.

1890—Feb., Great floods on Little Colorado r. and Silver Creek.

1891—Feb., large damage done by Salt r. floods.

1892—June 20, Lot Smith killed by Indians near Tuba City; July 3-4, general conference of Arizona Stakes at Pinetop; Dec. 8, Chas. L. Flake killed at Snowflake.

1893—Feb. 19, artesian flow struck at St. David.

1894—Feb. 24, C. I. Robson died at Mesa; May 10, C. R. Hakes president of Maricopa Stake.

1898—Jan. 29, St. Joseph Stake reorganized under Andrew Kimball; May 21, death of Chas. Shumway; Sept. 1, St. Joseph Stake Academy opened at Thatcher.

1903—Feb., Tuba settlers sell to Indian Bureau.

1904—Sept. 15, death of P. C. Merrill.

1905—May 1, breaking of St. Johns reservoir.

1906—June 5, death of Jesse N. Smith.

TRAGEDIES OF THE FRONTIER

It is notable that few were the Mormons who have met untimely death by violence in the Southwest. It is believed that the following brief record is, very nearly, complete:

George A. Smith, Jr.—Nov. 2, 1860. Killed by Navajos near Tuba City. See p. 66.

Dr. J. M. Whitmore and Robert McIntire—Jan. 8, 1866. Killed by Navajos near Pipe Springs. See p. 72.

Elijah Averett—Jan. 1866. Killed by Navajos near Paria Creek. Averett had been with the Capt. James Andrus expedition (see p. 72) after the Whitmore-McIntire murderers and had been sent back, with a companion, with dispatches from about the Crossing of the Fathers. He was killed on this return journey and his companion wounded.

Joseph Berry, Robert Berry and the latter's wife, Isabella—April 2, 1866. Killed by Paiutes at Cedar Knoll near Short Creek, west of Pipe Springs. The three were in a wagon and had attempted to escape by running their horses across country, but the Indians cut them off. They fought for their lives and one dead Indian was found near their bodies. In the woman's body was a circle of arrows.

Joseph Davidson, wife and son—June 12, 1869. Perished of thirst on Southern Nevada desert, in Muddy Valley section. See p. 119-20.

Lorenzo W. Roundy—May 24, 1876. Drowned in Colorado River. See p. 87.

Nathan B. Robinson—June 1, 1882. Killed by Apaches near Reidhead. See p. 172.

Nathan C. Tenney—June 24, 1882. Unintentionally shot by Mexicans in course of riot at St. Johns. See p. 181.

Jacob S. Ferrin—July 19, 1882. Killed by Apaches 12 miles east of San Carlos. See p. 253.

Mrs. W. N. Fife—Sept. 11, 1884. Murdered at her home in the Sulphur Springs Valley. She had given a Mexican dinner and was rewarded by a shot in the back. A 13-year-old daughter was saved by the timely arrival of a Mexican employe. The murderer, only known as Jesus, was captured the following day by a posse of settlers and, after full determination of guilt, was hanged to a tree. The murderer's skull now is in possession of Dr. Ezra Rich of Ogden, Utah.

Lorenzo and Seth Wright—Dec. 1, 1885. Ambushed by Apaches in Gila Valley. See p. 254.

Frank Thurston—May 23, 1886. Killed by Apaches six miles west of Pima. See p. 254.

Lot Smith—June 20, 1892. Killed by Navajos near Tuba. See p. 159-60.

Chas. L. Flake—Dec. 8, 1892. Killed by fugitive criminal at Snowflake. See p. 165.

Horatio Merrill and 14-year-old daughter, Eliza—Dec. 3, 1895. Killed by Apaches at Ash Springs, 30 miles east of Pima. This crime has been charged to the infamous Apache Kid.

Isaac Benj. Jones—May 12, 1897. Killed at El Dorado Canyon, near the Colorado River. While freighting ore to a mill, he was ambushed and shot from his wagon by a Paiute, Avote, who murdered several other whites before being run down and killed by Indians on Cottonwood Island, where he had taken refuge.

John Bleak—Jan. 26, 1899. Killed by Mexicans, near Hackberry, Mohave County. The body was found with many knife thrusts, with indications of a desperate resistance of two assailants.

Frank Lesueur and Augustus Andrew Gibbons—Mar. 27, 1900. Killed by outlaws near Navajo, eastern Apache County. They had been deserted by six Mexican members of a posse trailing American cattle thieves, who were fleeing northward from near St. Johns, and were ambushed in a mountain canyon. Lesueur was killed instantly by a shot in the forehead and Gibbons, already shot through the body, was killed by a shot in the head at very short range. The murderers were not apprehended.

Wm. T. Maxwell—1901. Killed by outlaws near Nutrioso. He was the son of a Mormon Battalion member.

Wm. W. Berry—Dec. 22, 1903. Murdered in Tonto Basin. John and Zach Booth, goat owners, were arrested for the crime. The latter was hanged and the former released after disagreement of the jury. The crime also embraced the murder of a 16-year-old boy, Juan Vigil, son of a herder. Berry at the time was in charge of a band of sheep.

Hyrum Smith Peterson—Nov. 12, 1913. Killed near Mesa. Peterson, city marshal, was shot down by thieves whom he was trying to arrest.

Frank McBride and Martin Kempton—Feb. 10, 1918. Killed 60 miles west of Pima. McBride was sheriff of Graham County and Kempton was deputy. The two sought arrest of the Powers brothers and Sisson, draft evaders, who were in a cabin in the Galiuro Mountains. With them was killed another deputy, Kane Wootan. In a following special session of the Legislature, the families of the three were given $17,500, to be invested for their benefit.

KILLED BY INDIANS

1—Geo. A. Smith, Jr.   2—Dr. Jas. M. Whitmore
3—Seth Wright 4—Jacob Ferrin 5—Eliza Merrill
6—Diana Davis Fife   7—Lorenzo Wright

KILLED BY OUTLAWS

1—Nathan C. Tenney   2—Chas. L. Flake   3—Frank Lesueur
4—Augustus Andrew Gibbons   5—Wm. Wiley Berry
6—Hyrum S. Peterson   7—R. Franklin McBride   8—Martin Kempton

INDEX

See Chronology 287-90, Mormon Settlement Place Names 281-86

A

Adair—Named for early resident 36
Adair, Samuel N.—Photo. 84
Adair, Wesley—Battalion member 36, photo. 21
Agriculture—Mormon pioneers in 2, first in N. Ariz. 117
Allen, Lt.-Col. Jas.—Commander Battalion 10, died 11
Allen, Rufus C.—Battalion member 36, to S. America 55, in Las Vegas section 106
Allen, W. C.—Heads L. Colorado party 138, photo. 188
Alma—Est. 218
Allred, Mrs. R. W.—With husband on Battalion march 36, photo. 29
Allred, Reuben W.—Battalion member 36, photo. 29
Alpine—Burial place of Jacob Hamblin 88, 187, est. 186
Ancient Races—Canal at Mesa 213-14, in Arizona 224-28, canals of, 213-14, 225-28, in Gila Valley 241
Andrus, Capt. Jas.—Led party against Indians 72
Apaches—Encroachments on Forest Dale 170-171, attack on Col. Carr's command 172, attack on Camp Apache 194-95, experiences with in Gila Valley 250-56, Chiricahua outbreaks 250-53, murders in Gila Valley 252-53
Arkansas Immigrants—At Taylor 148, on L. Colorado 151-52
Artesian Water—At St. David 238, wells in Gila Valley 259
Asay, Joseph—Aids Powell exp. 128-29
Atlantic & Pacific R. R.—Land grant 193-94

B

Ballenger, Jesse O.—Heads L. Colorado settlement 138
Ballenger's Camp (Brigham City)—Est. 140
Banta, A. F.—Arizona pioneer 178, 180, 184-85
Barbenceta—Navajo Chief 77-79
Barrus, Lt. Ruel—Battalion officer at San Luis Rey 28
Barth, Sol—On L. Colorado 177-79
Bartlett, John R.—At Tubac 56-57, in Texas 57-58
Bass, Willis W.—Grand Canyon guide 75
Beadle, J. H.—Visit to Lonely Dell and J. D. Lee 91-2
Beale, E. F.—At San Pascual 26, camel survey, carried dispatches east, advised Washington of discovery of gold 33

Beaver Dams—Early occupation 6, 101, settlement 117-18
Beebe, Nelson P.—Leader of Arkansas party 151
Bees—First in Utah 47
Bellamy, Edward—Study of United Order 131
Bennett, Capt. Frank F.—In great Navajo council 76-78
Berardo—At Horsehead Crossing 163
Berry, Mrs. Rachael—State legislator 106
Berry, Wm. Wiley—Killed by outlaws, photo. 291
Bibliography 279-80
Biggs, Thos.—Lehi settler 203, photo. 212
Bigler, Henry W.—At gold discovery 43-44, photo. 20
Bluewater, N. M.—Settlement 189
Blythe, John L.—Launched boat at Lee's Ferry 92, 94, at Moen Copie
    137, at Le Roux Spring 152, photo. 132
Bonelli, Daniel—Early ferryman 97-121, photo. 132
Boston Party—In L. Colorado Valley 149-51
Boyle, Henry G.—Battalion member 27, 36, outlined Mormon road 29,
    first president S. States Mission 36, photo. 29
Brannan, Samuel—Head of "Brooklyn" exp. 38-42, Wyoming confer-
    ence with Brigham Young, died in Mexico 42
Brigham City, Ariz.—Est. 140, naming 145, abandonment 147, photo.
    of old fort 140
Brigham City, Utah—Experiences in United Order 130
Brinkerhoff, Hyrum—Muddy r. and Gila v. pioneer 249, photo. 260
Brinkerhoff, Margaret—Muddy r. and Gila v. pioneer 249, photo. 261
Brizzee, H. W.—Battalion member 27, in Arizona 36, photo. 28
"Brooklyn"—Mormon immigrant ship 4, 38
Brown, Capt. Jas.—Led at Pueblo, Colo. 5, battalion officer 11-12,
    arr. Salt Lake, to Cal. for pay 29-30
Brown, Jas. S.—On Muddy r. 36, at Cal. gold discovery 44, head of
    1875 scouting party 137, battalion member 138, photo. 20
Bryce—Est. 249
Bryce, Ebenezer—Early Gila settler 249, photo. 260
Bushman, John V.—N. E. Ariz. settler 140, 144-45, 155, photo. 188

C

Call, Anson—Founded Callville 2, 113, photo. 132
Callville—Port on Colorado r. 44, est. 113-114, abandonment 116,
    county seat of Pah-ute Co. 123
Camels—Brought by Beale survey 33
Campbell, Gov. T. E.—Assistance in work iii, circumtoured Grand
    Canyon 69, Prest. League of the Southwest 110
Cannon, Angus M.—At Callville 72, on Colorado r. 114
Cannon, David H.—Baptism of Shivwits at St. George 67, photo. 117
Carson, Kit—Guide of Kearny exp. 25-26, carried dispatches east 33,
    campaign against Navajo 76
Carson Valley, Nev.—Settled by Mormons 5
Casa Grande—Ancient ruin 227
Cataract Canyon—Home of Hava-supai 69, entered by Hamblin 69,
    by Garces 69, by Ives 111
Central—Est. 249
Chemehuevis Indians—War band in Muddy r. district 109
Chronology 287-90

Chuichupa, Colonia—Mexican settlement 268

Claridge, Rebecca—Photo 261

Claridge, Samuel H.—Muddy and Gila r. pioneer 249, photo. 260

Cluff, Benjamin—At Las Vegas 105

Coal—Dug at San Diego by G. W. Sirrine 47

Cocheron, Augusta Joyce—Description of Yerba Buena 39

Cocopah Indians—Colorado r. deck hands 112

Colorado City—Est. on site of Yuma 111

Colorado River—Reached by Battalion 17, watershed embraced within
State of Deseret 50, ferries of 89-97, frozen over 95, transportation
110-116, efforts to utilize water and power, drainage area, flow,
water storage, navigation, watershed now barred for navigation
110-14

Colter, J. G. H.—At Round Valley 185

Concho—Hard living conditions 168, est. 183, naming 184

Cooke, Lt.-Col. P. St. George—Commander Mormon Battalion 11-12,
congratulatory order 15, story of march 18-19, left Santa Fe 25,
crossed Colorado r. 26, led Johnston's cavalry to Utah, resignation
32, photo. 20

Cooley, C. E.—Won Showlow in card game, sold 168

Cooperative Stores—Est. in many communities 133

Co-quap—Paiute killed at St. Thomas 108

Cotton—Raised by Maricopas 18, Pima long-staple 211

Crismon, Chas.—At San Bernardino 46, took first bees to Utah 47, at
founding of Mesa 212, photo. 213

Crosby, Geo. H. Sr.—Photo. 188

Crosby, Jesse W.—In re-settlement of Muddy 127

Crosby, Taylor—At Hopi 65

Crossing of the Fathers—Passed by Escalante and Dominguez 59,
Hamblin's was first crossing by white men since Spanish days 64,
early use of 89, photo., frontispiece

Curtis—Est. 248

Curtis, Elizabeth Hanks—Photo. 261, in Gila Valley 253

Curtis, Josephine—Photo. 189, in Gila Valley

Curtis, Martha—Photo. 189, in Gila Valley

Curtis, Moses M.—Gila Valley pioneer 247, at Eden 248

Curtis, Virginia—Photo. 189, in Gila Valley

Cushing, Frank H.—Southwestern ethnologist 213-14

Cutler, R. J.—Muddy settler 119, Rep. Pah-ute Co. in Ariz. 3d and 4th
legislatures 124, clerk Rio Virgen Co. 126

D

Davidson, Jas.—Death of family of thirst 119-120

Davis, Capt. Daniel C.—Battalion officer 28

Davis, Durias—Visit to Hopi 63

Day, Henry—In charge at Moen Copie 136

Defiance, Fort—Est. 5, great council with Navajo 76, settlement by
Hamblin of Indian troubles 86

Dellenbaugh, F. S.—Estimate of Mormon settlements 6, 128, wrote of
Navajo council 76

Deseret—State of, 48-52, map 51, origin of name 48, boundaries 49,
organization, legislature 52

Diaz, Colonia—Mexican settlement 267-68

Dixie, Utah's—Brigham Young in 81, ref. to 104
Dobson, Thos. F.—First settler at Fredonia 99
Dodge, Enoch—Fight with Navajos 71
Dominguez and Escalante—On Spanish Trail 53
Dublan, Colonia—Mexican settlement 268
Dykes, Geo. P.—Battalion officer 11, 21, 37, photo. 20, death 33

E

Eagar—Est. 185
Earthquake—At St. David 236
Eastern Arizona Stake—Est. 195-96
Eden—Est. 248
Ehrenberg—Military depot 111
El Dorado Canyon—At Cottonwood Island 114
Ellsworth, Edmund—Salt Lake Pioneer 106
Emory, W. H.—With Kearny exp. 25-26
Engelhardt, Father Z.—Estimate of Battalion members 31
Escalante-Dominguez—On Spanish Trail 53-54, at Crossing of the Fathers 89
"Explorer"—Ives' steamboat on Colorado r. 62, 111, photo. 68

F

Farish, Thos. E.—Former Arizona Historian iv
Ferrin, Jacob S.—Killed by Apaches 253, photo. 292
Fife, Diana Davis—Killed by Indians 291, photo. 292
Fife, J. D.—Sulphur Springs Valley pioneer, photo. 189
Fife, Wm. N.—Sulphur Springs Valley pioneer, photo. 189
Fish, Joseph—Early historian 166, photo. 172
Flagstaff—Naming of 151
Flake, Chas. L.—Killed by outlaw 165, photo. 293
Flake, Wm. J.—Land purchases at Snowflake 164, at Showlow 168, at Concho 183, at Springerville 185, at Nutrioso 185-86, photo. 188
Follett, Wm. A.—Battalion member 37, to Arizona 106, photo. 28
Foote, Jos. Warren—At St. Joseph, Nevada 118
Forest Dale—Est. 170-71, Indian encroachments, abandonment, claims for damages 170-73
Foreword iii-iv
Foutz, Joseph—Photo. 189
Franklin—Est. 250
Fredonia—Visited by Gov. Campbell 69, est., naming, description of 99-100, view 108
Fremont, John C.—Dissension in American forces 9, arrest and trial 32, on Spanish Trail 54

G

Garces, Father Francisco—Early Spanish priest 53, at Hopi 64
Garcia, Colonia—Mexican settlement 268
Gass, Octavius D.—Represented Mohave Co. in 2d legislature and Pah-ute Co. in 3d and 4th Legislatures 124, in 5th Legislature 125, floated down Colorado r. 125

Genoa—First American settlement in Nevada 5

Gibbons, Andrew S.—Investigated Welsh legend 64, took Hopi visitors home 69, shown sacred stone of Hopi 81, Salt Lake Pioneer 106, interpreter on Muddy 108-18, trip down Colorado r., in Ariz. Legislature from Pah-ute Co. 125, photo. 84

Gibbons, Mrs. A. S.—Photo. 189

Gibbons, Augustus A.—Killed by Indians 292, photo. 293

Gibbons, Richard—At Hopi village 82

Gibbons, Wm. H.—At Hopi village 82

Gila River—Barge made by Battalion 14, route of Battalion 17, land erosion 258, trouble with mill tailings 259

Gold—Battalion party present at discovery 43

Goodwin, Camp—In Gila Valley 251, abandonment 258

Graham—Est. 246

Graham County—Est. 250

Grand Canyon—Visited by Escalante-Dominguez 53-54, circumtoured by Hamblin 68, by Gov. Campbell 69, expl. by Powell 74-76, 90, 92, to be bridged 96

Grand Falls—Haight party at 92, view 156

Grand Wash—Ferry site 68, crossed by Hamblin 96

Grant—Early name of Luna 187

Grant Camp—Old and new, south of Gila 251

Grant, Heber J.—Church President iii, photo. 61, visit to St. Johns 195 Mexican trips 237, 267

Greeley, Lewis—With 1863 Hamblin party 69

Greer—Est. 186

H

Haight, Horton D.—Crossed river at Paria 92, first attempt at Arizona colonization 135-136, photo. 204

Hakes, Collins R.—At San Bernardino 45, President Maricopa Stake, at Bluewater, death 189, 221, photo. 220

Hall, Miss S. M.—Description of Lee's Ferry 93, of Fredonia 99, 100

Hamblin, Frederick—At Hopi 64, at Alpine 186, fight with bear 188, photo. 84

Hamblin, Jacob—Frontier guide 55, missionary to Indians, entry in Muddy section 59, Mountain Meadows massacre, saves wagon trains, photo. 60, at Las Vegas lead mines, encounter with Ives party 61-2, at Colorado r. 62, 114, trips to Hopi 63, 65-67, 70, 72, took Hopi visitors home 69, with Powell at Shivwits council 74-5, guide for Powell, council with Navajo 76-77, 91, error in date of great Navajo council 80, took provisions to second Powell exp., visited Fort Defiance 81, 1871-2-3 trips 82, ambassador to Navajo, in danger of death 83-86, located Grand Wash road, wagon route to Sunset, guide for D. H. Wells 1876 party, ordained Apostle to the Lamanites 86-87, moved to Arizona, death, monument inscription 87-88, 185, 187, first Colorado r. crossing at Ute ford, 1858, crossed at Paria on raft 90, located road to San Francisco mountains 92, in 1862 crossed river at Ute ford, in 1863 crossed at Grand Wash 96

Hamblin, Wm.—At Hopi 64, at naming of Pipe Springs 98

Hancock, Levi—Battalion poet 12

Hardy's Landing—Visited by Call 97, Callville visited by Hardy 114

Harris, Llewellyn—Welsh legend 64-65

Haskell, Thales—Investigated steamer on Colorado r. 62, at Hopi 65, 66, 68, 69, left Hopi 70, in Muddy district 107, with Paiutes 116, photo. 229

Hatch, Ira—With Paiutes 106-7, with Hopi 64, 70, at Meadows 184, photo. 229

Hatch, Lorenzo—Escape from drowning 87, at Taylor 167

Hava-supai Indians—See Cataract Canyon

Hawkins, Wm. R.—With Powell exp. 75

Hayden, C. T.—Visited by Jones party 198, assistance to settlers 207, est. Hayden's Ferry 219

Head, W. S.—Post trader at Verde 87

Heaton, Jonathan—Resident of Moccasin 98, photo. with sons 229

Heber—In Mogollons 155, in New Mexico 187

Holbrook—Naming 163

Holmes, Henry—Description of L. Colorado valley 136

Hopi—Visited by Father Garces 53, 64, by Escalante 54, by Jacob Hamblin 63-72, Welsh legend, composite language 63-64, snake dance, tribesmen taken to Salt Lake 68, threw Navajos from cliff 79, Tuba taken to Utah 80, sacred stone 81-82, southern origin 228

Hortt, Henry J.—Fredonia settler 99

Hubbard—Est. 249

Hubbell, J. L.—Investigated Utah Indian troubles 84

Hulett, Schuyler—Battalion member 37, photo. 28

Hunt—Est. 184

Hunt, Capt. Jefferson—Battalion officer 11, 24, 37

Hunt, John—Battalion member 37, Mormon road mail carrier 55, at Snowflake 164, photo. 21

Hunt, Marshall—Battalion member 37

Hunter, Capt. Jesse B.—Battalion officer 11

I

Idaho—Agricultural settlement 5

Index—To book 293

Irritaba—Mohave chief 62

Iverson, Alma—At LeRoux Spring 152

Ives, J. C.—Colorado r. exploration 62, 111

Ivins, Anthony W.—Indian warfare 72, crossed Colorado r. on the ice 95, agent for Mexican lands 267-68, 275, photo. 165

J

Jenson, Andrew—Assistant Church Historian iii, data on Callville 113, in Muddy Valley 127, in L. Colorado Valley 142-43, at Tuba City 158, photo. 173

Johnson, B. F.—At Tempe 219, at Nephi, death 220, photo. 189

Johnson, Warren M.—Escape from drowning 187, photo. of Lee's Ferry home 109

Johnson, W. H.—In charge of Virgin salt mines 127

Johnston, Capt. A. R.—Killed at San Pascual 25

Johnston, Gen. A. S.—Exp. to Utah 32

Johnston, Capt. Geo. A.—Ferried Beale camel exp. across river 97, 111, 112, offered to handle Salt Lake freight 115

Johnston, W. J.—Batt. member 37, gold disc. 44, photo. 20
Jones, D. W.—First exp. to Mexico 197-99, foundation of Lehi 201, 203-4, death 209, photos. 205, 212
Jones, Nathaniel V.—Battalion member 37, photo. 21
Jonesville—See Lehi
Jones, Wiley C.—With Jones party 197, photo. 205
Juarez, Colonia—Mexican settlement 267-68
Judd, Hyrum—Battalion member 37, photo. 28
Judd, Zadok K.—Battalion member 37, photo. 29
Junction City—On Colorado r. 118

K

Kaibab Plateau—Visited by Powell 91, view 101
Kanab—Passed in 1920 by Gov. Campbell 69, Powell exploration at 91, est. 97, 120
Kane, Col. Thos. L.—Introduction to Tyler history 19-20, conference with Paiutes 107
Kapurats—Paiute name for Maj. Powell 75
Kearny, Gen. S. W.—In command California invasion 9, 10, 25, 26
Kempton, Martin—Killed by outlaws 292, photo. 293
Kimball, Andrew—Prest. St. Joseph Stake 263, photo. 196
Kimball, Heber C.—Chief Justice of Deseret 52
Klineman, Conrad—Salt Lake Pioneer 106

L

Laguna Dam—Bars Colorado navigation 112-13
Lake, George—Leader on L. Colorado 136, 146, to Gila Valley 147, photo. 188
Land Grants—Atlantic & Pacific 192, 194, Reavis fraud 228-31, Texas-Pacific claim 229, 231, 259
Las Vegas, Nev.—Visited by P. P. Pratt 55, station on Mormon road 101, detail of missionaries 105, visited by Call 114
Las Vegas County—Creation asked 122
"Latter-day Saints"—Designation of 1
Layton—Est. 249-50
Layton, Christ.—Battalion member 24-5, 36-7, instructions to 260, biography 262-63, photo. 196
Layton, Elizabeth—Photo. 261
Lead mines—In Nevada 104
League of the Southwest—Water storage plans 110
Leavitt, Dudley—Smelted lead ore in Nevada 61, at Hopi 64, at naming of Pipe Springs 98
LeBaron, David T.—Tempe settler 219
Lee, John D.—Location on Paria 91-93, messenger for Battalion 92, residence on Canyon 93, capture, in Utah, execution 93, experience of wife with Indians 94, photo. of home at Moen Avi 149
Lee's Ferry—Visited by Gov. Campbell 69, passage of Roundy party 82, early crossings by Hamblin 90, Powell at 91-92, John D. Lee's residence at 91-93, ferry bought by Church 93, description of 93-94, river frozen 95, Stanton exp., main route into Arizona 94
Lehi—Map 202, est. 204-10, floods 210, arr. of Mesa party 213

Leithead, Jas.—In charge of Muddy settlements 12-21, built boat 125, supplied Powell exp. 129
Lemhi, Fort—Early settlement in Idaho 5
LeRoux, Antoine—Guide to Battalion 16, Arizona places named for 34, guide for Bartlett party 57
LeRoux Springs—History 150-51
Lesueur, Frank—Killed by outlaws 292, photo. 293
Lesueur, Jas. W.—President Maricopa Stake 221, photo. 220
Lesueur, John T.—President Maricopa Stake 221, photo. 220
Lewis, Samuel—Battalion member 37, photo. 21
List of Illustrations xi, xii
Little Colorado River—Irrigation difficulties 141-42, floods 143, view of crossing 140
Little Colorado Stake—Org. 195
Little Colorado Valley—Haight exp. 135, settlement 138, Arizona experiences 138-63, drought 190-91
Littlefield—Northwestern Arizona settlement 6, 101, 117-18, visited by Gov. Campbell 69
Lonely Dell—Lee's name for mouth of Paria 91
Los Angeles—Battalion experiences 22, Standage's description of, name 23-24, muster-out of Battalion 27
Los Muertos—Ancient city 213-214
Luna—Est. 187
Lund, A. H.—Church Historian iii
Lund, A. Wm.—Church Librarian iii
Lyman, Amasa M.—San Bernardino experiences 45, in Arizona 106, with Col. Kane on Muddy r. 107
Lyman, Francis M.—Exp. near St. Johns 182, at St. David 237

M

Macdonald—Est. 236
Macdonald, A. F.—Director of cattle company at Pipe Springs 98, President Maricopa Stake 98, 220, transfer to Mexico, death 221, named St. David 235, in Mexico 267, photo. 220
Malaria—At Obed 147, on San Pedro and Gila 233-34
Maps—State of Deseret 51, Pah-ute County 103, Northeastern Arizona 139, Plat of Lehi 202, Prehistoric canals 226, Southeastern Arizona 243, Arizona and Roads 309
Maricopa Indians—18
Maricopa Stake—Org. 220-21
Matthews—Est. 247
Maxwell, Wm. B.—Battalion member 37, at Moccasin Springs 97, photo. 29
Mazatzal City—Tonto Basin settlement 174
McBride, R. Franklin—Killed by outlaws 292, photo. 293
McClellan, Almeda—Photo. 189
McClellan, Wm. C.—Battalion member 37, photo. 21
McIntire, Robert—Killed by Indians 72
McIntyre, Wm.—Battalion surgeon 11
McConnell, Jehiel—At Hopi 66, 68-70
McMurrin, Jos. W.—At LeRoux Spring 152, photo. 165
Meadows—Purchase 179, occupied 184
Meeden, C. V.—Early Colorado r. pilot 112

Merrill, Eliza—Killed by Indians 292, photo. 292
Merrill, Philemon C.—Adjutant Battalion 21, 36-7, custodian of Utah stone, pioneer on San Pedro 33, 36, photos. 20, 212, in Lehi party 203, separation from Jones 207, est. of St. David 235
Mesa—Org. of "The Mesa Union" 133, est. 211, canal digging 213, building of first house 215, civic est., naming 216-17
Mesquite—Settlement on Virgin 119, 127
Mexico—Jones party trip 199, exploration for settlement 236, exploration 266, est. of colonies 267-270, flight from 270-274, repopulation 275
Mill Point—Est. on Muddy r. 118
Miller, Henry W.—At Beaver Dams 117, photo. 188
Miller, Jacob—Sec'y to Haight exp. 136, photo. 204
Milligan, Fort—Est. 88
Moabi—Near Moen Copie 137
Moccasin Springs—Occupation of 97, view 101
Moen Copie—Visited by Hamblin 82-3, Blythe location 137, mission post, Indian experiences 157, land bought by government 161, view 85
Mohave County—Embraced Nevada point 123
Mohave, Fort—Est. 5
Moody, Elizabeth—Photo. 261
Moody, John M.—First settler of Thatcher 249, photo. 260
Morelos, Colonia—Sonora settlement 268
Mormon Battalion—Reason for formation 7-8, muster at Council Bluffs 11, at San Bernardino ranch 13, 16, arr. Tucson 13, arr. Pima villages 14, left San Bernardino 16, experiences 24-25, muster-out 27, gold discovery 43
Mormon Battalion Monument—Arizona contributes 34-35, photo. 36
Mormon Dairy—Est. 154
Mormon Road—Broken by Boyle party 29, early travel 44, mail service 55, stations on 101
Moroni, Fort—Est. 152-53, use by John W. Young 153, named Fort Rickerson 154, photos. 157
Mountain Meadows—Massacre 45, Hamblin resident in 60
Mount Trumbull—Powell and Hamblin at Indian council 74, sawmill 155
Mowrey, Harley—Last Battalion survivor 34
Muddy Valley—Settlement 6, 117-129, population 122, Arizona Legislature protested separation 123, return of settlers 127
Munk, Dr. J. A.—Library of Arizoniana 166

N

Naraguts—Paiute guide 64
Navajo Indians—Fight near Pipe Springs 71, stole stock in Utah, great council with Powell and Hamblin 76, captured by Hopi, agreement to remain south of river 79, killing of three tribesmen in Utah 84
Nephi—Est. 220
Nevada—First American settlement by Mormons 5-6, jurisdiction over Muddy district 101, old mapping 102, Muddy abandoned 121-24, protest against separation from Arizona 123-24
New Hope—Early California colony 41
Northeastern Arizona—Map 139
Nutrioso—Est. 185-86
Nuttall, L. John—Exper. in crossing Colorado r. 87

O

P

Pratt, Helaman—Capt. of Muddy militia 109, in second southern exp. 199, photos 205
Prescott—Founded 5
Prows, Wm. C.—Battalion member 37, photo. 229
Pueblo—First Anglo-Saxon settlement in Colorado 5, Company ordered to winter at 12, Battalion sick sent to 21, departure of detachment 29-30
Pulsipher, David—Battalion member 37, photo. 28

R

Railroads—Construction northern Arizona 191-92, Atlantic & Pacific grant 193-94, construction through Gila Valley 256-57
Ramah, N. M.—Settlement 188-89
Ramsey, Ralph—Utah artist, moved to Ariz. 166
Reidhead—Est. 169
Reidhead, John—Woodruff settler 162
Richards, Joseph H.—L. Colorado settler 141, photos. 172, 173
Richards, Mary—Photos. 173, 189
Rioville—At mouth of Virgin 118
Roberts, B. H.—Story of Battalion 24-25, Utah historian 34
Robinson, Nathan B.—Killed by Apaches 172, photo. 229
Robson, Chas. I.—At founding of Mesa 211-12, President Maricopa Stake 220, death 221, photo. 220
Rogers, Henry C.—In Lehi party 203, 209, Church officer 220-21, photo. 212
Rogers, J. K.—Leader in Gila settlement 246, photo. 260
Rogers, Josephine Wall—Photo. 261
Rogers, Samuel H.—Battalion member 37, photo. 28
Roundy, Lorenzo W.—Led party across Colorado r. 82, drowned 87, photo. 204
Rusling, Gen. J. F.—Recommended use of Colorado r. as waterway 110

S

Safford—Est. 242, outlawry 255-56, first school house photo. 245
Safford, Gov. A. P. K.—At Tombstone 239, on Gila 242
Salt—From Virgin r. mines 111, description of deposit 127, Zuni salt lake, Hopi source of supply 156, central Arizona deposits 156-57
Salt Lake Pioneers—Later Arizonans 106
Salt River Valley—Visited by Jones party 198, Trejo description 200
San Bernardino (Cal.)—Settlement 5, est. 44-5, abandonment 46, Bartlett account of purchase 57
San Bernardino Ranch—Reached by Battalion 13, 16, Standage reference 21
San Diego—On route of Battalion, Standage reference to 22, arr. Kearny exp. 26, post of Battalion company 28, Battalion experiences 29
San Francisco—Arr. "Brooklyn" party 4, 38-41
San Jose, Colonia—Sonora settlement 272
San Pedro Valley—Battalion march 17-18, Standage description 21, settlement 231-35
Santa Cruz Valley—Earliest Spanish settlement 5
Santa Fe—On Battalion route 9, 10, 12

305

Thatcher—Est. 249, 262, photo. normal college 245
Thomas, Camp—In Gila Valley 251
Thompson, Samuel—Battalion member 37, photo. 28
Thurston, Frank—Killed by Apaches 254
To-ish-obe—Paiute Chief 108
Tombstone—Mining history 238-40
Tonto Basin—Settlement 173-74, abandonment authorized 176
Tragedies of the Frontier—List of Latter-day Saints killed by Indians or outlaws 291-92
Trejo, M. G.—Spanish missionary 197-201, photo. 205
Trueworthy, Thos. E.—Early Colorado r. pilot 111-12, steamboat trip up Colorado r. 115
Trumbull, Mount—Indian council 74, sawmill to Arizona 155
Tuba—Oraibi chief, with Hamblin to Utah 80, shows sacred stone 81, 82, returns to Oraibi 87, at Tuba City 159
Tuba City—Est. 158, woolen factory 159, killing of Lot Smith 159-60, sold to government 161
Tubac—Map 37, Mormon colony 5-6, 56-7, visited by second Mexican exp. 199
Tucson—Settlement 5, taking of by Battalion 10, Standage reference 21
Tumacacori—Est. of mission 5
Tyler, Daniel—Battalion history 18-19, 28
Tyler, Frank N.—Photo. 260

U

Udall, D. K.—Arr. at St. Johns 179-80, President St. Johns Stake 196, photo. first home 180, photo. 196
United Order—Est. in Muddy settlements 119, development 130-34, not a general Church movement 132, in Lehi 133, on L. Colorado r. 144-46, at Woodruff 162
Utah—Creation of Territory 52, seeks land north of Colorado r. 100
Utah, Camp—See Lehi
Utahville—See Lehi
Ute Ford—See Crossing of the Fathers

V

Vado de los Padres—See Crossing of the Fathers
Virden—Est. 250
Virgin River—Settlements on 6, 117, 129

W

Wallapai Indians—Visited Muddy Valley 110
Walnut Grove—Settled 184
Walpi—Hopi village, view 108
Weaver, Pauline—Principal guide to Battalion, gold discoveries, death 34
Wells, Daniel H.—Visited Arizona settlements 86-87, on L. Colorado r. 141, photo. 204
Welsh—Legend of the Hopi 63-65
West Point—Muddy settlement 101, 118
Wham robbery—Near Gila settlements 255